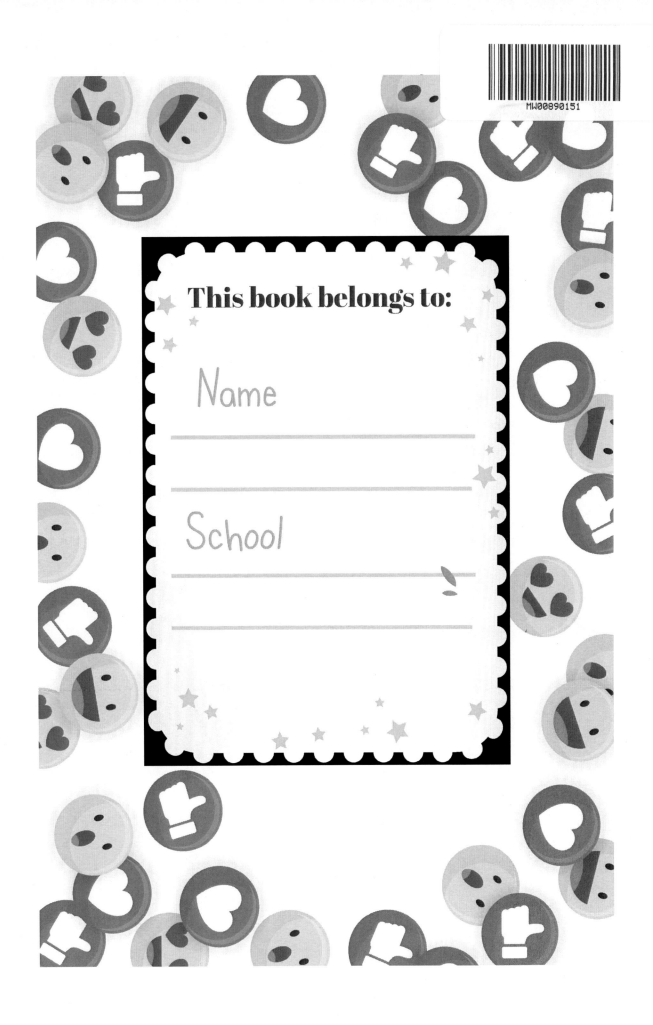

This book belongs to:

Name

_____

_____

School

_____

_____

Grammar: Personal Pronouns

Pronouns are words that are used to rename, stand-in for, refer to, or rename nouns (a person, place, thing, or idea). As a result, they frequently behave exactly like nouns in a sentence. Pronouns allow a speaker or writer to change how they refer to a noun, so pronouns are limited in meaning to the noun they are referring to. For instance, if someone is telling a story about a friend named Jim and says, "He went to the store," he is referring to Jim.

Without pronouns, relating information in writing or speech would feel stiff and repetitive. Assume an author wanted to write a story about a young man named Mike. Without pronouns, the author would have to refer to Mike by his first name or as "the boy." The plot could go something like this:

"Mike awoke at 8:30 a.m. every day. Mike dressed for the day, and then the boy ate breakfast. "Mike was always late for school."

Take note of how repetitive the story becomes when pronouns are removed. However, if pronouns are used instead of nouns, the story becomes less repetitive and wooden. As an example:

"Mike awoke at 8:30 a.m. every day. He put on his day's clothes and then ate breakfast. "He was always late for school."

The most well-known type of pronoun is the personal pronoun, which is used to identify oneself, people being spoken to, and people being spoken about. Personal pronouns have traditionally been classified as either subjective or objective, singular or plural, and first, second, or third person, as shown below.

First-person, singular -- I, my, mine, me.

Second person, singular -- you, your, yours.

Third-person, singular -- he, his, him, she, her, hers, it, its.

First-person, plural -- we, our, ours, us.

Second person, plural -- your, yours.

Third person, plural -- they, their, theirs, them

In short, personal pronouns are grammar's stunt doubles; they stand-in for the people (and possibly animals) who appear in our sentences. They allow us to speak and write more efficiently because they prevent us from repeating cumbersome proper nouns all day.

1. **Pronouns stand-in for the people and _____ .**
    a. animals
    b. nothing at all

2. **Using pronouns allows a speaker or writer to vary how they refer to a _____ .**
    a. adverb
    b. noun

3. **The tie is very special. ___ is a magic tie.**
    a. He
    b. It

4. **Charlie and I went to a pond. _____ saw two frogs.**
    a. They
    b. We

5. **The turtle is tired. _____ is rest under the tree.**
   a. Him
   b. It

6. **Tim and I saw the lion in the jungle. _____ were very afraid.**
   a. Their
   b. We

7. **The rabbit escaped from the trap and ran away. _____ was safe.**
   a. They
   b. It

8. **The farmer's wife saw a wolf. _____ shouted to the farmer for help.**
   a. She
   b. It

9. **The boys found a magic chain. _____ gave it to the queen.**
   a. They
   b. He

10. **_____ 20 years old.**
    a. Them
    b. She's

11. **_____ house is big.**
    a. He
    b. His

12. **_____ name's Farah.**
    a. Her
    b. She

13. **How old is she?**
    a. He's seven.
    b. She's seven.

14. **What's his name?**
    a. His name's Ali.
    b. Her name's Ali.

15. **Mia and Omar enjoy listening to Ree's singing. Becomes:**
    a. Them enjoy listening to Ree's singing.
    b. They enjoy listening to Ree's singing.

16. **Dana kicked the ball. Becomes:**
    a. She kicked the ball.
    b. He kicked the ball.

17. **The dog is barking. _____ is barking at someone.**
    a. He
    b. It

18. **My sister likes basketball. _____ plays everyday.**
    a. She
    b. He

Proofreading Skills: Volunteering

Score: _____

Date: _____

In this activity, you'll see lots of grammatical *errors*. Correct all the grammar mistakes you see.

> There are **10** mistakes in this passage. 3 capitals missing. 4 unnecessary capitals. 3 incorrect homophones.

Your own life can be changed and the lives of others, through volunteer work. to cope with the news that there has been a disaster, you can volunteer to help those in need. Even if you can't contribute financially, you can donate you're time instead.

Volunteering is such an integral part of the American culture that many high schools require their students to participate in community service to graduate.

When you volunteer, you have the freedom to choose what you'd like to do and who or what you think is most deserving of your time. Start with these ideas if you need a little inspiration. We've got just a few examples here.

Encourage the growth and development of young people. Volunteer as a Camp counselor, a Big Brother or Big Sister, or an after-school sports program. Special Olympics games and events are excellent opportunities to know children with special needs.

Spend the holidays doing good deeds for others. Volunteer at a food bank or distribute toys to children in need on Thanksgiving Day, and you'll be doing your part to help those in need. your church, temple, mosque, or another place of worship may also require your assistance.

You can visit an animal shelter and play with the Animals. Volunteers are critical to the well-being of shelter animals. (You also get a good workout when you walk rescued dogs.)

Become a member of a political campaign. Its a great way to learn more about the inner workings of politics if your curious about it. If you are not able To cast a ballot, you can still help elect your preferred candidate.

Help save the planet. Join a river preservation group and lend a hand. Participate in a park cleanup day in your community. Not everyone is cut out for the great outdoors; if you can't see yourself hauling trees up a hill, consider working in the park's office or education center instead.

Take an active role in promoting health-related causes. Many of us know someone afflicted with a medical condition (like cancer, HIV, or diabetes, for example). a charity that helps people with a disease, such as delivering meals, raising money, or providing other assistance, can make you Feel good about yourself.

Find a way to combine your favorite things if you have more than one. For example, if you're a fan of kids and have a talent for arts and crafts, consider volunteering at a children's hospital.

Weather and Climate

Score: _____

Date: _____

The difference between weather and climate is simply a matter of time. Weather refers to the conditions of the atmosphere over a short period of time, whereas climate refers to how the atmosphere "behaves" over a longer period of time.

When we discuss climate change, we are referring to changes in long-term averages of daily weather. Today's children are constantly told by their parents and grandparents about how the snow was always piled up to their waists as they trudged off to school. Most children today have not experienced those kinds of dreadful snow-packed winters. The recent changes in winter snowfall indicate that the climate has changed since their parents were children.

Weather is essentially the atmosphere's behavior, particularly in terms of its effects on life and human activities. The distinction between weather and climate is that weather refers to short-term (minutes to months) changes in the atmosphere, whereas climate refers to long-term changes. Most people associate weather with temperature, humidity, precipitation, cloudiness, brightness, visibility, wind, and atmospheric pressure, as in high and low pressure.

Weather can change from minute to minute, hour to hour, day to day, and season to season in most places. However, the climate is the average of weather over time and space. A simple way to remember the distinction is that climate is what you expect, such as a very hot summer, whereas weather is what you get, such as a hot day with pop-up thunderstorms.

Use the word bank to unscramble the words!

Pressure	Density	Cloudy	Latitude	Elevation	Weather
Absorb	Humid	Precipitation	Windy	Forecast	Climate
Sunshine	Temperature				

1. IUMHD   _ u _ _ _

2. UDLOYC   _ l _ u _ _

3. FSEATOCR   _ _ _ _ _ a _ t

4. UDLTITAE   L _ _ _ _ u _ _

5. IEOCAIIPPTRNT _ _ _ _ _ _ _ t _ _ _ o n

6. TEEERPAURMT   T _ _ _ e _ _ t _ _ _

7. RSEREUPS   _ r e _ _ _ _ _

8. LEICATM   _ _ i _ _ t _

9. SNNIEHUS   S _ _ _ _ _ i _ _

10. OBBASR   _ b s _ _ _

11. VETIEOANL   _ _ _ _ _ a t _ _ _

12. EATWRHE   W _ _ _ _ e _

13. NDWIY   _ _ _ _ y

14. TYNEIDS   _ _ _ _ _ i _ y

Test Your Mathematics Knowledge

1. To add fractions_____
   a. the denominators must be the same
   b. the denominators can be same or different
   c. the denominators must be different

2. To add decimals, the decimal points must be?
   a. column and carry the first digit(s)
   b. lined up in any order before you add the columns
   c. lined up vertically before you add the columns

3. When adding like terms_____
   a. the like terms must be same and they must be to the different power.
   b. the exponent must be different and they must be to the same power.
   c. the variable(s) must be the same and they must be to the same power.

4. The concept of math regrouping involves_____
   a. regrouping means that 5x + 2 becomes 50 + 12
   b. the numbers you are adding come out to five digit numbers and 0
   c. rearranging, or renaming, groups in place value

5. _____ indicates how many times a number, or algebraic expression, should be multiplied by itself.
   a. Denominators
   b. Division-quotient
   c. Exponent

6. _____is the numerical value of a number without its plus or minus sign.
   a. Absolute value
   b. Average
   c. Supplementary

7. Any number that is less than zero is called_____
   a. Least common multiple
   b. Equation
   c. Negative number

8. 23 = 2 x 2 x 2 = 8, 8 is the
   a. third power of 2
   b. first power of 2
   c. second power of 2

9. -7, 0, 3, and 7.12223 are
   a. all real numbers
   b. all like fractions
   c. all like terms

10. How do you calculate 2 + 3 x 7?
   a. 2 + 3 x 7 = 2 + 21 = 23
   b. 2 + 7 x 7 = 2 + 21 = 35
   c. 2 + 7 x 3 = 2 + 21 = 23

11. How do you calculate (2 + 3) x (7 - 3)?

    a. (2 + 2) x (7 - 3) = 5 x 4 = 32

    b. (2 + 3) x (7 - 3) = 5 x 4 = 20

    c. (2 + 7) x (2 - 3) = 5 x 4 = 14

12. The Commutative Law of Addition says_____

    a. positive - positive = (add) positive

    b. that it doesn't matter what order you add up numbers, you will always get the same answer

    c. parts of a calculation outside brackets always come first

13. The Zero Properties Law of multiplication says_____

    a. that any number multiplied by 0 equals 0

    b. mathematical operation where four or more numbers are combined to make a sum

    c. Negative - Positive = Subtract

14. Multiplication is when you_____

    a. numbers that are added together in multiplication problems

    b. take one number and add it together a number of times

    c. factor that is shared by two or more numbers

15. When multiplying by 0, the answer is always_____

    a. 0

    b. -0

    c. 1

16. When multiplying by 1, the answer is always the _____

    a. same as the number multiplied by 0

    b. same as the number multiplied by -1

    c. same as the number multiplied by 1

17. You can multiply numbers in_____

    a. any order and multiply by 2 and the answer will be the same

    b. any order you want and the answer will be the same

    c. any order from greater to less than and the answer will be the same

18. Division is____

    a. set of numbers that are multiplied together to get an answer

    b. breaking a number up into an equal number of parts

    c. division is scaling one number by another

19. If you take 20 things and put them into four equal sized groups

    a. there will be 6 things in each group

    b. there will be 5 things in each group

    c. there will be 10 things in each group

20. The dividend is_____

    a. the number you are multiplied by

    b. the number you are dividing up

    c. the number you are grouping together

21. The divisor is _____

    a. are all multiples of 3

    b. the number you are dividing by

    c. common factor of two numbers

22. The quotient is _____

    a. the answer

    b. answer to a multiplication operation

    c. any number in the problem

23. When dividing something by 1_____
    a. the answer is the original number
    b. the answer produces a given number when multiplied by itself
    c. the answer is the quotient

24. Dividing by 0_____
    a. the answer will always be more than 0
    b. You will always get 1
    c. You cannot divide a number by 0

25. If the answer to a division problem is not a whole number, the number(s) leftover_____
    a. are called the Order Property
    b. are called the denominators
    c. are called the remainder

26. You can figure out the 'mean' by_____
    a. multiply by the sum of two or more numbers
    b. adding up all the numbers in the data and then dividing by the number of numbers
    c. changing the grouping of numbers that are added together

27. The 'median' is the_____
    a. last number of the data set
    b. middle number of the data set
    c. first number of the data set

28. The 'mode' is the number_____
    a. that appears equal times
    b. that appears the least
    c. that appears the most

29. Range is the_____
    a. difference between the less than equal to number and the highest number.
    b. difference between the highest number and the highest number.
    c. difference between the lowest number and the highest number

30. Please Excuse My Dear Aunt Sally: What it means in the Order of Operations is____
    a. Parentheses, Exponents, Multiplication and Division, and Addition and Subtraction
    b. Parentheses, Equal, Multiplication and Decimal, and Addition and Subtraction
    c. Parentheses, Ellipse, Multiplication and Data, and Addition and Subtraction

31. A ratio is_____
    a. a way to show a relationship or compare two numbers of the same kind
    b. short way of saying that you want to multiply something by itself
    c. he sum of the relationship a times x, a times y, and a times z

32. Variables are things_____
    a. that can change or have different values
    b. when something has an exponent
    c. the simplest form using fractions

33. Always perform the same operation to_____of the equation.
    a. when the sum is less than the operation
    b. both sides
    c. one side only

34. The slope intercept form uses the following equation:
    a. $y = mx + b$
    b. $y = x + ab$
    c. $x = mx + c$

35. The point-slope form uses the following equation:

    a. $y - y_1 = m(y - x_2)$

    b. $y - y_1 = m(x - x_1)$

    c. $x - y_2 = m(x - x_1)$

36. Numbers in an algebraic expression that are not variables are called____

    a. Square

    b. Coefficient

    c. Proportional

37. A coordinate system is _____

    a. a type of cubed square

    b. a coordinate reduced to another proportion plane

    c. a two-dimensional number line

38. Horizontal axis is called_____

    a. h-axis

    b. x-axis

    c. y-axis

39. Vertical axis is called____

    a. v-axis

    b. y-axis

    c. x-axis

40. Equations and inequalities are both mathematical sentences____

    a. has y and x variables as points on a graph

    b. reduced ratios to their simplest form using fractions

    c. formed by relating two expressions to each other

Occupation **Lawyer, university administrator, writer,**

BORN DATE: **January 27, 1954**   Nationality **American**

DEATH DATE: **still alive and well**   Education **Princeton & Harvard University**   Children **2 girls**

Childhood and Family Background Facts

Born as Mary Robinson in Chicago, Illinois.

Dad's name John Robinson III & mom's name Rose Robinson.

One brother named Malcolm Robinson, he's a college basketball coach.

Her great-great-great-grandmother, Cindy Shields, was born into slavery in South Carolina.

Her childhood home was in New York.

Her great-aunt who was a piano teacher, taught her how to play the piano.

Work and Career Facts

- First job was babysitting.
- Mary majored in sociology at Princeton, where she graduated with honors, and went to Harvard Law School.
- She once worked in public service as an assistant to the mayor.
- She was the Vice President of Community and External Affairs at the University of Chicago Medical Center.

Friends, Social Life and Other Interesting Facts

- When she was a teen, she became friends with Kim Jackson.
- Her college bestie Suzanne Alele died from cancer at a young age in 1990.
- Her two favorite children's books: "Goodnight Moon" and "Where the Wild Things Are."
- Celebrity Crush: Denzel & Will Smith

Children, Marriage or Significant Relationships

- She suffered a heartbreaking miscarriage.
- Gave birth to two beautiful daughters Monica and Jennifer.
- She met her husband Tom when she was assigned to be his mentor when he was a summer associate at the law firm she worked at.

Did you enjoy researching this person?

Rating: ☆ ☆ ☆ ☆ ☆

RESEARCH: Galileo Galilei

DATE_____

Occupation _____

BORN DATE:_____ Nationality_____

DEATH DATE:_____ Education _____ #Children _____

Childhood and Family Background Facts

Work and Career Facts

Children, Marriage and or Significant Relationships

Friends, Social Life and Other Interesting Facts

Did you enjoy researching this person?

Give a Rating: ☆ ☆ ☆ ☆ ☆

Step 1: Double-check that the bottom numbers (the denominators) are the same.
Step 2: Add the top numbers (the numerators), then place that answer over the denominator
Step 3: Reduce the fraction to its simplest form (if possible)

Score : _____

Date : _____

Adding Fractions

1) $\dfrac{5}{7} + \dfrac{4}{7} = \dfrac{9}{7} = 1\dfrac{2}{7}$

2) $\dfrac{2}{8} + \dfrac{5}{8} =$

3) $\dfrac{6}{7} + \dfrac{4}{7} =$

4) $\dfrac{5}{4} + \dfrac{3}{4} =$

5) $\dfrac{1}{8} + \dfrac{3}{8} =$

6) $\dfrac{2}{6} + \dfrac{5}{6} =$

7) $\dfrac{2}{6} + \dfrac{2}{6} =$

8) $\dfrac{5}{4} + \dfrac{3}{4} =$

9) $\dfrac{8}{8} + \dfrac{6}{8} =$

10) $\dfrac{3}{7} + \dfrac{5}{7} =$

11) $\dfrac{7}{9} + \dfrac{1}{9} =$

12) $\dfrac{3}{9} + \dfrac{6}{9} =$

13) $\dfrac{2}{7} + \dfrac{4}{7} =$

14) $\dfrac{3}{6} + \dfrac{2}{6} =$

15) $\dfrac{3}{6} + \dfrac{5}{6} =$

The factors of a number are the numbers that add up to the original number when multiplied together. Factors of 8, for example, could be 2 and 4 because 2 * 4 equals 8.

Find the Greatest Common Factor for each number pair.

1)   15 , 3   ___3___

2)   24 , 12   _____

3)   10 , 4   _____

4)   40 , 4   _____

5)   8 , 40   _____

6)   10 , 4   _____

7)   12 , 20   _____

8)   5 , 20   _____

9)   8 , 2   _____

10)   24 , 40   _____

11)   6 , 8   _____

12)   10 , 3   _____

13)   8 , 6   _____

14)   24 , 10   _____

15)   24 , 12   _____

16)   40 , 24   _____

17)   8 , 10   _____

18)   10 , 20   _____

19)   2 , 3   _____

20)   6 , 12   _____

Step 1: List or write ALL the factors of each number.

Step 2: Identify the common factors.

Step 3: After identifying the common factors, select or choose the number which has the largest value. This number will be your Greatest Common Factor (GCF).

Example:
12, 18

Factors of 12: 1, 2, 3, 4, 6, 12
Factors of 18: 1, 2, 3, 6, 9, 18

What is the Greatest Common Factor?
The GCF of 12 and 18 is 6. That's it!

GRADE_____

DATE_____   **RESEARCH: Marie Curie**

Occupation _____

BORN DATE:_____   Nationality_____

DEATH DATE:_____   Education_____   #Children_____

Childhood and Family Background Facts

Work and Career Facts

Children, Marriage and or Significant Relationships

Friends, Social Life and Other Interesting Facts

Did you enjoy researching this person?

Give a Rating: ☆ ☆ ☆ ☆ ☆

The factors of a number are the numbers that add up to the original number when multiplied together. Factors of 8, for example, could be 2 and 4 because 2 * 4 equals 8.

List All of the Prime Factors for each number.

1) 38   **2, 19** _____

2) 49   _____

3) 35   _____

4) 25   _____

5) 15   _____

6) 44   _____

7) 32   _____

8) 48   _____

9) 22   _____

10) 21   _____

11) 30   _____

12) 20   _____

13) 39   _____

14) 14   _____

15) 12   _____

16) 26   _____

17) 46   _____

18) 40   _____

19) 24   _____

20) 10   _____

The term "prime factorization" refers to the process of determining which prime numbers multiply to produce the original number.

Step 1 : Divide the given number in two factors.

Step 2 : Now divide these two factors into other two multiples.

Step 3 : Repeat the step 2 until we reach all prime factors.

Step 4 : All the prime factors so obtained collectively known as prime factors of given number. In order to cross check; multiply all the prime factors, you must get the given number.

Find the Prime Factors of the Numbers

1)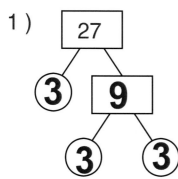

Prime Factors

_ x _ x _ = 27

2)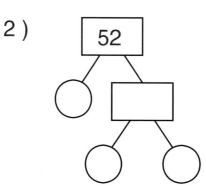

Prime Factors

_ x _ x _ = 52

3)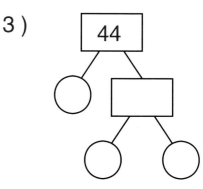

Prime Factors

_ x _ x _ = 44

4)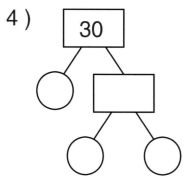

Prime Factors

_ x _ x _ = 30

5)

Prime Factors

_ x _ x _ x _ = 24

6)

Prime Factors

_ x _ x _ = 28

DATE_____   **RESEARCH: Andrew Jackson**

Occupation _____

BORN DATE:_____   Nationality_____

DEATH DATE:_____   Education_____   #Children _____

Childhood and Family Background Facts

Work and Career Facts

Children, Marriage and or Significant Relationships

Friends, Social Life and Other Interesting Facts

Did you enjoy researching this person?

Give a Rating: ☆ ☆ ☆ ☆ ☆

Numerical Cognition Exercise
Rearranging Digits

Rearrange each set of numbers to produce the largest possible number.

1) 399   **993**   _____

2) 744   _____

3) 488   _____

4) 616   _____

5) 734   _____

6) 846   _____

7) 844   _____

8) 345   _____

9) 959   _____

10) 559   _____

Rearrange each set of numbers to make the smallest number possible.

1) 897   **789**   _____

2) 696   _____

3) 825   _____

4) 135   _____

5) 751   _____

6) 149   _____

7) 862   _____

8) 212   _____

9) 557   _____

10) 675   _____

Numerical Cognition Exercise
Rearranging Digits

Rearrange each set of numbers to produce the largest possible number.

1) 1,182 **8,211** _____

2) 1,549 _____

3) 5,366 _____

4) 3,869 _____

5) 2,853 _____

6) 7,769 _____

7) 7,521 _____

8) 8,146 _____

9) 8,161 _____

10) 7,769 _____

Rearrange each set of numbers to make the smallest number possible.

1) 7,816 **1,678** _____

2) 3,827 _____

3) 4,946 _____

4) 5,938 _____

5) 1,627 _____

6) 6,636 _____

7) 8,176 _____

8) 9,222 _____

9) 2,172 _____

10) 5,366 _____

GRADE_____

DATE_____ **RESEARCH: King Arthur**

Occupation _____

BORN DATE:_____ Nationality_____

DEATH DATE:_____ Education_____ #Children _____

Childhood and Family Background Facts

Work and Career Facts

Children, Marriage and or Significant Relationships

Friends, Social Life and Other Interesting Facts

Did you enjoy researching this person?

Give a Rating: ☆ ☆ ☆ ☆ ☆

TIME

What time is on the clock?   _____

What time was it 1 hour ago?   _____

What time was it 3 hours and 40 minutes ago?   _____

What time will it be in 4 hours and 20 minutes?   _____

What time is on the clock?   _____

What time was it 2 hours ago?   _____

What time will it be in 3 hours ?   _____

What time will it be in 4 hours and 20 minutes?   _____

What time is on the clock?   _____

What time was it 1 hour ago?   _____

What time was it 3 hours and 20 minutes ago?   _____

What time will it be in 2 hours ?   _____

What time is on the clock?   _____

What time will it be in 3 hours and 20 minutes?   _____

What time was it 2 hours ago?   _____

What time was it 1 hour ago?   _____

Find the Missing Addends.

1) $59 = \_\_ + 40$

2) $19 + \_\_ = 36$

3) $34 + \_\_ = 51$

4) $14 + \_\_ = 41$

5) $\_\_ + 28 = 53$

6) $33 = \_\_ + 18$

7) $57 = \_\_ + 40$

8) $27 + \_\_ = 42$

9) $\_\_ + 10 = 45$

10) $65 = 34 + \_\_$

11) $27 + \_\_ = 53$

12) $47 = \_\_ + 27$

13) $43 = \_\_ + 15$

14) $11 + \_\_ = 24$

15) $40 = \_\_ + 15$

16) $\_\_ + 36 = 58$

17) $72 = 33 + \_\_$

18) $38 = 16 + \_\_$

19) $\_\_ + 21 = 37$

20) $13 + \_\_ = 50$

21) $\_\_ + 23 = 51$

22) $\_\_ + 18 = 46$

23) $\_\_ + 32 = 52$

24) $57 = 22 + \_\_$

25) $37 + \_\_ = 75$

26) $34 = \_\_ + 19$

27) $28 = 10 + \_\_$

28) $66 = 33 + \_\_$

29) $20 + \_\_ = 53$

30) $29 = 19 + \_\_$

TIME

What time is on the clock?   _____

What time will it be in 7 hours and 15 minutes?   _____

What time was it 3 hours and 45 minutes ago?   _____

What time will it be in 1 hour and 30 minutes?   _____

What time is on the clock?   _____

What time will it be in 7 hours ?   _____

What time was it 4 hours and 45 minutes ago?   _____

What time will it be in 6 hours and 15 minutes?   _____

What time is on the clock?   _____

What time will it be in 9 hours and 45 minutes?   _____

What time was it 8 hours ago?   _____

What time will it be in 1 hour and 30 minutes?   _____

What time is on the clock?   _____

What time will it be in 2 hours ?   _____

What time was it 7 hours and 15 minutes ago?   _____

What time will it be in 1 hour and 45 minutes?   _____

GRADE_____

DATE_____   **RESEARCH: Mother Teresa**

Occupation _____

BORN DATE:_____   Nationality_____

DEATH DATE:_____   Education_____   #Children _____

Childhood and Family Background Facts

Work and Career Facts

Children, Marriage and or Significant Relationships

Friends, Social Life and Other Interesting Facts

Did you enjoy researching this person?

Give a Rating: ☆ ☆ ☆ ☆ ☆

Social Studies Vocabulary 8

Choose the best answer to each question.

1. The workplace where people labor long hours for very low pay.
   a. Factory
   b. Sweatshop

2. To make plain or understandable; to give reasons for.
   a. Explain
   b. Interpret

3. What is the meaning of the word "Evaluate"?
   a. to examine and judge the significance, worth or condition of or value of
   b. to observe or inspect carefully or critically

4. The process by which an immigrant becomes a citizen.
   a. Dual Citizenship
   b. Naturalization

5. What is the meaning of the word "Draft"?
   a. selection of people who would be forced to serve in the military
   b. a person who enlists in military service by free will

6. A conference between the highest-ranking officials of different nations.
   a. Diplomatic Conference
   b. Summit Meeting

7. Select the correct meaning of the word "Identify".
   a. to recognize by or divide into classes
   b. to establish the essential character of

8. A person who flees his or her homeland to seek safety elsewhere.
   a. Immigrant
   b. Refugee

9. To make clear or obvious by using the examples or comparisons.
   a. Illustrate
   b. Demonstrate

10. To investigate closely; to examine critically
    a. Scrutinize
    b. Analyze

11. Select the correct meaning of the word "Laissez Fair".
    a. literally means "hands off"; business principle advocating an economy free of governmental business regulations
    b. an economic system whereby monetary goods are owned by individuals or companies.

12. The theory that Earth's atmosphere is warming up as a result of air pollution, causing ecological problems.
    a. Global Warming
    b. Climate Change

Social Studies Vocabulary IV

Choose the best answer to each question.

1. Political movement of the late 1800's favoring greater government regulation of business, graduated income tax and greater political involvement by the people
   a. Socialism
   b. Populism

2. To arrange in a systematic way.
   a. Manage
   b. Organize

3. Protests in which people sit in a particular place or business and refuse to leave.
   a. Strike
   b. Sit-In

4. An index based on the amount of goods, services, education, and leisure time that a people have.
   a. Standard of Living
   b. Quality of Life

5. Combination of businesses joining together to limit competition within an industry.
   a. Trust
   b. Monopolies

6. The factors that cause people to leave an area. (e.x. famine, war, political upheaval).
   a. Push factors
   b. Pull factors

7. The factors that attract people to a new area (e.x. jobs, freedom, family).
   a. Pull factors
   b. Push factors

8. What is the meaning of the word "Stock"?
   a. a legal entity that holds and manages assets on behalf of another individual or entity
   b. a share in a business

9. What is the meaning of the word "Suburb"?
   a. a community located within commuting distance of a city
   b. a community that's in a city or town

10. What is the meaning of the word "Recession"?
    a. a short term mild depression in which business slows and some workers lose their jobs
    b. an increase in the price of products and services over time in an economy

11. The movement of population from farms to city.
    a. Industrialization
    b. Urbanization

12. A belief that one's own ethnic group is superior to others.
    a. Ethnocentrism
    b. Ethnorelativism

Social Studies Vocabulary II

Choose the best answer to each question.

1	Solar Energy	an idea that supreme governing power belongs to the voters.	A
2	Naturalization	person who works to reduce pollution and protect the natural environment.	B
3	Restate	nonviolent opposition to a government policy or law by refusing to comply with it.	C
4	Totalitarian State	paper money issued by the federal government during the Civil War.	D
5	Inflation	program in areas such as employment and education to provide more opportunities for members of groups that faced discrimination in the past.	E
6	Environmentalist	manufacturing process, developed by Henry Ford in the 1920's, whereby factory workers engage in specific and repetitive tasks.	F
7	Greenbacks	power source derived from the sun.	G
8	Assembly Line	sharp rise in prices and decrease in the value of money.	H
9	Détente	easing of tensions between nations.	I
10	Affirmative Action	a country where a single party controls the government and every aspect of the loves of people.	J
11	Civil Disobedience	to say again in a slightly different way.	K
12	Popular Sovereignty	The process by which an immigrant becomes a citizen.	L

GRADE_____

DATE_____   **RESEARCH: Eli Whitney**

Occupation _____

BORN DATE:_____   Nationality_____

DEATH DATE:_____   Education_____   #Children _____

Childhood and Family Background Facts

Work and Career Facts

Children, Marriage and or Significant Relationships

Friends, Social Life and Other Interesting Facts

Did you enjoy researching this person?

Give a Rating: ☆ ☆ ☆ ☆ ☆

Social Studies Vocabulary XV

Score: _____

Date: _____

Choose the best answer to each question.

1	Primary source	products made in one country and going to another.	A
2	Rural	Two house law-making body.	B
3	Bicameral Legislature	Central government	C
4	Act	group of elected officials that make laws (each state has two).	D
5	Suffrage	Native American word to describe the Iroquois people.	E
6	Tariff	law	F
7	Senate	highly developed level of cultural and technological development.	G
8	Federal	to make a country larger.	H
9	Haudenosaunee	firsthand information about people or events.	I
10	Import	tax	J
11	Civilization	vote	K
12	Exports	country or farmland.	L
13	Expansion	trade product brought into a country.	M

Shakespeare: Romeo and Juliet

Across

1. an enemy or opponent
2. something surrendered or subject to surrender as punishment for a crime, an offense, an error, or a breach of contract
3. loathsome; disgusting
7. to expel or banish a person from his or her country
8. to feel sorry for; regret
12. a small container, as of glass, for holding liquids
15. long and tiresome

Down

3. boldly courageous; brave; stout-hearted
5. to express disapproval of; scold; reproach
6. a musician, singer, or poet
9. an expression of grief or sorrow
10. to flood or to overwhelm
11. a malicious, false, or defamatory statement or report
13. infliction of injury, harm, humiliation, or the like, on a person by another who has been harmed by that person; violent revenge
14. to read through with thoroughness or care

VALIANT   LAMENT   SLANDER
MINSTREL   PERUSE
TEDIOUS   CHIDE   EXILE
VILE   FORFEIT   INUNDATE
REPENT   ADVERSARY   VIAL
VENGEANCE

GRADE_____

DATE_____

RESEARCH: Nikola Tesla

Occupation _____

BORN DATE:_____ Nationality _____

DEATH DATE:_____ Education _____ #Children _____

Childhood and Family Background Facts

Work and Career Facts

Children, Marriage and or Significant Relationships

Friends, Social Life and Other Interesting Facts

Did you enjoy researching this person?

Give a Rating: ☆ ☆ ☆ ☆ ☆

Science Vocabulary 6

Choose the best answer to each question.

1	Precipitation	Earth's solid, rocky surface.	A
2	Inner Core	The movement of the Earth's continents relative to each other by appearing to drift across the ocean bed	B
3	Continental Drift	Process of water vapor changing to liquid water	C
4	Crust	Inner most layer composed of solid iron and nickel. Stays solid due to the pressure of the layers above it.	D
5	Asthenosphere	Continuous movement of water from the air to the earth and back again.	E
6	Condensation	Made up of mostly molten (melted) iron and nickel.	F
7	Mantle	Process of water falling from clouds to earth in the form of rain, sleet, show, or hail	G
8	Core	Solid layer of the mantle beneath lithosphere; made of mantle rock that flows very slowly allowing tectonic plates to move on top of it.	H
9	Plate Tectonics	Scientific theory that describes the large-scale motions of Earth's lithosphere.	I
10	Water Cycle	The layer of Earth beneath the crust.	J

Science Vocabulary 5

Choose the best answer to each question.

1. Energy that all objects have that increases as the object's temperature increases.
   a. Thermal Energy
   b. Potential Energy

2. Energy carried by electric current.
   a. Electrical Energy
   b. Radiant Energy

3. Transfer of heat by the flow of material. Heat rises and cool air sinks.
   a. Conduction
   b. Convection

4. What is the meaning of the word "Radiant Energy"?
   a. Energy that all objects have that increases as the object's temperature increases.
   b. Energy carried by light.

5. Transfer of energy that occurs when molecules bump into each other.
   a. Convection
   b. Conduction

6. The crust and the rigid part of Earth's mantle. Divided into tectonic plates.
   a. Lithosphere
   b. Asthenosphere

7. What is the meaning of the word "Potential Energy"?
   a. Energy stored in an object due to its position.
   b. Energy stored in chemical bonds.

8. Energy contained in atomic nuclei; splitting uranium nuclei by nuclear fission.
   a. Nuclear Energy
   b. Thermal Energy

9. States that energy can change its form but is never created or destroyed.
   a. Law of Conservation of Mass
   b. Law of Conservation of Energy

10. What is the meaning of the word "Chemical Energy"?
    a. Energy stored in chemical bonds.
    b. Energy stored in an object due to its position.

GRADE_____

DATE_____   **RESEARCH:**

Occupation _____

BORN DATE:_____   Nationality_____

DEATH DATE:_____   Education_____   #Children _____

Childhood and Family Background Facts

Work and Career Facts

Children, Marriage and or Significant Relationships

Friends, Social Life and Other Interesting Facts

Did you enjoy researching this person?

Give a Rating: ☆ ☆ ☆ ☆ ☆

Science Vocabulary 4

Choose the best answer to each question.

1. Family of elements in the periodic table that have similar physical or chemical properties.
   a. Group
   b. Subgroup

2. Table of elements organized into groups and periods by increasing atomic number.
   a. Periodic Table
   b. Chemical Elements

3. It is the property of many substances that give the ability to do work; many forms of energy (i.e., light, heat, electricity, sound)
   a. Energy
   b. Power

4. Number of protons in the nucleus of an atom of a given element.
   a. Mass Number
   b. Atomic Number

5. The sum of neutrons and protons in the nucleus of an atom.
   a. Mass Number
   b. Atomic Number

6. Force of attraction between all objects in the universe.
   a. Gravity
   b. Friction

7. What is the meaning of the word "Isotope"?
   a. Atoms of the same element that have different numbers of neutrons.
   b. An atom or molecule with a positive or negative charge.

8. What is the meaning of the word "Period"?
   a. Vertical row of elements in the periodic table.
   b. Horizontal row of elements in the periodic table.

9. What is the meaning of the word "Tides"?
   a. Rise and fall of ocean water levels.
   b. Ae formed because of the winds blowing over the surface of the ocean.

10. What is the meaning of the word "Kinetic Energy"?
    a. Energy an object has due to its motion.
    b. A form of energy that has the potential to do work but is not actively doing work or applying any force on any other objects.

Science: Titanium (Ti) Element

Titanium is the first element in the periodic table's fourth column. It is a transition metal. Titanium atoms contain 22 protons and 22 electrons.

Titanium is a complex, light, silvery metal under normal conditions. It can be brittle at room temperature, but it becomes more bendable and pliable as the temperature rises.

Titanium's high strength-to-weight ratio is one of its most desirable properties. This means it is both extremely strong and lightweight. Titanium is double the strength of aluminum but only 60% heavier. It is also as strong as steel but weighs a fraction of the weight.

Compared to other metals, titanium is relatively non-reactive and highly resistant to corrosion caused by different metals and chemicals such as acids and oxygen. As a result, it has relatively low thermal and electrical conductivity.

Titanium is not found in nature as a pure element but rather as a compound found in the Earth's crust as a component of many minerals. According to the International Atomic Energy Agency, it is the ninth most prevalent element in the Earth's crust. Rutile and ilmenite are the two most essential minerals for titanium mining. Australia, South Africa, and Canada are the top producers of these ores.

Titanium is mostly used in the form of titanium dioxide (TiO2). Tio2 is a white powder used in various industrial applications such as white paint, white paper, white polymers, and white cement.

Metals like iron, aluminum, and manganese are combined with titanium to create strong and lightweight alloys that can be utilized in spacecraft, naval vessels, missiles, and armor plating. Due to its corrosion resistance, it is particularly well-suited for seawater applications.

The biocompatibility of titanium is another valuable property of the metal. This indicates that the human body will not reject it. Together with its strength, durability, and lightweight, titanium is a good material for medical applications. It is utilized in various applications, including hip and dental implants. Titanium is also utilized in the manufacture of jewelry, such as rings and watches.

Reverend William Gregor recognized titanium as a new element for the first time in 1791. As a hobby, the English clergyman was fascinated by minerals. He coined the term menachanite for the element. M.H. Kalproth, a German chemist, eventually altered the name to titanium. M. A. Hunter, an American scientist, was the first to create pure titanium in 1910.

Titanium is named after the Greek gods Titans.

Titanium has five stable isotopes: titanium-46, titanium-47, titanium-48, titanium-49, and titanium-50. The isotope titanium-48 accounts for the vast bulk of titanium found in nature.

1. Titanium has five stable ____.
   a. isotopes
   b.

2. Titanium is the first element in the periodic table's ____ column.
   a. 4rd
   b. fourth

3. Titanium is a transition ____.
   a. metal
   b.

4. Titanium is mostly used in the form of ____ (TiO2).
   a. titanium dioxide
   b. dioxide oxygen

DATE_____   **RESEARCH:**

Occupation _____

BORN DATE:_____ Nationality_____

DEATH DATE:_____ Education_____ #Children _____

Childhood and Family Background Facts

Work and Career Facts

Children, Marriage and or Significant Relationships

Friends, Social Life and Other Interesting Facts

Did you enjoy researching this person?

Give a Rating: ☆ ☆ ☆ ☆ ☆

Proofreading Interpersonal Skills: Peer Pressure

In this activity, you'll see lots of grammatical *errors*. Correct all the grammar mistakes you see.

> There are **30** mistakes in this passage. 3 capitals missing. 5 unnecessary capitals. 3 unnecessary apostrophes. 6 punctuation marks missing or incorrect. 13 incorrectly spelled words.

Tony is mingling with a large group of what he considers to be the school's cool kids. Suddenly, someone in the group begins mocking Tony's friend Rob, who walks with a limp due to a physical dasability.

They begin to imitate rob's limping and Call him 'lame cripple' and other derogatory terms. Although Tony disapproves of their behavior, he does not want to risk being excluded from the group, and thus joins them in mocking Rob.

Peer pressure is the influence exerted on us by member's of our social group. It can manifest in a variety of ways and can lead to us engaging in behaviors we would not normally consider such as Tony joining in and mocking his friend Rob.

However, peer pressure is not always detrimental. Positive peer pressure can motivate us to make better chioces, such as studying harder, staying in school, or seeking a better job. Whan others influence us to make poor Choices, such as smoking, using illicit drugs, or bullying, we succumb to negative peer pressure. We all desire to belong to a group and fit in, so Developing strategies for resisting peer pressure when necessary can be beneficial.

Tony and his friends are engaging in bullying by moking Rob. Bullying is defined as persistent, unwanted. aggressive behavior directed toward another person. It is moust prevalent in school-aged children but can also aphfect adults. Bullying can take on a variety of forms, including the following:

· Verbil bullying is when someone is called names, threatened, or taunted verbally.
· Bullying is physical in nature - hitting spitting, tripping, or poshing someone.
· Social Bullying is intentionally excluding Someone from activities spreading rumors, or embarrassing sumeone.

· Cyberbullying is the act of verbally or socially bullying someone via the internet, such as through social media sites.

Peer pressure exerts a significant influence on an individual's decision to engage in bullying behavoir. In Tony's case, even though Rob is a friend and tony would never consider mocking his disability, his desire to belong to a group outweighs his willingness to defend his friend

Peer pressure is a strong force that is exerted on us by our social group members. Peer pressure is classified into two types: negative peer pressure, which results in poor decision-making, and positive peer pressure, which influences us to make the correct choices. Adolescents are particularly susceptible to peer pressure because of their desire to fit in

Peer pressure can motivate someone to engage in bullying behaviors such as mocking someone, threatening to harm them, taunting them online, or excluding them from an activity. Each year, bullying affect's an astounding 3.2 million school-aged children. Severil strategies for avoiding peer pressure bullying include the following:

- consider your actions by surrounding yourself with good company.
- Acquiring the ability to say no to someone you trust.

Speak up - bullying is never acceptable and is taken extramely seroiusly in schools and the workplace. If someone is attempting to convince you to bully another person, speaking with a trusted adult such as a teacher, coach, counselor, or coworker can frequently help put thing's into perspective and highlight the issue.

Julius Caesar Roman Dictator

Julius Caesar played a big part in the rise of the Roman Empire and made social and governmental changes. Caesar was not a noble when he was born in Rome, Italy, in July of 100 BC. His parents were not powerful people in politics, and they were not rich. Caesar's story of how he went from being a low-class citizen to becoming a Dictator is one of hard work, inspiration, and personal triumph.

The Rome of Caesar's youth was not stable at all. A few years after leaving Rome and joining the military, Caesar returned to Rome to get involved in politics. This is how it worked: He became a public speaker and advocated for the law. Because of his passionate speech, he was well-known. Most of the time, he spoke out against corrupt politicians. It took a long time, but Caesar was eventually elected to the government office. He started working his way up the political ladder.

He was chosen to be the Chief Priest of the Roman state religion when he was first chosen for the job. Afterward, he was chosen to run Spain in 62 BC. This was a big success. While in Spain, he overthrew two tribes and finished his time there well.

Caesar returned to Rome to run a counsel electoral campaign. During that election, Caesar worked closely with Pompey, a former military officer, and Crassus, one of the wealthiest men in Rome, to help them win. This partnership worked out well for Caesar because it gave him power and money. The First Triumvirate was the name given to the three men because of how close they were.

Caesar was elected easily and made a lot of laws that people liked. He was chosen to run Northern Italy and parts of southeast Europe in the next step.

The 13 Legione led Caesar to conquer Gaul, now France and Belgium. He also punished his enemies by cutting off their hands to show them that they were not welcome in the city. In the end, Caesar was known for the way he treated his enemies.

In 50 BC, the Senate, led by Pompey, told Caesar to go home because his term as governor had ended, so he had to leave. It took Pompey a long time to change his mind about Caesar, but he did.

Caesar went to war with Pompey. Caesar took over Italy and pushed Pompey into Egypt, where Pompey was killed. When Caesar was in Egypt, he had an affair with Cleopatra, who gave birth to Caesar's only known biological son, Caesarion, born after the affair.

Crassus was defeated and killed in a battle in Syria.

They overthrew their king in 509 BC, who had all the power and could rule without the Senate or citizen votes. A system of checks and balances like the US one was put into place to make sure the new government worked well in Rome, which was democratic at one point. However, the Roman founders also included an "emergency clause" that said that the Senate could vote to give absolute power to one man as a dictator when the country was in trouble. This way, the Senate could have strong leaders to help them get through that time. Many people were talking about war and chaos in Rome by 48 BC. Much political corruption took place. Finally, the Senate agreed that Caesar should be made the new ruler.

During Caesar's time as ruler, he made significant progress for Rome. Caesar changed the debt laws in Rome, which freed up a lot of money for the people. In addition, Caesar changed the Senate and election rules.

Most importantly, Caesar made changes to the Roman calendar. The calendar used to be based on the phases of the moon. There were more months in the calendar in this newly updated Julian Calendar. It was set to have 365 days and had a leap day every four years at the end of February. It's almost the same as the Western calendar we use today.

During his time as dictator, Caesar became more and more interested in power. They were worried that Caesar would not step down as dictator when the time came. Then, Marcus Brutus came up with a plan to kill Caesar on the Ides of March (the 15th) in 44 BC. Caesar was going to be killed at a meeting of the Senate at the Theater of Pompey.

It is thought that 60 or more men were involved. Caesar was stabbed 23 times on the Senate floor, and it is thought that there were more than 60 people involved.

During the years following the death of Caesar, there were five civil wars. These wars helped to form the Roman Empire.

Caesar was swiftly martyred and, two years later, became the first Roman to be worshiped.

When Caesar was alive, he was married three times. He married Cornelia Cinnilla for the first time when he was 18. (married 83 BC - 69 BC.) Afterward, Julia married Pompey and gave birth to a child, but she didn't live long enough to see it grow up. She was his second wife (married 67 BC - 61 BC.) His third wife was Calpurnia Pisonis, and they had a daughter together (married 59 BC - 44 BC.) Caesar had an affair with Cleopatra, which led to a son named Caesarion. Since it was an extramarital relationship, Caesarion was never recognized as Caesar's son by the Roman government.

Caesar named his great-nephew Octavian in his will. Octavian became the first Roman emperor, Augustus Caesar, in the end.

1. **Caesar made changes to the Roman _____.**
   a. history
   b. calendar

2. **Julius Caesar parents were the most powerful people in politics.**
   a. True
   b. False

3. **Julius Caesar became a public speaker and advocated for the _____.**
   a. government
   b. law

4. **Julius was chosen to run Spain in _____ BC**
   a. 62
   b. 32

5. **Caesar worked closely with _____, a former military officer, and _____, one of the wealthiest men in Rome**
   a. Crassus, Poindexter
   b. Pompey, Crassus

6. **Caesar changed the debt laws in ___.**
   a. Rome
   b. Egypt

7. **_____ came up with a plan to kill Caesar on the Ides of March.**
   a. Marcus Brutus
   b. Mark Buccaning

8. **What wars helped to form the Roman Empire?**
   a. civil wars
   b. World War II

GRADE_____

DATE_____   **RESEARCH: Charles Darwin**

Occupation _____

BORN DATE:_____ Nationality_____

DEATH DATE:_____ Education_____ #Children _____

Childhood and Family Background Facts

Work and Career Facts

Children, Marriage and or Significant Relationships

Friends, Social Life and Other Interesting Facts

Did you enjoy researching this person?

Give a Rating: ☆ ☆ ☆ ☆ ☆

Jackie Robinson: The First African-American Player In MLB

Score: _____

Date: _____

First, read over the entire passage(s). Then go back and fill in the blanks. You can skip the blanks you're unsure about and come back to them later.

Roosevelt	general	Pasadena	paved	Dodgers
honorable	Rookie	major	Texas	enthusiast
League	prejudice	batting	military	football

On January 31, 1919, in Cairo, Georgia, Jack _____ Robinson was born. There were five children in the family, and the youngest one was him. After Jackie was born, Jackie's father left the family, and he never returned. His mother, Millie, took care of him and his three brothers and one sister when they were young.

The family moved to _____, California, about a year after Jackie was born. Jackie was awed by his older brothers' prowess in sports as a child. Meanwhile, his brother Mack rose to prominence as a track star and Olympic silver medalist in the 200-meter dash.

Jackie was an avid sports _____. Like his older brother, he competed in track and field and other sports like football, baseball, and tennis. Football and baseball were two of his favorite sports to play. Throughout high school, Jackie was subjected to racism daily. Even though white teammates surrounded him, he felt like a second-class citizen off the field.

After high school, Jackie went to UCLA, where he excelled in track, baseball, _____, and basketball. To his credit, he was the first player at UCLA to receive all four varsity letters in the same season. The long jump was another event where he excelled at the NCAA level.

With the outbreak of World War II, Robinson's football career was over before it began. He was called up for _____ service. Jackie made friends with the legendary boxing champion Joe Lewis at basic training. Robinson was accepted into officer training school thanks to Joe's assistance.

After completing his officer training, Jackie was assigned to the 761st Tank Battalion at Fort Hood, _____. Only black soldiers were assigned to this battalion because they could not serve alongside white soldiers. When Jackie refused to move to the back of an army bus one day, he got into trouble. In 1944, he was discharged with an _____ discharge after nearly being expelled from the military.

Robinson began his professional baseball career with the Kansas City Monarchs soon after he was discharged from the military. The Negro Baseball _____ was home to the Monarchs. Black players were still not allowed to play in Major League Baseball at this time. Jackie performed well on the field. He was an outstanding shortstop, hitting .387 on average.

While playing for the Monarchs, Branch Rickey, the Dodgers' _____ manager, approached Jackie. Branch hoped that the Dodgers could win the pennant by signing an African-American player. Branch warned Robinson that he would encounter racial _____ when he first joined the Dodgers. Branch was looking for a person who could take insults without reacting. This famous exchange between Jackie and Branch occurred during their first conversation:

Jackie: "Are you looking for a Negro who is afraid to fight back, Mr. Rickey?"
Jackie: "Are you looking for a Negro who is afraid to fight back, Mr. Rickey?" Robinson, I'm looking for a baseball player who has the guts not to fight back."

For the Montreal Royals, Jackie first played in the minor leagues. He was constantly confronted with racism. Because of Jackie, the opposing team would occasionally fail to show up for games. Then there were the times when people would verbally abuse or throw objects at him. In the midst of all this, Jackie remained calm and focused on the game. He had a .349 batting average and was named the league's most valuable player.

Robinson was called up to play for the Brooklyn _____ at the start of the 1947 baseball season, and he did. On April 15, 1947, he became the first African-American to play in the sport's major leagues. Racially charged taunts were once again directed at Jackie from both fans and fellow players alike. Death threats were made against him. But Jackie had the courage not to fight back. He kept his word to Branch Rickey and dedicated himself solely to the game of baseball. The Dodgers won the pennant that year, and Jackie was named the team's _____ of the Year for his achievements.

Jackie Robinson was one of the best _____ league baseball players for the next ten years. During his lengthy career, his _____ average stood at.311, and he hit 137 home runs while also stealing 197 bases. Six times he was selected to the All-Star team, and in 1949 he was named the National League MVP.

Because of Jackie Robinson's groundbreaking work, other African-American players could play in the major leagues. He also _____ the way for racial integration in different facets of American life. He was inducted into the Baseball Hall of Fame in 1962. On October 24, 1972, Robinson suffered a heart attack and died.

GRADE_____

DATE_____

RESEARCH: Ludwig van Beethoven

Occupation _____

BORN DATE:_____ Nationality_____

DEATH DATE:_____ Education_____ #Children _____

Childhood and Family Background Facts

Work and Career Facts

Children, Marriage and or Significant Relationships

Friends, Social Life and Other Interesting Facts

Did you enjoy researching this person?

Give a Rating: ☆ ☆ ☆ ☆ ☆

Flamingo Bird Facts

Score: _____

Date: _____

First, read over the entire passage(s). Then go back and fill in the blanks. You can skip the blanks you're unsure about and come back to them later.

females	algae	vivid	coast	diet
prey	theory	top-heavy	wading	mudflats

Flamingos are the show stoppers of the avian world. Their long legs, bending beaks, and _____ orange hue make them a sight to behold. They're a popular attraction at zoos and nature preserves because they are fascinating to see up close.

Phoenicopterus ruber is the scientific name for the American Flamingo. They reach a height of 3 to 5 feet and a weight of 5 to 6 pounds at maturity. Males tend to be larger than _____ in general. Feathers of the common flamingo are typically pinkish red. Additionally, their pink feet and pink and white bill, which has a black tip, distinguish them.

Central and South America and the Caribbean are home to the American Flamingo. It can also be found in the Bahamas and Cuba, and the Yucatan Peninsula of Mexico's Caribbean coast. As far as Brazil, there are some that can be found on the northern _____. In addition, the Galapagos Islands have a population.

Lagoons and low-lying _____ or lakes are the preferred environments for the Flamingos. They like seeking food by wading across the water. They form enormous flocks, sometimes numbering in the tens of thousands.

Flamingos come in a variety of colors, including pink and orange. Carotenoids are responsible for the orange hue of several foods, such as carrots. Carrots would turn your skin and eyes orange if you just ate them. Flamingoes appear pink or orange because they eat _____ and small shellfish rich in carotenoids. They would lose their vibrant hue if they switched to a different _____.

Is it possible for flamingoes to fly? Yes. Flamingos can fly, even though we usually associate them with _____ in the water. Before they can take off, they have to run to build up their speed. They often fly in big groups.

Scientists don't know why Flamingos stand on one leg, but they have a few ideas. There is a rumor that it is to keep one leg warm. Because it's cold outside, they can keep one leg near their body to keep it warm. Another _____ is that they are drying out one leg at a time. A third idea argues that it aids them in deceiving their _____, as one leg resembles a plant more than two.

It doesn't matter the reason; these _____ birds can stand on one leg for long periods. They even sleep with one leg balanced on the ground!

Financial: Money, Stocks and Bonds

Tip: First, read the entire passage. After that, go back and fill in the blanks. You can skip the blanks you're unsure about and finish them later.

barter	coins	valuable	principal	exchange
obligation	gold	issued	shareholders	NASDAQ
economy	bankruptcy	golden	monetary	conditions

Three important _____ must be met in order for something to qualify as a financial asset. It has to be:

Something you can have
Something monetary in nature
A contractual claim provides the basis for that monetary value

That last condition may be difficult to grasp at first, but it will become clear in a few minutes.

As a result, financial assets differ from physical assets such as land or _____. You can touch and feel the actual physical asset with land and gold, but you can only touch and feel something (usually a piece of paper) that represents the asset of value with financial assets.

Money is a government-defined official medium of _____ that consists of cash and _____. Money, currency, cash, and legal tender all refer to the same thing. They are all symbols of a central bank's commitment to keeping money's value as stable as possible. Money is a financial asset because its value is derived from the faith and credit of the government that issued it, not from the paper or metal on which it is printed.

Money is obviously a _____ financial asset. We would all have to _____ with one another without a common medium of exchange, trading whatever goods and services we have for something else we need, or trade what we have for something else we could then trade with someone else who has what we need. Consider how complicated that can become!

Stock is another crucial financial asset in the US _____. Stock, like money, is simply a piece of paper that represents something of value. The something of value' represented by stock is a stake in a company. Stock is also known as 'equity' because you have a stake in its profits when you own stock in a company.

Consider little Jane's lemonade stand as the most basic example. Jane only has $4 to begin her business, but she requires $10. Jane's parents give her $3 in exchange for 30% of her business, a friend gives her $1 for 10%, and her brother gives her $2 in exchange for 20%. Jane, her parents, a friend, and her brother are now all _____ in her company.

That example, as simple as it is, accurately describes stock. The complexities arise when we attempt to assign a _____ value to that stock. A variety of factors determines a stock's value. One share of stock in one company does not equal one share of stock in another. The number of shares issued by each company, as well as the size and profitability of each company, will affect the value of your share. Anything that has an impact on a business, good or bad, will affect the stock price.

These are the most basic and fundamental factors that can influence the value of a share of stock. Individual stock prices are affected by macroeconomic trends as well. Thousands of books have been written in an attempt to discover the _____ rule that determines the exact value of a share of stock.

The value of a stock can fluctuate from minute to minute and even second to second. The New York Stock Exchange and _____ were the world's two largest stock exchanges in 2014. (both located in the United States).

Bonds are the final financial asset we'll look at. Bonds are, in essence, loans. When an organization, such as a company, a city or state, or even the federal government, requires funds, bonds can be _____. Bonds come in various forms, but they are all debt instruments in which the bondholder is repaid their _____ investment, plus interest, at some future maturity date.

The only way a bondholder's money is lost is if the entity that issued the bond declares _____. Bonds are generally safer investments than stocks because they are a legal _____ to repay debt, whereas stocks represent ownership, which can make or lose money.

GRADE_____

DATE_____

RESEARCH: Harriet Beecher Stowe

Occupation _____

BORN DATE:_____ Nationality _____

DEATH DATE:_____ Education _____ #Children _____

Childhood and Family Background Facts

Work and Career Facts

Children, Marriage and or Significant Relationships

Friends, Social Life and Other Interesting Facts

Did you enjoy researching this person?

Give a Rating: ☆ ☆ ☆ ☆ ☆

Boston Tea Party

First, read over the entire passage(s). Then go back and fill in the blanks. You can skip the blanks you're unsure about and come back to them later.

cargo	Indians	protest	hefty	leader
Parliament	displeasure	favorite	Harbor	pounds

Was it a big, boisterous tea party? Not at all. There was tea in the mix, but no one was drinking it. It was a _____ by the American Colonists against the British government that resulted in the Boston Tea Party. They boarded three trade ships in Boston _____ and threw the ships' _____ of tea into the ocean to show their anger at the government. Into the water, they threw 342 chests of tea. Some of the colonists dressed up as Mohawk _____, but they fooled no one. The British knew who had thrown away the tea.

First, it might seem like a silly idea to throw tea into the ocean dressed as Mohawks. But the people who lived in colonial America knew why they did this. Among the British, tea was a _____ drink. People who worked for the East India Trading company made a lot of money from it. They were told they could only buy tea from this one company in the colonies. This was a British company. They were also informed that the tea would be taxed at a _____ rate. The Tea Act was the name given to the tax that was levied on the sale of tea.

People in the colonies didn't think this was fair because they weren't represented in British _____ and didn't say how taxes were done. They asked that the tea be returned to Great Britain since they refused to pay taxes on it. As a result, they decided to toss the tea into the ocean as a form of protest against Britain's excessive taxes.

Historians wouldn't know for sure if the protest was planned or not. People in the town had met earlier that day to talk about the tea taxes and fight them. Samuel Adams was in charge of the meeting, which was significant. Samuel Adams was a key revolutionary _____ in Boston. Many people liked him because he could use public _____ with Parliament's power to tax the colonies to do good things for the country. The tea was destroyed, but no one is sure if Samuel Adams planned to do this. Instead, a group of people did it on their own because they were angry. In the future, Samuel Adams said that it was people defending their rights, not a group of people who were mad at each other. Although Adams did not participate in the Boston Tea Party, he was undoubtedly one of its planners.

It was, in fact, a lot of tea. The 342 containers had 90,000 _____ of tea in them! In today's money, that would be equivalent to around one million dollars in tea.

GRADE_____

DATE_____

RESEARCH: Captain James Cook

Occupation _____

BORN DATE:_____ Nationality _____

DEATH DATE:_____ Education _____ #Children _____

Childhood and Family Background Facts

Work and Career Facts

Children, Marriage and or Significant Relationships

Friends, Social Life and Other Interesting Facts

Did you enjoy researching this person?

Give a Rating: ☆ ☆ ☆ ☆ ☆

GRADE_____

DATE_____

RESEARCH: Benedict Arnold

Occupation _____

BORN DATE:_____ Nationality_____

DEATH DATE:_____ Education _____ #Children _____

Childhood and Family Background Facts

Work and Career Facts

Children, Marriage and or Significant Relationships

Friends, Social Life and Other Interesting Facts

Did you enjoy researching this person?

Give a Rating: ☆ ☆ ☆ ☆ ☆

Single Quadrant Ordered Pairs

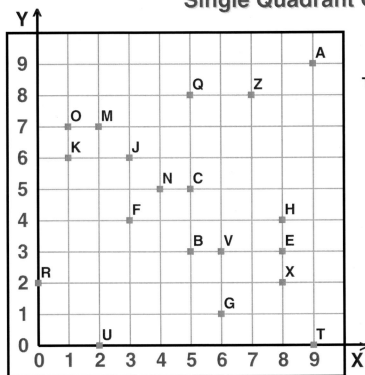

Tell what point is located at each ordered pair.

1) (8,3) _____   6) (1,6) _____

2) (9,9) _____   7) (4,5) _____

3) (8,2) _____   8) (0,2) _____

4) (6,3) _____   9) (9,0) _____

5) (6,1) _____   10) (5,8) _____

Write the ordered pair for each given point.

11) **B** _____   14) **Z** _____   17) **O** _____

12) **M** _____   15) **J** _____   18) **U** _____

13) **C** _____   16) **H** _____   19) **F** _____

Plot the following points on the coordinate grid.

20) **W** (7,6)   22) **L** (8,6)   24) **Y** (7,5)

21) **S** (7,1)   23) **D** (3,2)   25) **P** (4,8)

What is the Fraction of the Shaded Area ?

1) _____

2) _____

3) _____

4) _____

5) _____

6) _____

7) _____

8) _____

9) _____

10) _____

Shade the Figure with the Indicated Fraction.

11) $\dfrac{1}{2}$

12) $\dfrac{1}{4}$

13) $\dfrac{1}{5}$

14) $\dfrac{5}{8}$

15) $\dfrac{2}{8}$

16) $\dfrac{4}{8}$

17) $\dfrac{4}{5}$

18) $\dfrac{1}{8}$

19) $\dfrac{2}{4}$

20) $\dfrac{4}{5}$

Visually Adding Simple Fractions

1)

$$\frac{3}{11} \quad + \quad \frac{4}{11} \quad = \quad \text{———}$$

2)

$$\frac{1}{10} \quad + \quad \frac{6}{10} \quad = \quad \text{———}$$

3)

$$\frac{4}{11} \quad + \quad \frac{5}{11} \quad = \quad \text{———}$$

4)

$$\frac{3}{12} \quad + \quad \frac{6}{12} \quad = \quad \text{———}$$

5)

$$\frac{1}{4} \quad + \quad \frac{2}{4} \quad = \quad \text{———}$$

GRADE_____

DATE_____

RESEARCH: Dwight D. Eisenhower

Occupation _____

BORN DATE:_____ Nationality_____

DEATH DATE:_____ Education_____ #Children_____

Childhood and Family Background Facts

Work and Career Facts

Children, Marriage and or Significant Relationships

Friends, Social Life and Other Interesting Facts

Did you enjoy researching this person?

Give a Rating: ☆ ☆ ☆ ☆ ☆

ARTS Vocabulary Terms 3

Choose the best answer to each question.

1	India ink		A movement in the 19th century which bridged the "realist" tradition with the modern movements of the 20th century. The focus was on light and atmosphere.	A
2	Impressionism		A painting either on a wall or on a surface to be attached to a wall.	B
3	Kiln		Design, motif or symbol repeated over and over.	C
4	Linear perspective		French word for "small model". Used particularly by sculptors as a "sketch" of their work.	D
5	Marquette		A waterproof ink made from lampblack.	E
6	Medium		Light and dark tones of a singular color.	F
7	Monochrome		Oil based crayons.	G
8	Mural		Creating the illusion of depth on a picture plane with the use of lines and a vanishing point.	H
9	Newsprint		The surface used to dispense and mix paint on.	I
10	Oil pastel		A large "oven" used for firing clay work.	J
11	Palette		Newspaper stock used for sketching, preliminary drawings and printing.	K
12	Pattern		The process or material used in a work of art.	L

ARTS Vocabulary Terms 2

Choose the best answer to each question.

| 1 | Computer art | | Art made on a grand scale, involving the creation of a man-made environment such as architecture, sculpture, light or landscape. | A |

| 2 | Diptych | | Painting, usually an altarpiece, made up of hinged panels. | B |

| 3 | Earth colors | | Artwork based on the human form. | C |

| 4 | Eye-level | | Art made with the use of a computer program. | D |

| 5 | Environmental art | | Applying gold leaf to a painting or other surface. | E |

| 6 | Facade | | The horizontal line that distinguishes the sky from the earth, or the ground from the wall. The eye-level of the artists view. Also, where the vanishing point lies in a perspective drawing. | F |

| 7 | Figurative | | Dried clay forms that have not been fired. | G |

| 8 | Foreshortening | | Pigments made using earth (dirt) that contain metal oxides mixed with a binder such as glue | H |

| 9 | Gilding | | The front or face of a building. | I |

| 10 | Greenware | | A binder used in watercolors made from the gum of an acacia tree. | J |

| 11 | Gum Arabic | | The artists' view of where the perceived line or perspective came from. | K |

| 12 | Horizon line | | A rule in perspective to create the illusion of coming forward or receding into space | L |

GRADE_____

DATE_____

RESEARCH: Eleanor Roosevelt

Occupation _____

BORN DATE:_____ Nationality _____

DEATH DATE:_____ Education _____ #Children _____

Childhood and Family Background Facts

Work and Career Facts

Children, Marriage and or Significant Relationships

Friends, Social Life and Other Interesting Facts

Did you enjoy researching this person?

Give a Rating: ☆ ☆ ☆ ☆ ☆

ARTS Vocabulary Terms 1

Choose the best answer to each question.

1	The arrangement of the parts of a work of art.	Binder	A
2	Coarse cloth or heavy fabric that must be stretched and primed to use for painting, particularly for oil paintings.	Chiaroscuro	B
3	The use of found objects or three-dimensional objects to create a work of art.	Assemblage	C
4	Colors next to each other on the color wheel.	Analogous colors	D
5	An arrangement of shapes adhered to a background.	Bisque	E
6	The organization of colors on a wheel. Used to help understand color schemes.	Canvas	F
7	The "glue" the holds pigment together and makes it stick to a surface.	Composition	G
8	Originally the study of beautiful things; currently refers to the study or understanding of anything that is visually pleasing or "works" within the boundaries of the principles of art.	Collagraph	H
9	A print made from a collage of assorted pasted materials such as papers, cardboards, string etc.	Collage	I
10	The art principle which refers to the arrangement of elements in an art work. Can be either formal symmetrical, informal asymmetrical or radial.	Balance	J
11	Italian word for "light-shade". The use and balance of light and shade in a painting, and in particular the use of strong contrast.	Color wheel	K
12	Clay objects that have been fired one time. (unglazed).	Aesthetics	L

Alice & The Rabbit-Hole

First, read the entire story. After that, go back and fill in the blanks. You can skip the blanks you're unsure about and finish them later.

sister	courageous	tunnel	pictures	hurry
dark	jar	feet	Rabbit	remarkable

ALICE was growing tired of sitting beside her _____ on the bank and having nothing to do: she had peeped into the book her sister was reading once or twice, but it was lacking _____ or words; "and what use is a book," Alice argued, "without pictures or conversations?" Thus, she was wondering in her mind (as best she could, given how sleepy and foolish she felt due to the heat) whether the pleasure of creating a cute daisy chain was worth the difficulty of getting up and gathering the daisies when a white _____ with pink eyes darted nearby her.

There was nothing _____ about that; nor did Alice consider it strange to hear the Rabbit exclaim to itself, "Oh no! Oh no! I will arrive too late!" (On reflection, she should have been surprised, but at the time, it seemed perfectly natural). Still, when the Rabbit actually removed a watch from its waistcoat-pocket, examined it, and then hurried on, Alice jumped to her _____, for it flashed across her mind that she had never seen a rabbit with either a waistcoat-pocket or a watch to remove from it, and burning with curiosity, she ran across the field after it. Alice saw the Rabbit go down a hole under the hedge. Alice followed it down in a _____, never once thinking how she would get out again.

The rabbit-hole continued straight ahead like a _____ for some distance and then suddenly dipped down, so quickly that Alice had no time to think about stopping herself before falling into what appeared to be a very deep well.

Either the well was really deep, or she dropped very slowly, as she had plenty of time to look around her and ponder on what might happen next. She first attempted to glance down and see what she was approaching, but it was too _____ to see anything; then, she discovered the sides of the well were lined with cupboards and bookcases; here and there, she observed maps and images hung on hooks. She removed a _____ from one of the shelves as she passed; it was labeled "ORANGE MARMALADE," but it was empty; she did not want to drop the jar for fear of killing someone beneath, so she managed to stuff it into one of the cupboards as she passed it.

"Perfect!" Alice exclaimed to herself. "After such a tumble, I shall have no worries about falling downstairs! How _____ they will all believe I am at home!

GRADE_____

DATE_____   **RESEARCH:** Nelson Mandela

Occupation _____

BORN DATE:_____   Nationality_____

DEATH DATE:_____   Education _____   #Children _____

Childhood and Family Background Facts

Work and Career Facts

Children, Marriage and or Significant Relationships

Friends, Social Life and Other Interesting Facts

Did you enjoy researching this person?

Give a Rating: ☆ ☆ ☆ ☆ ☆

Addition Worksheet

53125	893724	7754653	40034
58540	759775	8766279	70732
79810	403688	7714657	43161
+ 11737	+ 200969	+ 4524724	+ 41196

192189	2241377	84097	413796
965026	7928905	19687	877734
531938	5984195	69704	997766
+ 385320	+ 8264879	+ 21157	+ 742703

7059169	86799	636053	6947438
5369228	28259	120921	8770263
9985601	90783	897238	9488267
+ 8707044	+ 14295	+ 447023	+ 9910513

35283	189936	7019570	24476
17919	753760	1010287	75122
61158	617906	5621292	61687
+ 49632	+ 863520	+ 5479675	+ 55646

GRADE_____

DATE_____

RESEARCH: Davy Crockett

Occupation _____

BORN DATE:_____ Nationality_____

DEATH DATE:_____ Education_____ #Children _____

Childhood and Family Background Facts

Work and Career Facts

Children, Marriage and or Significant Relationships

Friends, Social Life and Other Interesting Facts

Did you enjoy researching this person?

Give a Rating: ☆ ☆ ☆ ☆ ☆

GRADE_____

DATE_____

RESEARCH: William Cullen

Occupation _____

BORN DATE:_____ Nationality_____

DEATH DATE:_____ Education_____ #Children _____

Childhood and Family Background Facts

Work and Career Facts

Children, Marriage and or Significant Relationships

Friends, Social Life and Other Interesting Facts

Did you enjoy researching this person?

Give a Rating: ☆ ☆ ☆ ☆ ☆

A Community Garden Letter

First, read the questions. Then read the letter. Answer the questions by circling the correct letter.

Jill Kindle
780 Billings St.
Riverstide, MB
J9K 5G9

June 5, 2018

Dear Andrew,

Thank you for your letter asking about gardening plots in a community garden. There are two plots available in the Greendale Community Garden at 678 Warren Drive. The fee for the 10 x 10 plot is $45.00 per year and the 10 x 12 plot is $55.00 per year. The water is included. There are a couple gardening tools, but it is best to bring your own. I suggest you talk to Dawn Clover to get a key for the shed. You can write your name on your tools and keep them in the shed. Dawn is the coordinator and her phone number is 693-555-9009. Please send your cheque to:

> Greendale Community Garden
> c/o Dawn Clover
> 789 Gibbons St.
> Riverstide, MB
> J8K 4G9

Thank you for your interest in the community garden program. We hope you have a fun time gardening this season.

Please let me know if you have any more questions.

Best regards,

Jill Kindle

Director of Community Gardens
City of Riverstide

A Community Garden Letter
Questions

1. Who sent this letter?
    a. Andrew Fitzgerald
    b. Jill Kindle
    c. Dawn Clover

2. Who is the letter for?
    a. Jill Kindle
    b. Dawn Clover
    c. Andrew Fitzgerald

3. How much is the 10 x 12 plot per year?
    a. $90.00
    b. $45.00
    c. $55.00

4. What is Dawn Clover's phone number?
    a. 693-555-9006
    b. 963-555-9669
    c. 693-555-9009

5. What job does Jill Kindle have?
    a. Community Garden Person
    b. Director of Community Gardens
    c. Garden Coordinator

6. What town or city is this community garden in?
    a. Gibbons
    b. Billings
    c. Riverstide

7. Where is the Greendale Community Garden?
    a. 678 Warren Drive
    b. 780 Billings St.
    c. 789 Gibbons St.

8. How many plots are available?
    a. 2
    b. 10
    c. 12

9. The water costs extra.
    a. True
    b. False

10. When was this letter written?
    a. June 5, 2018
    b. June 5, 2019
    c. June 9, 2015

Science: Protists

First, read the entire passage. After that, go back and fill in the blanks. You can skip the blanks you're unsure about and finish them later.

unclassifiable	tiny	consume	enormous	cell
Amoebas	acellular	cellular	tail	color
scoot	reproduce	oxygen	energy	molds

Protists are organisms that are classified under the biological kingdom protista. These are neither plants, animals, bacteria, or fungi, but rather _____ organisms. Protists are a large group of organisms with a wide variety of characteristics. They are essentially all species that do not fit into any of the other categories.

Protists as a group share very few characteristics. They are eukaryotic microorganisms with eukaryote _____ structures that are pretty basic. Apart from that, they are defined as any organism that is not a plant, an animal, a bacteria, or a fungus.

Protists can be classified according to their mode of movement.

Cilia - Certain protists move with _____ hair called cilia. These tiny hairs can flap in unison to assist the creature in moving through water or another liquid.

Other protists have a lengthy _____ known as flagella. This tail can move back and forth, aiding in the organism's propulsion.

Pseudopodia - When a protist extends a portion of its cell body in order to _____ or ooze. Amoebas move in this manner.

Different protists collect _____ in a variety of methods. Certain individuals consume food and digest it internally. Others digest their food through the secretion of enzymes. Then they _____ the partially digested meal. Other protists, like plants, utilize photosynthesis. They absorb sunlight and convert it to glucose.

Algae is a main form of protist. Algae are photosynthesis-capable protists. Algae are closely related to plants. They contain chlorophyll and utilize _____ and solar energy to generate food. However, they are not called plants because they lack specialized organs and tissues such as leaves, roots, and stems. Algae are frequently classified according on their _____, which ranges from red to brown to green.

Slime _____ are distinct from fungus molds. Slime molds are classified into two types: cellular and plasmodial. Slime molds of Plasmodium are formed from a single big cell. They are also referred to as _____. Even though these organisms are composed of only one cell, they can grow quite _____, up to several feet in width. Additionally, they can contain several nuclei inside a single cell. Cellular slime molds are little single-celled protists that can form a single organism when combined. When combined, various _____ slime molds will perform specific activities.

_____ are single-celled organisms that move with the assistance of pseudopods. Amoebas have no structure and consume their food by engulfing it with their bodies. Amoebas _____ by dividing in two during a process called mitosis.

GRADE_____

DATE_____   **RESEARCH: Davy Crockett**

Occupation _____

BORN DATE:_____ Nationality_____

DEATH DATE:_____ Education_____ #Children_____

Childhood and Family Background Facts

Work and Career Facts

Children, Marriage and or Significant Relationships

Friends, Social Life and Other Interesting Facts

Did you enjoy researching this person?

Give a Rating: ☆ ☆ ☆ ☆ ☆

DATE_____

RESEARCH: William Cullen

Occupation _____

BORN DATE:_____ Nationality _____

DEATH DATE:_____ Education _____ #Children _____

Childhood and Family Background Facts

Work and Career Facts

Children, Marriage and or Significant Relationships

Friends, Social Life and Other Interesting Facts

Did you enjoy researching this person?

Give a Rating: ☆ ☆ ☆ ☆ ☆

Science: Black Hole

Black holes are one of the universe's most mysterious and powerful forces. A black hole is a region of space where gravity has become so strong that nothing, not even light, can escape. A black hole's mass is so compact or dense that the force of gravity is so strong that even light cannot escape.

Black holes are entirely invisible. Because black holes do not reflect light, we cannot see them. Scientists can detect black holes by observing light and objects in their vicinity. Strange things happen in the vicinity of black holes due to quantum physics and space-time. Even though they are authentic, they are a popular subject for science fiction stories.

When giant stars explode at the end of their lives, black holes form, this type of explosion is known as a supernova. If a star has enough mass, it will collapse in on itself and shrink to a tiny size. Because of its small size and massive mass, the gravity will be so strong that it will absorb light and turn into a black hole. As they continue to absorb light and mass around them, black holes can grow enormously large. They can absorb other stars as well. Many scientists believe that supermassive black holes exist at the centers of galaxies.

An event horizon is a special boundary that exists around a black hole. At this point, everything, including light, must gravitate toward the black hole. Once you've crossed the event horizon, there's no turning back!

In the 18th century, two scientists, John Michell and Pierre-Simon Laplace, proposed the concept of a black hole. The term "black hole" was coined in 1967 by physicist John Archibald Wheeler.

1. Black holes are _____.
   a. can be seen with telescope
   b. invisible
   c. partial visible

2. Black holes are one of the most mysterious forces in the ____.
   a. near the moon
   b. under the stars
   c. universe

3. A black hole is where _____ has become so strong that nothing around it can escape.
   a. black dust
   b. gravity
   c. the sun

4. We can't actually see black holes because they don't ____.
   a. need sun
   b. reflect light
   c. have oxygen

5. Black holes are formed when _____ explode at the end of their lifecycle.
   a. giant stars
   b. planets
   c. Mars

6. Black holes can grow incredibly huge as they continue to absorb____.
   a. stars
   b. other planets
   c. light

Science Multiple Choice
Quiz: Noble Gases

Score: _____

Date: _____

Select the best answer for each question.

1. The noble gases are located to the far right of the periodic table and make up the _____.
   a. 16th column
   b. 18th column
   c. 17th column

2. Noble gases are _____, meaning each molecule is a single atom and almost never react with other elements.
   a. diatomic
   b. polyatomic
   c. monoatomic

3. The six noble gases are:
   a. Chlorine, bromine, iodine, astatine, tennessine
   b. Helium, hydrogen, radon, lithium, krypton, neon
   c. helium, neon, argon, krypton, xenon, and radon.

4. Helium is the second most abundant element in the universe after _____.
   a. radon
   b. hydrogen
   c. Argon

5. Xenon gets its name from the _____ word "xenos" which means "stranger or foreigner."
   a. Greek
   b. Latin
   c. Spanish

6. _____ has the lowest melting and boiling points of any substance.
   a. Neon
   b. Radon
   c. Helium

7. All of the noble gases except for _____ have stable isotopes.
   a. radon
   b. argon
   c. neon

8. This element is non-flammable and it is much safer to use in balloons than hydrogen.
   a. Krypton
   b. Helium
   c. Xenon

9. Many of the noble gases were either discovered or isolated by _____ chemist _____.
   a. Scottish, Sir William Ramsay
   b. Russian, Dmitri Mendeleev
   c. German, Robert Bunsen

10. Krypton gets its name from the _____ word "kryptos" meaning "_____".
    a. Greek; "sweet"
    b. Greek; "the hidden one."
    c. Greek; "lazy"

11. _____ , mixed with nitrogen, is used as a filler gas for incandescent light bulbs.
    a. Carbon monoxide
    b. Hydrogen
    c. Argon

12. _____, a highly radioactive element and is only available in minute amounts, is utilized in radiotherapy.
    a. Radon
    b. Carbon
    c. Uranium

Science Multiple Choice
Quiz: Alkali Metals

Score: _____

Date: _____

Select the best answer for each question.

1. **The elements of the alkali metals include _____, _____, _____, _____, _____, and _____.**

    a. magnesium, calcium, Radium, beryllium, silicon,and lithium

    b. lithium, sodium, potassium, rubidium, cesium, and francium

    c. radium, beryllium, lithium, sodium, calcium, and francium

2. **The alkali metals are all in the _____ of the periodic table except for hydrogen.**

    a. 1st column

    b. 2nd column

    c. 16th column

3. **Alkali Metals have a _____ when compared to other metals.**

    a. high density

    b. low density

    c. light density

4. **The word "alkali" comes from the _____ word meaning "ashes."**

    a. German

    b. Arabic

    c. Greek

5. **_____ is the most important alkali metal.**

    a. lithium

    b. sodium

    c. potassium

6. **Alkali metals are generally stored in _____.**

    a. oil

    b. soil

    c. water

7. **All alkali metals have _____ atomic numbers.**

    a. even

    b. odd

    c. prime

8. **Potassium's atomic number is ____ and its symbol is _____.**

    a. 19 and P

    b. 19 and K

    c. 11 and Na

9. **Alkali metals are the _____in group one of the periodic systems.**

    a. non metals

    b. chemical elements

    c. late transition metals

10. **_____ is the lightest known metal.**

    a. Sodium

    b. Lithium

    c. Francium

Organisms Multiple Choice
Quiz: Domestic Pig

Select the best answer for each question.

1. **Domestic pigs are often _____ but small pigs kept as pets (pot-bellied pigs) are often other colors.**
   a. white
   b. black
   c. pink

2. **The dental formula of adult pigs is 3.1.4.3/3.1.4.3, giving a total of _____ teeth.**
   a. 36
   b. 44
   c. 50

3. **Pigs are_____ in the genus Sus**
   a. reptiles
   b. amphibians
   c. mammals

4. **_____ of piglet fatalities are due to the mother attacking, or unintentionally crushing, the newborn pre-weaned animals.**
   a. 60%
   b. 50%
   c. 30%

5. **The ancestor of the domestic pig is the _____, which is one of the most numerous and widespread large mammals.**
   a. wild boar
   b. babirusa
   c. warthog

6. **Pigs are _____, which means that they consume both plants and animals.**
   a. omnivores
   b. herbivores
   c. carnivores

7. **Pigs need a _____, _____ under a roof to sleep, and they should not be crowded.**
   a. warm, muddy area
   b. warm, clean area
   c. cold, clean area

8. **Piglets weigh about _____ at birth, and usually double their weight in one week.**
   a. 1.5 kilograms
   b. 2.2 kilograms
   c. 1.1 kilograms

9. **Pigs often roll in _____ to protect themselves from sunlight.**
   a. water
   b. mud
   c. grass

10. **Pigs are among the smartest of all domesticated animals and are even smarter than _____.**
    a. dogs
    b. cats
    c. birds

Math: Linear Equation

Score: _____

Date: _____

What exactly is a linear equation?

First, consider the word equation. An equation is a mathematical statement containing the equals sign. Of course, linear means "in a straight line."

A linear equation is an equation with degree 1 -, which means that the highest exponent on all variables in the equation is 1. It turns out that if you plot the solutions to a linear equation in a coordinate system, they form a straight line.

A linear equation resembles an equation (there must be an equals sign) with variables that all have an exponent of one (in other words, no variable is raised to a higher power, and no variable is under a square root sign).

These equations are linear: y=2x+9 or 5x=6+3y

1. Which of the following is a solution to both y - 3x = 6 and y - 6x = 3?

   a. (6,9)

   b. (3,6)

   c. (1,9)

2. Different plans are available from two cellphone carriers. AT&K charges a monthly flat rate of $100 plus $10 for each gigabyte of data used. Verikon Communications does not have a flat rate, but instead charges $40 for each gigabyte of data used. Let c represent your total cost and d represent the data used. What is the equation system that represents these two plans?

   a. V = 100 + 10d and A = 40d

   b. A = 100d and V = 40d

   c. c = 100 + 10d and c = 40d

3. Solve the following system of equations 3x + y = 1 and -x + 2y = 2

   a. (2, 1)

   b. (3, 1)

   c. (0, 1)

4. What is the slope of a line with a graph that moves one place to the right by going up three places on a coordinate plane?

   a. -3

   b. 3

   c. 2

5. Find the slope of the line 2x - y = 6.

   a. 6

   b. 2

   c. -2

6. Which of the following linear equations has a y-intercept of 3 and a graph that slopes upward from left to right?

   a. -4x + 2y - 6 = 0

   b. -4x + 2y + 6 = 0

   c. 4x + y + 3 = 0

7. What are the x and y-intercepts of 3x + 4y = 12?

   a. (0, 12) and (3, 0)

   b. (4, 0) and (0, 3)

   c. (12, 4) and (4, 3)

8. Which linear equation has the solutions (1, 3) and (3, 9)?

   a. x = 1y

   b. y = 9x + 2

   c. y = 3x

Math: Inequalities

Mathematics isn't always about "equals"; sometimes all we know is that something is greater or less than another. An inequality is a mathematical equation that uses greater or less than symbols and is useful in situations where there are multiple solutions.

For example: Alexis and Billy compete in a race, and Billy wins!

What exactly do we know?

We don't know how fast they ran, but we do know Billy outpaced Alexis:

Billy was quicker than Alexis. That can be written down as follows: b > a

(Where "b" represents Billy's speed, ">" represents "greater than," and "a" represents Alex's speed.)

Do you require any other assistance? Try looking for instructional videos on Pre-Calculus Functions on YouTube.

1. A truck is driving across a bridge that has a weight limit of 50,000 pounds. The front of the truck weighs 19,800 pounds when empty, and the back of the truck weighs 12,500 pounds. How much cargo (C), in pounds, can the truck carry and still cross the bridge?

   a. C ≤ 10000
   b. C ≤ 17700
   c. C ≤ 7700

2. Monica wants to buy a phone, and the cheapest one she's found so far is $15. Monica has $4.25 set aside for a cell phone. How many hours (H) will Monica have to work to afford a mobile phone if she earns $2.15 per hour?

   a. H ≥ 3.75
   b. H ≥ 5.50
   c. H ≥ 5

3. Solve the inequality 4x + 8 > 5x +9

   a. x < 8
   b. x > 2
   c. x < -1

4. Solve the following inequality - 4|2 - x| - 4 < -28

   a. x > 8 or x < -4
   b. x < 8 or x > -4
   c. x > 4 or x < 28

5. Which of the following best describes the appearance of these two inequalities when graphed together? 2y - 9 ≥ 4x and 4 < x + y

   a. both boundary lines will be solid or dotted
   b. both boundary lines will be dotted
   c. one boundary line will be solid and one will be dotted

6. Which compound inequality has the solution x < -8 ?

   a. x + 2 > 16 OR x + 6 < 8
   b. 6 - 2x > 22 OR 3x + 14 < -10
   c. 4x + 2 > 7 AND 2 - 6x > -1

7. If 2x - 8 ≥ 2, then

   a. x ≤ 4
   b. x ≥ 5
   c. x ≤ 8

8. Which of the following is an example of an inequality?

   a. 70 - 2(15) = 88
   b. 60 + 2x < 120
   c. 70 + 3x = 80

Math: Domain and Range

Score: _____

Date: _____

The collection of all input values on which a function is defined is known as the domain. If a value is entered into the function, the function will remain defined regardless of what value is entered. A function's range is defined as the set of all possible output values for the function. It can also be thought of as the collection of all possible values that the function will accept as input.

1. Which of the following describes a collection of a function's outputs?

    a. Domain

    b. Inputs

    c. Range

2. What is the range of the function: $g(x) = |x| + 1$

    a. $R = \{1 \geq x\}$

    b. $R = \{x \geq 1\}$

    c. $R = \{y \geq 1\}$

3. A set of ordered pairs is called what?

    a. the domain

    b. a function

    c. a relation

4. What is the domain of a relation?

    a. the set of all y-values

    b. the set of all y + x values

    c. the set of all x-values

5. Which is the set of all y-values or the outputs?

    a. Domain

    b. Function

    c. Range

6. For the function $\{(0,1), (1,-3), (2,-4), (-4,1)\}$, write the domain and range.

    a. D:{0, 1, 2, -4} R:{1, -3, -4}

    b. D: {1, -3, -4,} R: {0, 1, 2, -4}

    c. D:{0, 1, 2, 3, 4} R:{1, -3, -4}

7. Identify the range of the following function when given the domain { 2, 3, 10}: $y = 4x - 12$

    a. -10, 0, 28

    b. -4, 0, 28

    c. 4, 5, 20

8. Which set of ordered pairs is not a function?

    a. (-9, 4), (-6, 3), (-2, 8), (0, 21)

    b. (1, 2), (3, 5), (6, 9), (7, 11)

    c. (2, 3), (4, 9), (3, 8), (4, 15)

9. What variable does Domain represent?

    a. Range

    b. X

    c. output

10. Which is the set of all y-values or the outputs?

    a. Range

    b. Domain

    c. Relation

Language: Technology

Score: _____

Date: _____

Match the English and German words. Use Google translate.

#	English		German	
1	☐	mouse	Nachricht	A
2	☐	touch	Handy	B
3	☐	screen	Maus	C
4	☐	Wi-Fi	Schoß	D
5	☐	message	Spiel	E
6	☐	game	berühren	F
7	☐	website	Rechner	G
8	☐	mobile	Bildschirm	H
9	☐	smart	Schreibtischplatte	I
10	☐	computer	Tastatur	J
11	☐	desktop	klug, intelligent	K
12	☐	lap	WLAN	L
13	☐	net	Netz	M
14	☐	app(lication)	App, Anwendung	N
15	☐	keyboard	Webseite	O

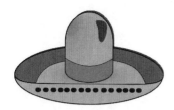

Language: Spanish

Score: _____

Date: _____

Use Google to help translate.

1. You would answer: ¡Muy bien! to which of the following questions in Spanish?

    a. 'Cómo te llamas?

    b. 'De dónde eres?

    c. 'Cómo estás?

2. What does Soy de Virginia means?

    a. I am from Virginia

    b. My name is Virginia

    c. I am Virginia

3. Buenas tardes is a Spanish greeting for which time of the day?

    a. Good night

    b. Good morning

    c. Afternoon

4. You would answer: Me llamo Antonio to which of the following questions in Spanish?

    a. 'A quién llamas?

    b. 'Cómo te llamas?

    c. 'Cuándo llamas?

5. You would answer: Soy de Carolina to which of the following questions in Spanish?

    a. 'De dónde eres?

    b. 'Dónde vas?

    c. 'Cómo te llamas?

6. How would you say 'Good morning' to a store clerk?

    a. Buenos días

    b. Hola

    c. My llamo

7. 'Soy de California.

    a. 'She from California.

    b. 'I am from California.

    c. 'I live in California.

8. Which of the following persons would you address by using the pronoun 'Tú'?

    a. a teacher

    b. Your aunt

    c. Your sibling

9. What would be the best greeting for the nighttime?

    a. Buenas tardes

    b. Soy

    c. Buenas noches

10. Which of the following is NOT a way to tell someone your name?

    a. Soy de...

    b. Me llamo...

    c. Mi nombre es...

11. Which two words mean 'you?'

    a. Tú and Usted

    b. Yo and Cómo

    c. Usted and Nónde

12. Buenos días, señor. ?

    a. Good night sir. ?

    b. Good morning sir. ?

    c. Good afternoon sir. ?

13. Cómo se llama ud.?'

    a. What's your name.?'

    b. What time is it.?'

    c. Where are you?

14. Where it is?'

    a. Me rónde es?'

    b. De dónde es?'

    c. Re dónde see?'

History: Age of Discovery

Tip: After you've answered the easy ones, go back and work on the harder ones.

valuable	Navigator	Middle	Discovery	Columbus
voyage	Africa	tobacco	sugar	sailed

Early in the 14th century, the Age of _____ (also known as the Age of Exploration) began. It lasted until the mid-1600s. European nations began to explore the globe during this time period. A large part of the Far East and the Americas were found as well as new routes to India and the _____ East. The Renaissance occurred at the same time as the Age of Exploration.

The process of preparing for an expedition can be costly and time-consuming. Many ships _____ away and never came back. So what was it about exploration that piqued the interest of Europeans? Answering this question is as easy as saying "money." Despite the fact that some explorers went on expeditions to acquire notoriety or to have an exciting experience, the primary goal of an organization was to make money.

New trade routes discovered by expeditions brought quite a lot of money for their countries. Many traditional routes to India and China were closed after the Ottoman Empire took Constantinople in 1453. Spices and silk were brought in via these trading routes, making them extremely _____. New explorers were seeking oceangoing routes to India and the Far East. Gold and silver were discovered by some journeys, including the Spanish ones to the Americas, which made them wealthy. They also found fresh territory to create colonies and cultivate crops like _____, cotton, and _____.

Henry the _____, a Portuguese explorer, kicked off the Age of Exploration in the country. Henry dispatched a fleet of ships to map and investigate the continent's western coast. They explored a large portion of west _____ for the Portuguese after traveling further south than any previous European expedition had. Portuguese explorer Bartolomeu Dias discovered the southern tip of Africa and into the Indian Ocean in 1488

The Spanish urgently needed a trade route to Asia. The famed European explorer, Christopher _____, believed he might reach China by sailing west over the Atlantic Ocean. He turned to the Spanish for funding after failing to secure it from the Portuguese. Isabella and Ferdinand, the monarchs of Spain, agreed to foot the bill for Columbus' _____. Columbus made his voyage to the New World in 1492 and discovered the Americas.

Financial: Money, Stocks and Bonds

Score: _____

Date: _____

Tip: First, read the entire passage. After that, go back and fill in the blanks. You can skip the blanks you're unsure about and finish them later.

asset	gold	stake	coins	paper
bankruptcy	economy	trade	currency	principal
shareholders	NASDAQ	barter	conditions	monetary
obligation				

Three important _____ must be met in order for something to qualify as a financial asset. It has to be:

Something you can have
Something monetary in nature
A contractual claim provides the basis for that monetary value

That last condition may be difficult to grasp at first, but it will become clear in a few minutes.

As a result, financial assets differ from physical assets such as land or gold. You can touch and feel the actual physical asset with land and _____, but you can only touch and feel something (usually a piece of _____) that represents the asset of value with financial assets.

Money is a government-defined official medium of exchange that consists of cash and _____. Money, _____, cash, and legal tender all refer to the same thing. They are all symbols of a central bank's commitment to keeping money's value as stable as possible. Money is a financial asset because its value is derived from the faith and credit of the government that issued it, not from the paper or metal on which it is printed.

Money is obviously a valuable financial _____. We would all have to _____ with one another without a common medium of exchange, trading whatever goods and services we have for something else we need, or _____ what we have for something else we could then trade with someone else who has what we need. Consider how complicated that can become!

Stock is another crucial financial asset in the US _____. Stock, like money, is simply a piece of paper that represents something of value. The something of value' represented by stock is a _____ in a company. Stock is also known as 'equity' because you have a stake in its profits when you own stock in a company.

Consider little Jane's lemonade stand as the most basic example. Jane only has $4 to begin her business, but she requires $10. Jane's parents give her $3 in exchange for 30% of her business, a friend gives her $1 for 10%, and her brother gives her $2 in exchange for 20%. Jane, her parents, a friend, and her brother are now all _____ in her company.

That example, as simple as it is, accurately describes stock. The complexities arise when we attempt to assign a _____ value to that stock. A variety of factors determines a stock's value. One share of stock in one company does not equal one share of stock in another. The number of shares issued by each company, as well as the size and profitability of each company, will affect the value of your share. Anything that has an impact on a business, good or bad, will affect the stock price.

These are the most basic and fundamental factors that can influence the value of a share of stock. Individual stock prices are affected by macroeconomic trends as well. Thousands of books have been written in an attempt to discover the golden rule that determines the exact value of a share of stock.

The value of a stock can fluctuate from minute to minute and even second to second. The New York Stock Exchange and _____ were the world's two largest stock exchanges in 2014. (both located in the United States).

Bonds are the final financial asset we'll look at. Bonds are, in essence, loans. When an organization, such as a company, a city or state, or even the federal government, requires funds, bonds can be issued. Bonds come in various forms, but they are all debt instruments in which the bondholder is repaid their _____ investment, plus interest, at some future maturity date.

The only way a bondholder's money is lost is if the entity that issued the bond declares _____. Bonds are generally safer investments than stocks because they are a legal _____ to repay debt, whereas stocks represent ownership, which can make or lose money.

Art: Pablo Picasso

Score: _____

Date: _____

depressed	suicide	features	Carlos	newspapers
blue	historians	circuses	collaborated	sand
painter	Madrid	prestigious	Spanish	French

Pablo Picasso was born on October 25, 1881, in Spain and grew up there. His father was a

_____ who also taught art. Pablo has always enjoyed drawing since he was a child.

According to legend, his first word was "piz," which is _____ for "pencil." Pablo quickly

demonstrated that he had little interest in school but was an extremely talented artist. Pablo enrolled in

a _____ art school in Barcelona when he was fourteen years old. He transferred

to another school in _____ a few years later. Pablo, on the other hand, was dissatisfied with

the traditional art school teachings. He didn't want to paint in the manner of people from hundreds of

years ago. He wished to invent something new.

Pablo's close friend _____ Casagemas committed _____ in 1901. Pablo became

_____. He began painting in Paris around the same time. For the next four years, the

color _____ dominated his paintings. Many of the subjects appeared depressed and solemn. He

depicted people with elongated _____ and faces in his paintings. Poor People on the

Seashore and The Old Guitarist are two of his paintings from this time.

Pablo eventually recovered from his depression. He also had feelings for a _____ model. He

began to use warmer colors such as pinks, reds, oranges, and beiges in his paintings. The Rose

Period is a term used by art _____ to describe this period in Pablo's life. He also

started painting happier scenes like _____. The Peasants and Mother and Child are two

of his paintings from this time period.

Picasso began experimenting with a new painting style in 1907. He _____

with another artist, Georges Braque. By 1909, they had developed a completely new painting style

known as Cubism. Cubism analyzes and divides subjects into different sections. The sections are then reassembled and painted from various perspectives and angles.

Picasso began combining Cubism and collage in 1912. He would use _____ or plaster in his paint to give it texture in this area. He would also add dimension to his paintings by using materials such as colored paper, _____, and wallpaper. Three Musicians and the Portrait of Ambroise Vollard are two of Picasso's Cubism paintings.

Although Picasso continued to experiment with Cubism, he went through a period of painting more classical-style paintings around 1921. He was influenced by Renaissance painters such as Raphael. He created strong characters that appeared three-dimensional, almost like statues. The Pipes of Pan and Woman in White are two of his works in this style.

Pablo became interested in the Surrealist movement around 1924. Surrealist paintings were never meant to make sense. They frequently resemble something out of a nightmare or dream. Although Picasso did not join the movement, he did incorporate some of its ideas into his paintings. This period was dubbed "Monster Period" by some. Guernica and The Red Armchair are two examples of surrealism's influence on Picasso's art.

Pablo Picasso is widely regarded as the greatest artist of the twentieth century. Many consider him to be one of the greatest artists in all of history. He painted in a variety of styles and made numerous unique contributions to the world of art. He painted several self-portraits near the end of his life. Self-Portrait Facing Death, a self-portrait done with crayons on paper, was one of his final works of art. He died a year later, on April 8, 1973, at the age of 91.

Geography Multiple Choice
Quiz: Antarctic

Score: _____

Date: _____

Select the best answer for each question.

1. _____ is the fifth-largest continent in terms of total area.
   a. Antarctic
   b. Artic
   c. Antarctica

2. _____ is composed of older, igneous and metamorphic rocks.
   a. Lesser Antarctica
   b. Greater Antarctica
   c. Antarctica

3. Antarctica is:
   a. Nearly all exposed land with some glaciers
   b. About half ice and half exposed land
   c. Mainly ice, with a few areas of exposed land

4. Antarctica has the world's largest?
   a. Mountains
   b. Ice
   c. Desert

5. In 1983, the coldest temperature ever recorded in Antarctica is?
   a. -108.5°F
   b. -118.0°F
   c. -128.6°F

6. The Antarctic region has an important role in _____.
   a. global climate processes
   b. Earth's heat balance
   c. Earth's atmosphere

7. The _____ is one of the driest _____ in the world.
   a. Antarctic desert and deserts
   b. Antarctic continent and deserts
   c. Antarctic archipelago and continent

8. One of the apex, or top, predators in Antarctica is the?
   a. penguin
   b. sperm whales
   c. leopard seal

9. _____ study climate patterns, including the "ozone hole" that hovers over the Antarctic.
   a. Climatologists
   b. Meteorologists
   c. Geographers

10. _____ is the largest single piece of ice on Earth.
    a. Antarctic Ice Sheet
    b. Glacial Ice
    c. Ross Ice Shelf

11. _____, is part of the "Ring of Fire," a tectonically active area around the Pacific Ocean.
    a. Antarctica
    b. Greater Antarctica
    c. Lesser Antarctica

12. _____ in the Antarctic is hard to measure as it always falls as snow.
    a. Evaporation
    b. Condensation
    c. Precipitation

Biology: Famous Biologists Research

Oswald Avery was a biologist who discovered that DNA contains genetic information passed down from generation to generation.

Rachel Carson: This biologist made a breakthrough in the field of environmental biology by discovering the impact of chemicals on the environment and the food we eat.

Marie Curie: This biologist made a discovery related to the elements that we now see on the periodic table, and she was among the first to experiment with radiation and tumor treatment. Today, this experiment is widely used to treat cancers and tumors, demonstrating the significance of this discovery.

Charles Darwin: This biologist studied the concept of species evolution as well as the origins of species.

William Harvey: This biologist discovered that blood leaves the heart and travels around the body before returning to the heart, forming a circuit.

Research each biologist and write 2 amazing facts about them

Biology: Excretory System

chloride	pressure	bladder	filtering	bloodstream
molecules	concentrate	urine	muscular	detoxifies
kidneys	substances	glomeruli	reabsorbing	converts

Toxins are present in all animals' bodies and must be eliminated. The human liver _____ and

modifies dangerous _____ so that they can be quickly and easily removed from the body. For

example, ammonia is very toxic, so the liver _____ it to urea, which is far less toxic and easily

removed from the body.

The _____ are the organs responsible for _____ waste products from the blood and

regulating blood composition and pressure. The outer layer of the kidneys contains structures known as

_____, which are ball-like structures made up of very porous capillaries. Large amounts of water

and small molecules, including urea, are forced out through the pores by the blood _____ in these

capillaries, but blood cells and larger _____ that are too large to fit through the pores remain in the

_____.

The glomeruli are surrounded by the ends of the renal tubules, which are long, looping tubes in the kidney that

collect blood filtrate and _____ it into the urine. The filtrate travels through the tubules,

_____ nutrients, water, and sodium _____ from the renal tubules and returning them

to the blood. Waste products are concentrated in the tubules and become urine as water and nutrients are

reabsorbed. Urine is stored in the _____ after the kidneys have concentrated it. Most people can

control when they empty their bladder by controlling a _____ valve at the exit point. When this valve

is opened and the bladder muscles contract, _____ enters the urethra, where it travels before

exiting the body.

History Reading Comprehension: George Washington

You've probably seen him on a one-dollar bill. The capital of the United States is named after him.

George Washington was born on February 22, 1732, and died on December 14, 1799. As the son of wealthy plantation owners, he grew up in Colonial Virginia. A plantation is a large farm that is tended by a large number of people. George's father died when he was 11 years old, so he was raised primarily by his older brother, who ensured he received a basic education and learned how to be a gentleman. George's teeth had deteriorated over time, necessitating the use of dentures (fake teeth). They eventually turned a dingy brown color, and many people assumed they were made of wood, but they weren't. Imagine attempting to eat corn on the cob with wooden teeth.

George married the widow Martha Custis, who had two children from her previous marriage when he was an adult. A widow is someone whose husband has died, which is why she was able to marry George later in life. George became a plantation owner while also serving in the Virginia legislature, which meant he helped write and pass laws in Virginia. He was a very busy man!

The United States had not yet been formed at this point, and the British still ruled and owned the colonies. George and his fellow plantation owners became enraged because they felt they were being treated unfairly by their British rulers. A group of people from each town or colony met and decided that the colonies would fight the British together.

George Washington was elected as the first President of the United States of America in 1789. He had the option of becoming king, but he believed that no one should be in power for too long. A president in the United States is elected or chosen by popular vote, and George Washington decided not to run for reelection after his second term. Almost all American presidents followed in his footsteps, but the two-term (or eight-year) limit was not established until the 1950s.

George Washington served as president during peaceful times, and he was instrumental in establishing the new government and leadership of the United States. He was also a member of the leadership that aided in the adoption of the Constitution. The United States Constitution is the law of the land, and it guarantees the people of our country basic freedoms. However, freedom does not imply the ability to do whatever you want. Even free countries have laws and rules that must be followed.

Washington caught a cold just a few years after leaving the presidency. He became ill quickly with a cold and died on December 14, 1799.

Fun Facts

He was the only president who was elected unanimously.

He never served as president in the capital named after him, Washington, D.C. The capital was in New York City during his first year, then moved to Philadelphia, Pennsylvania.

He stood six feet tall, which was unusual for the 1700s.

George Washington did not have wooden teeth, but he did wear ivory dentures.

In his will, Washington freed his slaves.

1. George Washington was born on _____.
   a. 02-22-1732
   b. February 24, 1732

2. The United States Constitution is the law of the _____.
   a. land
   b. world

3. George's _____ had deteriorated.
   a. teeth
   b. feet

4. George Washington can be seen on a _____.
   a. one-dollar bill
   b. five-dollar bill

5. George's father died when he was 20 years old.
   a. True
   b. False

6. George was a plantation owner.
   a. True
   b. False

7. George married the widow _____.
   a. Martha Custis
   b. Mary Curtis

8. In his will, Washington freed his _____.
   a. children
   b. slaves

9. George served in the _____ legislature.
   a. Virginia
   b. Maryland

10. George Washington was elected as the _____ President of the USA.
    a. forth
    b. first

11. A widow is someone whose husband has died.
    a. True
    b. False

12. George died on December 14, 1699.
    a. True
    b. False

13. George grew up in _____.
    a. Washington DC
    b. Colonial Virginia

14. The capital of the United States is named after George.
    a. True
    b. False

15. A plantation is a town that is tended by a large number of officials.
    a. True
    b. False

16. Washington caught a _____ just a few years after leaving the presidency.
    a. cold
    b. flight

Health: Immune System

white	defends	cell-mediated	cells	Immune
external	Macrophages	signals	foreign	invading

Your immune system _____ you against harmful intruders. _____ responses occur when your body's immune system detects threats.

Your immune system, which detects and eliminates _____ invaders, provides this tremendous service. An immunological reaction occurs when your body's immune system detects _____ intruders. Your immune system is a great asset that selflessly protects you from antigens, or foreign intruders.

Immunity by Cells

Antibody-mediated immunity is one of your immune system's two arms. The other arm is _____ immunity, which helps the body get rid of undesired cells like infected, cancerous, or transplanted cells. _____ consume antigens in this sort of immunity. If you split down macrophages, you can remember it easily. Big indicates macro- and phages means 'eaters.' So macrophages are voracious consumers of antigens. The macrophage then chews up the antigen and displays the fragments on its surface.

When helper T cells encounter macrophages, they give out _____ that activate other _____ blood _____, such as cytotoxic or killer T cells. These killer T cells multiply fast, forming an army ready to battle and eliminate the _____ cell that prompted the immune response.

Health: Check Your Symptoms

Score: _____

Date: _____

Healthy habits aid in the development of happy and healthy children as well as the prevention of future health issues such as diabetes, hypertension, high cholesterol, heart disease, and cancer.

Chronic diseases and long-term illnesses can be avoided by leading a healthy lifestyle. Self-esteem and self-image are aided by feeling good about yourself and taking care of your health.

Maintain a consistent exercise schedule.

No, you don't have to push yourself to go to the gym and do tough workouts, but you should be as active as possible. You can maintain moving by doing simple floor exercises, swimming, or walking. You can also remain moving by doing some domestic chores around the house.

What matters is that you continue to exercise. At least three to five times a week, devote at least twenty to thirty minutes to exercise. Establish a regimen and make sure you get adequate physical activity each day.

Be mindful of your eating habits.

You must continue to eat healthily in order to maintain a healthy lifestyle. Eat more fruits and vegetables and have fewer carbs, salt, and harmful fat in your diet. Don't eat junk food or sweets.

Avoid skipping meals since your body will crave more food once you resume eating. Keep in mind that you should burn more calories than you consume.

1. **I've got a pain in my head.**
   a. Stiff neck
   b. headache

2. **I was out in the sun too long.**
   a. Sunburn
   b. Fever

3. **I've got a small itchy lump or bump.**
   a. Rash
   b. Insect bite

4. **I might be having a heart attack.**
   a. Cramps
   b. Chest pain

5. **I've lost my voice.**
   a. Laryngitis
   b. Sore throat

6. **I need to blow my nose a lot.**
   a. Runny nose
   b. Blood Nose

7. **I have an allergy. I have a**
   a. Rash
   b. Insect bite

8. **My shoe rubbed my heel. I have a**
   a. Rash
   b. Blister

9. **The doctor gave me antibiotics. I have a/an**
   a. Infection
   b. Cold

10. **I think I want to vomit. I am**
    a. Nauseous
    b. Bloated

11. **My arm is not broken. It is**
    a. Scratched
    b. Sprained

12. **My arm touched the hot stove. It is**
    a. Burned
    b. Bleeding

13. **I have an upset stomach. I might**
    a. Cough
    b. Vomit

14. **The doctor put plaster on my arm. It is**
    a. Sprained
    b. Broken

15. **If you cut your finger it will**
    a. Burn
    b. Bleed

16. **I hit my hip on a desk. It will**
    a. Burn
    b. Bruise

17. **When you have hay-fever you will**
    a. Sneeze
    b. Wheeze

18. **A sharp knife will**
    a. Scratch
    b. Cut

Spelling: How Do You Spell It?
Part II

Score: _____

Date: _____

Write and circle the correct spelling for each word.

		A	B	C	D
1.	_____	compllain	complian	complain	compllian
2.	_____	negattyve	negatyve	negative	negattive
3.	_____	importance	importence	imporrtance	imporrtence
4.	_____	encourragement	encouragement	encourragenment	encouragenment
5.	_____	shallves	shelves	shellves	shalves
6.	_____	mixture	mixttore	mixtore	mixtture
7.	_____	honorrable	honorable	honorible	honorrible
8.	_____	lagall	legall	lagal	legal
9.	_____	manar	mannar	manner	maner
10.	_____	encyllopedia	encyclopedia	encyllopedai	encyclopedai
11.	_____	repllacement	replacenment	repllacenment	replacement
12.	_____	medycie	medycine	medicine	medicie
13.	_____	experriance	experience	experiance	experrience
14.	_____	hunger	hunjer	hungerr	hunjerr
15.	_____	sallote	sallute	salote	salute
16.	_____	horrizon	hurizon	hurrizon	horizon
17.	_____	sestion	session	setion	sesion
18.	_____	shorrten	shurten	shorten	shurrten
19.	_____	fuacett	faucett	fuacet	faucet
20.	_____	haadache	haadace	haedache	headache
21.	_____	further	furrther	forrther	forther
22.	_____	injurry	injory	injury	injorry
23.	_____	disstance	distence	distance	disstence
24.	_____	rattio	ratio	rattoi	ratoi
25.	_____	independense	independence	independance	independanse

Spelling: How Do You Spell It?
Part I

Write and circle the correct spelling for each word.

		A	B	C	D
1.	_____	grade	grrada	grrade	grada
2.	_____	elementary	elenmentary	ellenmentary	ellementary
3.	_____	marks	marrcks	marrks	marcks
4.	_____	repurt	reporrt	report	repurrt
5.	_____	schedolle	schedule	schedole	schedulle
6.	_____	timetible	timetable	timettable	timettible
7.	_____	highlight	highllight	hyghllight	hyghlight
8.	_____	foell	foel	fuell	fuel
9.	_____	instrucsion	insstruction	instruction	insstrucsion
10.	_____	senttence	sentance	senttance	sentence
11.	_____	vaccination	vacination	vaccinasion	vacinasion
12.	_____	proof	prwf	prouf	proph
13.	_____	mandatury	mandattury	mandatory	mandattory
14.	_____	final	fynall	finall	fynal
15.	_____	envellope	envelope	envellupe	envelupe
16.	_____	equattor	eqauttor	eqautor	equator
17.	_____	bllanks	blanks	blancks	bllancks
18.	_____	honorible	honorrable	honorable	honorrible
19.	_____	scaince	sceince	science	sciance
20.	_____	mussic	mosic	muscic	music
21.	_____	history	hisstory	hisctory	histury
22.	_____	lissten	liscten	lysten	listen
23.	_____	entrence	enttrance	enttrence	entrance
24.	_____	especialy	especailly	especaily	especially
25.	_____	mariage	maraige	marraige	marriage

Reading Comprehension: Law Enforcement Dogs

Police dogs are dogs that assist cops in solving crimes. In recent years, they have grown to be an essential part of law enforcement. With their unique abilities and bravery, police dogs have saved many lives. They are often regarded as an important and irreplaceable part of many police departments because they are loyal, watchful, and protective of their police officer counterparts.

Today, police dogs are trained in specific areas. They could be considered experts in their field. Some of the particular police dog roles are as follows:

Tracking: Tracking police dogs use their keen sense of smell to locate criminal suspects or missing people. Tracking dogs are trained for years and can track down even the most elusive criminal. Without police tracking dogs, many suspects would be able to elude capture.

Substance Detectors: Like tracking dogs, these police dogs use their sense of smell to assist officers. Substance dogs are trained to detect a specific substance. Some dogs are trained to detect bombs or explosives. These brave dogs are trained not only to detect explosives but also to respond (very carefully!) and safely alert their officer partner to the explosive location. Other dogs may be drawn to illegal drugs. By quickly determining whether an illegal substance is nearby, these dogs save officers from searching through luggage, a car, or other areas by hand.

Public Order - These police dogs assist officers in keeping the peace. They may pursue a criminal suspect and hold them until an officer arrives, or they may guard an area (such as a jail or prison) to prevent suspects from fleeing.

Cadaver Dogs: Although it may sound disgusting, these police dogs are trained to locate dead bodies. This is a critical function in a police department, and these dogs perform admirably.

A police dog is not just any dog. Police dogs require very special and specialized training. There are numerous breeds of dogs that have been trained for police work. What breed they are often determined by the type of work they will do. German Shepherds and Belgian Malinois are two of the most popular breeds today, but other dogs such as Bloodhounds (good for tracking) and Beagles (good for drug detection) are also used. Police dogs, regardless of breed, are typically trained to do their job from the time they are puppies.

Typically, police dogs are regarded as heroes. They frequently go to live with their human partner police officer. They've known this person for years and have grown to consider them family, which works out well for both the officer and the dog.

1. Tracking police dogs use their _____ to locate criminal suspects or missing people.
   a. keen sense of training
   b. keen sense of taste
   c. keen sense of smell

2. Some substance dogs are trained to detect _____.
   a. runaway children
   b. bombs or explosives
   c. metal and iron

3. Police dogs are trained in ___ areas.
   a. many
   b. a few
   c. specific

4. Police dogs are dogs that assist cops in solving _____.
   a. littering
   b. homelessness
   c. crimes

5. Substance dogs are trained to detect a specific _____.
   a. substance
   b. person
   c. other police dogs

6. What type of police dog is trained pursue a criminal suspect and hold them until an officer arrives?
   a. Crime Fighting dog
   b. Tracking dog
   c. Public Order dog

7. These police dogs are trained to locate dead bodies
   a. Law and Order dogs
   b. Cadaver dogs
   c. Deadly Substance dogs

8. What are the two most popular police dogs used today?
   a. German Shepherds and Belgian Malinois
   b. Bloodhounds and German Shepherds
   c. Belgian Malinois and Rottweiler

Geography: Mountain Range

A mountain range is a collection of connected mountains that often form a long line of mountains. Large mountain ranges are frequently composed of smaller mountain ranges known as subranges. The Smokey Mountain Range, for example, is a section of the Appalachian Mountain Range. It is a subdivision of the Appalachian Mountains.

The Himalayas are the world's highest mountain range, while the Andes are the world's longest.

The Himalayas span 1,491 miles across a large portion of central Asia. They travel from Afghanistan and Pakistan to Bhutan via India, Nepal, and China. In addition to the Himalayas, the Karakoram and Hindu Kush mountain ranges are included.

The Himalayas are renowned for their lofty peaks. The Himalayas are home to most of the world's tallest mountains, including the world's two tallest peaks, Mount Everest at 29,035 feet and K2 at 28,251 feet.

The Himalayas have played a significant role in Asia's history. Many religions, including Buddhism and Hinduism, regard Tibet's mountains and high peaks as sacred.

The Andes Mountains, approximately 4,300 miles in length, is the world's longest mountain range. The Andes Mountains run north to south across a large portion of South America, passing through Argentina, Chile, Peru, Bolivia, Venezuela, Colombia, and Ecuador. Mount Aconcagua, at 22,841 feet, is the Andes' tallest peak. The Andes played a critical role in South America's history. Machu Picchu, the Inca's famous ancient city, was built high in the Andes.

The Alps are a significant mountain range that runs through central Europe. They traverse through several nations in Europe, including France, Germany, Switzerland, Italy, Austria, and Slovenia. Mont Blanc, at 15,782 feet, is the highest summit in the Alps, located on the French-Italian boundary.

Over time, the Alps cemented their position in history. Perhaps the most famous instance occurred during the Punic Wars when Hannibal of Carthage crossed the Alps to attack Rome.

The Rocky Mountains span western North America from north to south. They connect Canada and the United States of America's state of New Mexico. Mount Elbert, at 14,440 feet, is the tallest peak in the Rockies.

The Sierra Nevada Mountain Range runs parallel to the Rockies in the United States but further west. Beautiful national parks, like Yosemite and Kings Canyon, are located here. Mount Whitney, at 14,505 feet, is the tallest mountain in the contiguous United States.

On the eastern coast of the United States, the Appalachian Mountains stretch parallel to the Atlantic Ocean.

In western Russia, the Ural Mountains run north to south. The eastern edge of these mountains is frequently seen as the dividing line or border between Europe and Asia.

The Pyrenees, Tian Shan, Transantarctic Mountains, Atlas, and the Carpathians are also significant world mountain ranges.

Remember that there may be some question-answer relationship (QAR) questions, so please keep that in mind when answering the questions below.

1. A _____ includes geological features that are in the same region as a mountain range.
   a. mountain passes
   b. mountain chain
   c. mountain system

2. _____ are smaller mountain ranges that can be found within larger mountain ranges.
   a. Hill ranges
   b. Subranges
   c. Micro ranges

3. **The world's tallest mountain ranges form when pieces of the Earth's crust, known as _____, collide.**

    a. core

    b. mantle

    c. plates

5. **Mountain ranges usually include highlands or _____.**

    a. mountain passes and valleys

    b. valleys and rifts

    c. mountain peaks and edges

7. **_____ is a scientific theory that explains how major landforms are created as a result of Earth's subterranean movements.**

    a. Erosion

    b. Plate tectonics

    c. Sedimentation

9. **What is the highest peak in the Rocky Mountain Range that is 14,440 feet tall?**

    a. Mt. Everest

    b. Mt. Elbert

    c. Mt. Mayon

11. **The _____ runs somewhat parallel to the Rockies, but further west in the United States.**

    a. Sierra Nevada Mountain Range

    b. Appalachian

    c. Himalayas

4. **The tallest mountain range in the world is the _____ and the longest is the _____.**

    a. Himalayas, Andes

    b. Andes, Mt. Vinson

    c. Mt. Everest, Manaslu

6. **The Andes Mountains are the world's longest mountain range, stretching approximately _____.**

    a. 4,300 miles

    b. 5,000 miles

    c. 2,000 miles

8. **The Himalayas run 1,491 miles across much of _____.**

    a. Central Europe

    b. South America

    c. Central Asia

10. **The majority of geologically young mountain ranges on Earth's land surface are found in either the _____ or the _____.**

    a. Alpide belt, Oceanic Ridge belt

    b. Pacific Ring of Fire, Alpide Belt

    c. Oceanic Ridge belt, Circum-Pacific Seismic Belt

12. **Mountains often serve as _____ that define the natural borders of countries.**

    a. enclosure

    b. geographic features

    c. barriers

English: Tenses

Verbs are classified into three tenses: past, present, and future. The term "past" refers to events that have already occurred (e.g., earlier in the day, yesterday, last week, three years ago). The present tense is used to describe what is happening right now or what is ongoing. The future tense refers to events that have yet to occur (e.g., later, tomorrow, next week, next year, three years from now).

borrowed	went	eat	play	go	giving
read	give	gave	will eat	yelled	seeing
will have	had	reading	will go	do	will borrow
playing	doing	yelling	did	will yell	will do
will give	fight	borrow	yell	will fight	will play
borrowing	played	fighting	read	have	will see
going	see	will read	read	eating	ate
saw	having		fought		

Simple Present (11)	Present Progressive (IS/ARE +) (11)	Past (11)	Future (11)

English: Personal Pronouns

Score: _____

Date: _____

Personal pronouns are words that are used to replace the subject or object of a sentence to make it easier for readers to understand.

To give a brief, personal pronouns are:

1. Replace nouns and other pronouns to make sentences easier to read and understand.

2. A sentence's subject or object can be either. For example, 'I' is the first-person subject pronoun, whereas 'me' is the first-person object pronoun.

3. It is possible to use the singular or plural form.

4. They must agree on gender and number with the words they are substituting.

1. Which of the following sentences has a plural subject pronoun and a plural object pronoun?
   a. She wants to live as long as she can, as long as she have someone by her side.
   b. While Tom believe everything will be fine, many don't agree with him.
   c. Whether we lived or died, it didn't matter to us either way.

2. Which of the following words would make the following sentence grammatically correct? '6th graders should check with their teachers before you leave the classroom.'
   a. Replace 'their' with 'they'
   b. Replace 'you' with 'they'
   c. Replace '6th graders' with 'they'

3. The pronoun 'my' is a . . .
   a. 1st person possessive pronoun
   b. 3rd person nominative pronoun
   c. 2nd person possessive pronoun

4. Which of the following correctly identifies the subjective and objective pronouns in the sentence here? 'Run away from the dinosaurs with the giant feet?' she asked. 'You don't have to tell me twice.'
   a. she - subject pronoun; you - subject pronoun; me - object pronoun
   b. she - object pronoun; you - object pronoun; me - object pronoun
   c. she - object pronoun; you - subject pronoun; me - object pronoun

5. The pronoun 'your' is a . . .
   a. 2nd person possessive pronoun
   b. 1st person possessive pronoun
   c. 2nd person objective pronoun

6. Which pronouns are found in the following sentence? 'I kept telling her that we would go back for John, but I knew we had left him behind. '
   a. I, we, knew, we, him
   b. I, her, we, I, we, him
   c. I, we, I, we, him

7. Kevin likes playing basketball. _____ is a very good player.
   a. Him
   b. He
   c. Their

8. The pronoun 'its' is a . . .
   a. 3rd person possessive pronoun
   b. 2nd person possessive pronoun
   c. 3rd person objective pronoun

9. The pronoun 'their' is a . . .
   a. 2nd person possessive pronoun
   b. 3rd person objective pronoun
   c. 3rd person possessive pronoun

10. Kimmy is a very good cook. _____ can cook any kind of food.
    a. She
    b. Hey
    c. Their

English: Nouns, Verbs, Adjectives, Adverbs

A noun is defined as a person, place, thing, or idea that has been used for thousands of years in all spoken languages.

An action verb is a word that shows action. 'What did they do in the sentence?' is one way to find the action verb. Action verbs are necessary for descriptive and informative writing.

Adjectives are descriptive words for nouns. We use them to provide our audience with a more complete and detailed picture of the noun we are describing. What words would you use to describe yourself? Would you describe yourself as intelligent or amusing? Is your room cluttered or neat? When describing something, adjectives are used.

An adverb is a word that modifies another word, such as a verb, adjective, or adverb. Adverbs improve the precision and interest of writing. Adverbs answer these questions:

- When?
- Where?
- In what manner?
- To what extent?

1. Which of the following is NOT a noun?
   a. place
   b. person
   c. action

2. A verb is a(n) _____.
   a. action
   b. word that describes a noun
   c. person, place, thing, or idea

3. True or False: An adjective describes a verb.
   a. True
   b. False

4. Adverbs describe or modify _____.
   a. adverbs
   b. adjectives
   c. verbs

5. What is the adverb in the sentence? Peter neatly wrote a shopping list.
   a. Peter
   b. wrote
   c. neatly

6. Which sentence shows the proper use of an adverb?
   a. Jim quick walked.
   b. Jim walked quickly.
   c. Jim walked quick.

7. Which of the following words is a common noun identifying a person?
   a. Dr. Jones
   b. doctor
   c. Mr. Jones

8. Which of the following nouns is a proper noun?
   a. Cat
   b. Central Park
   c. Fireman

9. Which sentence part contains an action verb?
   a. baseball or soccer
   b. eat an ice cream cone
   c. to the top of the hill and back

10. Adjectives are words that describe what?
    a. nouns
    b. other adjectives
    c. verbs

11. Which adjective would best describe a cat?
    a. sharp
    b. furry
    c. cold

12. Which sentence gives the clearest picture using adjectives?
    a. The tall, fast lady runs.
    b. The lady runs fast.
    c. The sleek, slender, funny little lady runs.

More Spelling Words

Fill in the blanks with the correct spelling word.

drank	personal	equipment	I've	heavy
Arkansas	spaghetti	direction	moral	twenty
exist	choose	Wednesday	growls	Japanese
junior	wouldn't	empty		

1. You will make _____ dollars per day.

2. My dog _____ at everyone.

3. We sat outside and _____ tea.

4. We have a _____ obligation to do the right thing.

5. There is an _____ lot for sale.

6. The painting is much too _____ to carry by myself.

7. She said we could have lunch on _____.

8. My favorite food is _____.

9. My uncle has a cabin in _____.

10. I didn't even know that they still _____.

11. There's no need to get _____.

12. My best friend is _____.

13. She is a _____ partner in the law firm.

14. Our _____ is old and broken.

15. A palindrome can be read in either _____ like the word mom.

16. I just can't _____ between these shoes.

17. He _____ tell the secret to anyone.

18. _____ always loved to walk on the beach.

Score: _____

Date: _____

More Spelling Words IV

Fill in the blanks with the correct spelling word.

reminded	yesterday	frozen	district	frilly
excellent	terrible	surface	scoop	Florida
present	extent	professors	numb	arrived
mistletoe	graduation			

1. The ground is still _____.

2. We are planning a _____ party.

3. Your blue dress is so _____.

4. I will _____ out some beans into this bag.

5. The flower was near dead when it _____.

6. The ideas that Kevin had were _____.

7. This _____ will vote at the main office.

8. My hand was almost _____.

9. The picture _____ me of how much fun we had.

10. The _____ of the damage was unknown.

11. We will buy the teacher a _____.

12. The _____ was smooth and cold.

13. I told you about the test _____.

14. This program was created by _____.

15. My haircut looks _____.

16. My mom will hang _____ over the door.

17. _____ is a peninsula.

Spelling Words Lesson

Score: _____

Date: _____

Write and circle the correct spelling for each word.

		A	B	C	D
1.	_____	grravity	grraviti	graviti	gravity
2.	_____	jewelri	jewellri	jewellry	jewelry
3.	_____	obstroct	obstruct	obsctruct	obsstruct
4.	_____	trompet	trrumpet	trumpet	trrompet
5.	_____	imigrant	imygrant	immygrant	immigrant
6.	_____	oxygen	oxygfn	oxyjen	oxyjtn
7.	_____	sensse	sence	sense	sensce
8.	_____	judje	juqje	judge	judne
9.	_____	altitode	alltitude	alltitode	altitude
10.	_____	December	Decemberr	Desember	Desemberr
11.	_____	tolerable	tolerible	tollerible	tollerable
12.	_____	acttive	actyve	acttyve	active
13.	_____	aware	awarre	awarra	awara
14.	_____	trryple	tryple	trriple	triple
15.	_____	exselent	excelent	exsellent	excellent
16.	_____	adaptible	adapttible	adaptable	adapttable
17.	_____	Ausstralia	Ausstralai	Australai	Australia
18.	_____	syngle	singlle	single	synglle
19.	_____	launch	luanch	laonch	loanch
20.	_____	smyled	smilled	smiled	smylled
21.	_____	finanse	finance	finense	finence
22.	_____	climb	cllymb	cllimb	clymb
23.	_____	introducsion	inttroduction	introduction	inttroducsion
24.	_____	Japanece	Japanese	Japanesse	Japanesce
25.	_____	speciallize	specialize	specailize	specaillize
26.	_____	gulible	gullible	gulable	gullably

Spelling Words Lesson IV

Write and circle the correct spelling for each word.

		A	B	C	D
1.	_____	enttared	entered	enttered	entared
2.	_____	ignorant	ignurrant	ignurant	ignorrant
3.	_____	brilaint	brilliant	briliant	brillaint
4.	_____	wonder	wonderr	wunder	wunderr
5.	_____	horable	horible	horrable	horrible
6.	_____	horicane	huricane	horricane	hurricane
7.	_____	Aprryl	April	Apryl	Aprril
8.	_____	respirasion	respiration	resspiration	resspirasion
9.	_____	information	infformasion	infformation	informasion
10.	_____	crruel	croel	cruel	crroel
11.	_____	January	Janaurry	Janaury	Januarry
12.	_____	buttom	botom	bottom	butom
13.	_____	bicycle	bicicle	bicyclle	biciclle
14.	_____	cumett	comett	comet	cumet
15.	_____	recieved	reseived	received	recyeved
16.	_____	students	sttudents	sttodents	stodents
17.	_____	movenment	movenmentt	movementt	movement
18.	_____	cumpay	cumpany	company	compay
19.	_____	disclike	disslike	dislicke	dislike
20.	_____	sheepish	shepysh	shepish	sheapish
21.	_____	surprise	surrprise	surprice	surrprice
22.	_____	politicain	polliticain	pollitician	politician
23.	_____	senator	senattur	senatur	senattor
24.	_____	endoy	enjoy	enjyy	enjuy
25.	_____	pattroit	pattriot	patriot	patroit
26.	_____	brruise	bruice	bruise	brruice
27.	_____	sleeve	sleve	seeave	tlave

Science: Temperate Forest Biome

There are many trees in all forests, but there are different types of forests. They are frequently referred to as different biomes. One of the most noticeable differences is where they are in relation to the equator and the poles. Forest biomes are classified into three types: rainforest, temperate forest, and taiga. Rainforests are found near the equator in the tropics. Taiga forests are found in the far north. Temperate rainforests are found in the middle.

Temperature - Temperate means "in moderation" or "not to extremes." Temperate refers to the temperature in this context. The temperate forest never gets extremely hot (as in the rainforest) or extremely cold (as in the Taiga). The temperature ranges between -20 and 90 degrees Fahrenheit.

Four distinct seasons - Winter, spring, summer, and fall are the four distinct seasons. Each season lasts roughly the same amount of time. Plants have a long growing season with only a three-month winter.

Lots of rain - Throughout the year, there is a lot of rain, usually between 30 and 60 inches. Fertile soil - Rotted leaves and other decaying matter create a rich, deep soil that allows trees to grow strong roots.

Temperate forests come in a variety of forms. Here are a few examples:

Coniferous forests are dominated by conifer trees such as cypress, cedar, redwood, fir, juniper, and pine. These trees have cones instead of flowers and grow needles instead of leaves.

Broad-leafed forests are made up of broad-leafed trees like oak, maple, elm, walnut, chestnut, and hickory. The leaves on these trees are large and change color in the fall.

Mixed coniferous and broad-leaved forests - These forests contain a mixture of conifers and broad-leaved trees.

Major temperate forests can be found all over the world, including:

Eastern North America
Southeast Australia
New Zealand
Eastern China
Europe
Japan

The plants in the forests grow in layers. The canopy is the top layer, which is made up of fully grown trees. Throughout the year, these trees form an umbrella, providing shade for the layers below. The understory refers to the middle layer. Smaller trees, saplings, and shrubs make up the understory. The forest floor, which is made up of wildflowers, herbs, ferns, mushrooms, and mosses, is the lowest layer.

The plants that grow here share some characteristics.

They shed their leaves - Many of the trees that grow here are deciduous, which means they shed their leaves in the winter. There are a few evergreen trees that keep their leaves throughout the winter.

Sap - sap is used by many trees to help them survive the winter. It keeps their roots from freezing and is then used as energy to start growing again in the spring.

Animals that live here include black bears, mountain lions, deer, fox, squirrels, skunks, rabbits, porcupines, timber wolves, and a variety of birds. Mountain lions and hawks, for example, are predators. Many animals, such as squirrels and turkeys, rely on the nuts from the many trees to survive.

Each animal species has adapted to survive the winter.

Stay active - Some animals remain active throughout the winter. There are rabbits, squirrels, foxes, and deer, all of which are active.

Some are simply good at finding food, whereas others, such as squirrels, store and hide food in the fall so that they can eat it during the winter.

Migrate - Some animals, such as birds, migrate to warmer areas for the winter and then return home in the spring.

Hibernate - During the winter, some animals hibernate or rest. They basically sleep all winter and survive on fat stored in their bodies.

Many insects die and lay eggs because they cannot survive the winter, but they lay eggs that can. In the spring, their eggs will hatch.

Remember that there may be some question-answer relationship (QAR) questions, so please keep that in mind when answering the questions below.

1. _____ are found in Northern Hemisphere regions with moist, warm summers and cold winters, primarily in eastern North America, eastern Asia, and western Europe.
   a. Wild forests
   b. Rainforests
   c. Deciduous forests

2. How many types of forest biomes are there?
   a. 2
   b. 3
   c. 4

3. Temperate forests emerged during the period of global cooling that began at the beginning of the _____.
   a. Medieval Era
   b. Paleozoic Era
   c. Cenozoic Era

4. Major temperate forests are located in the following areas, except for:
   a. Japan
   b. Korea
   c. Eastern China

5. What makes a forest a temperate forest?
   a. Temperature, Two seasons, Tropics, and Clay soil.
   b. Temperature, Climate, Wet season, and Loam soil.
   c. Temperature, Four seasons, Lots of rain, and Fertile soil.

6. The three main types of forest biomes are: the rainforest, the temperate forest, and the _____.
   a. Taiga
   b. Broad-leafed
   c. Coniferous

7. Many trees rely on _____ to get through the winter.
   a. temperature
   b. sap
   c. rain

8. Temperate forests are usually classified into two main groups, and these are: _____ and _____.
   a. Indigenous, Evergreen
   b. Deciduous, Evergreen
   c. Coniferous, Deciduous

9. Deciduous is a Latin word that means _____.
   a. "to subside"
   b. "to rise up"
   c. "to fall off"

10. Certain trees in a temperate forest can grow up to how many feet?
    a. 50 feet tall
    b. 90 feet tall
    c. 100 feet tall

11. _____ forests are made up mostly of conifer trees such as cypress, cedar, redwood, fir, juniper, and pine trees.
    a. Coniferous
    b. Broad-leafed
    c. Mixed coniferous and broad-leafed

12. The animals that live in temperate forests have _____ that allow them to _____ in different kinds of weather.
    a. adaptations, survive
    b. conformity, thrive
    c. compatibility, survive

Science: Mallard Duck

First, read the entire passage. After that, go back and fill in the blanks. You can skip the blanks you're unsure about and finish them later.

plants	habitats	female	bodies	quacking
North	hatch	foods	waddle	colors

The Mallard Duck is what most people think of when they think of ducks. The Mallard is a common duck that can be found throughout _____ America, Europe, and Asia. Central America, Australia, and New Zealand are also home to the Mallard Duck. Anas Platyrhynchos is the scientific name for the Mallard Duck. It belongs to the Dabbling Ducks family. Mallard Ducks enjoy the water and are commonly found near rivers, ponds, and other _____ of water.

Mallard ducks can grow to be about two feet long and weigh about two and a half pounds. The _____ Mallard Duck has tan feathers all over, whereas the male Mallard Duck has a green head, darker back and chest feathers, and a white body. Some people breed domestic Mallard Ducks in order to get different _____.

Mallards are omnivorous birds. This means that they consume both _____ and other animals. They primarily feed on the water's surface, consuming various seeds, small fish, insects, frogs, and fish eggs. They also enjoy some human _____, particularly grain from human crops.

Female Mallard ducks are well-known for their "quack." When you were a kid and learned that ducks make a _____ sound, you were hearing the female Mallard. Females quack to attract other ducks, usually their ducklings. This call is also known as the "hail call" or "decrescendo call." This call can be heard for miles by the ducklings.

Like many other birds, Mallard ducks migrate in flocks from the north to the south for the winter and then back north for the summer. This way, they're always where it's warm, and there's food. These ducks are also adaptable in other ways. They thrive even when humans destroy their natural _____. This is not to say that we should destroy their habitat, but they have not been endangered due to human interaction thus far.

Ducklings are young Mallards. A mother duck will typically lay 10 to 15 eggs. She cares for the eggs in a nest by herself. The mother duck will lead the ducklings to the water shortly after they _____ from the eggs. They usually do not return to the nest after that. Baby ducklings are ready to go just a few hours after hatching. They can swim, _____, feed themselves, and find food quickly. For the next few months, their mother will keep an eye on them and protect them. The ducklings will be able to fly and become self-sufficient after about two months.

Science Multiple Choice Quiz: Tyrannosaurus Rex

Score: _____

Date: _____

Tyrannosaurus Rex, one of the most famous and notable dinosaurs, is a theropod dinosaur. Many Tyrannosaurus fossils have been discovered, allowing scientists to learn more about how big it was, how it hunted, and how it lived.

Tyrannosaurus rex was a land predator dinosaur that was one of the largest. The T-rex could grow to be 43 feet long and weigh up to 7.5 tons. Because of its size and overall fearsome image, the dinosaur is frequently used in movies and films such as Jurassic Park.

Tyrannosaurus rex was a two-legged dinosaur. This means it could walk and run on two legs. These two legs were large and strong enough to support the dinosaur's massive weight. The T-arms, rex's, on the other hand, were relatively small. However, it is believed that the small arms were powerful to hold onto prey.

The Tyrannosaurus' massive skull and large teeth are among its most terrifying features. T-rex skulls as long as 5 feet have been discovered! Other evidence suggests that the Tyrannosaurus had a powerful bite that allowed it to crush other dinosaurs' bones easily when combined with sharp teeth.

The Tyrannosaurus Rex ate meat from other animals and dinosaurs. Still, it is unclear whether it was a predator (hunted and killed its food) or a scavenger (meaning it stole food from other predators). Many scientists believe the dinosaur did both. Much is dependent on how fast the dinosaur was. Some claim that the T-Rex was fast and capable of catching its prey. Others argue that the dinosaur was slow and used its fearsome jaws to frighten other predators and steal their prey.

There are numerous significant Tyrannosaurus specimens in museums around the world. "Sue" at the Field Museum of Natural History in Chicago is one of the largest and most comprehensive. "Stan," another significant T-Rex specimen, can be found at the Black Hills Museum of Natural History Exhibit in Hill City, South Dakota. Also on display at the American Museum of Natural History in New York, paleontologist Barnum Brown's largest Tyrannosaurus find (he discovered five in total). The only known Tyrannosaurus Rex track can be found at Philmont Scout Ranch in New Mexico.

_____

Remember that there may be some **question-answer relationship (QAR)** questions, so please keep that in mind when answering the questions below.

1. The T-rex usually measures up to _____ and weighs as much as _____.
   a. 43 feet, 2 tons
   b. 43 feet, 7.5 tons

2. The Tyrannosaurus rex was a _____ dinosaur.
   a. quadrupedal
   b. bipedal

3. The T-rex is a member of the dinosaur subgroup _____, which includes all the flesh-eating dinosaurs.
   a. Thyreophora
   b. Theropoda

4. The Tyrannosaurus rex lived in North America between 65 and 98 million years ago, during the late _____ period.
   a. Cretaceous
   b. Triassic

5. Where could we find the only documented track of a Tyrannosaurus Rex?
   a. at Philmont Scout Ranch in New Mexico
   b. at the Field Museum of Natural History in Chicago

6. Which of the following is the largest and most complete T-rex specimen that can be found on display at the Field Museum of Natural History in Chicago?
   a. Stan
   b. Sue

7. The Tyrannosaurus had a life span of around _____.
   a. 30 years
   b. 50 years

8. It is one of the most ferocious predators to ever walk the Earth.
   a. Giganotosaurus
   b. Tyrannosaurus rex

9. Tyrannosaurus rex was also adept at finding its prey through its keen sense of _____.
   a. smell
   b. sight

10. Tyrannosaurus rex (rex meaning "_____" in Latin).
    a. king
    b. master

Reading Storytime: The Frog

Score: _____

Date: _____

First, read the entire passage. After that, go back and fill in the blanks. You can skip the blanks you're unsure about and finish them later.

Frog	dinner	beautiful	castle	door
ball	cried	companion	fountain	swimming

When wishing was a thing, there was a King whose daughters were all _____, but the youngest was so stunning that even the sun, which has seen so much, was taken aback whenever it shone in her face.

A large dark forest lay close to the King's _____, and a fountain was hidden beneath an old lime tree in the woods. When it was a hot day, the King's Child went out into the forest and sat by the cool fountain, and when she was bored, she took a golden ball, threw it up in the air, and caught it. And the ball was her favorite toy.

Now, one day, the King's Daughter's golden _____ fell onto the ground and rolled straight into the water rather than into the little hand she was holding up for it. The King's Daughter pursued it with her eyes, but it vanished, and the well was deep, so deep that the bottom could not be seen. She began to cry, and she screamed louder and louder, and she could not be consoled.

And as she sobbed, someone asked her, "What ails you, King's Daughter?" You weep so much that even a stone would feel sorry for you."

When she turned around to the side from which the voice had come, she saw a _____ sticking its thick, ugly head out of the water. "Ah! "Is it you, old water-splasher?" she asked, "I am weeping for my golden ball, which has fallen into the fountain."

"Be quiet and do not weep," the Frog replied, "I can help you." But what will you give me if I bring up your toy again?"

"Whatever you want, dear Frog," she said, "my clothes, my pearls, and jewels, even the golden crown I'm wearing."

"I don't care for your clothes, pearls, and jewels, or your golden crown," the Frog replied, "but if you will love me and let me be your _____ and playfellow, and sit by you at your little table, and eat off your little golden plate, and drink out of your little cup, and sleep in your little bed-if you promise me this, I will go down below and bring your golden ball up again."

"Oh, yes," she said, "I promise you everything you want if you just bring my ball back." "How the silly

Frog does talk!" she thought. He lives in the water with the other frogs and croaks and can't be a human's companion!"

But, having received this promise, the Frog plunged his head into the water and sank. He quickly came _____ up with the ball in his mouth, and threw it on the grass. The King's Daughter was thrilled to see her pretty plaything again, and she quickly picked it up and ran away with it.

"Wait, wait," the Frog said. "Bring me along. I can't run as fast as you." But what good did it do him to scream his croak, croak, croak, croak, croak, croak! She ignored it and ran home, quickly forgetting the poor Frog, who was forced to return to his _____.

The next day, as she sat at the table with the King and all the courtiers, eating from her little golden plate, something crept up the marble staircase, splish splash, splish splash. When it reached the top, it knocked on the _____ and cried out:

"Youngest King's Daughter."
"Please open the door!"

She dashed outside to see who was there, but when she opened the door, the Frog was standing in front of it. Then she hurriedly slammed the door, sat down to _____ again, and was terrified.

"My Child, what are you so afraid of?" said the King, seeing her heart beating furiously. Is there a Giant outside looking to take you away?"

"Ah, no," she replied, "it's a disgusting Frog, not a Giant."

"What exactly does the Frog want from you?"

"Ah, dear Father, my golden ball fell into the water yesterday while I was sitting by the fountain in the forest, playing." Because I _____ so much, the Frog brought it out for me again. And because he insisted, I promised him he could be my companion, but I never imagined he'd be able to get out of the water! And now he's here, wanting to come in."

Meanwhile, it knocked a second time and cried:

"Youngest King's Daughter!"
Allow me to enter!
Don't you remember yesterday and everything you said to me, besides the cooling fountain's spray?
Youngest King's Daughter!
"Let me in!"

Music: The Piano

Score: _____

Date:_____

Bartolomeo Cristofori was the first to successfully develop a hammer-action keyboard instrument and hence deserves to be regarded as the creator of the piano.

Cristofori was dissatisfied with musicians' lack of control over the harpsichord's loudness level. Around 1700, he is credited for replacing the plucking mechanism with a hammer and thus creating the modern piano. Initially, the instrument was dubbed "clavicembalo con piano e forte" (literally, a harpsichord that can play soft and loud noises). This was later abbreviated to the now-common term "piano."

The piano possesses the characteristics of both a string and percussion instrument. A hammer strikes a string inside the piano (much like a percussion instrument). The piano's sounds and notes are produced by the vibration of these strings (like a string instrument).

The piano is commonly referred to as a keyboard instrument. This is because it is performed similarly to several other keyboard instruments, including the organ, harpsichord, electronic keyboards, and synthesizers.

The organ was the first keyboard instrument, dating back to the third century. However, the organ did not begin to use keys until much later. The harpsichord was invented in the 14th century and quickly gained popularity throughout Europe. The harpsichord plucked a string and resembled modern pianos in appearance. However, plucking the string did not allow for the playing of various volumes and expressions.

The term piano is derived from the Italian phrase pianoforte, which translates as "loud and soft." This is because you may now adjust the volume of notes played on the keyboard.

The grand piano and the upright piano are the two primary types of pianos.

Grand piano - a grand piano's strings and primary frame are horizontal. This enables longer strings and also aids in the piano's mechanics. However, grand pianos can consume a significant amount of room.

Upright piano - This piano style is more compact, making it ideal for use in a home. The strings and mainframe are arranged vertically.

Additionally, there are electronic pianos. While the keyboard and playing technique is typically identical to a standard piano, the sound is frequently quite different.

1. This piano style is more compact, making it ideal for use in a home.
   a. Upright piano
   b. Downright piano

2. A _____ strings and primary frame are horizontal.
   a. organ piano's
   b. grand piano's

3. The term piano is derived from the_____phrase pianoforte.
   a. English
   b. Italian

4. The _____ was invented in the 14th century.
   a. pianiochord
   b. harpsichord

5. The piano is commonly referred to as a _____ instrument.
   a. singer
   b. keyboard

6. The organ and harpsichord are keyboard instruments.
   a. organ
   b. guitar

Music: Jimi Hendrix

First, read the entire passage. After that, go back and fill in the blanks. You can skip the blanks you're unsure about and finish them later.

guitar	odd	acoustic	mother	Animals
guitarist	stage	Seattle	rock	childhood

Jimi Hendrix, a _____, singer, and songwriter, wowed audiences in the 1960s with his outrageous electric guitar skills and experimental sound.

Jimi Hendrix began playing guitar as a teenager and grew up to become a _____ legend known for his innovative electric guitar playing in the 1960s. His performance of "The Star-Spangled Banner" at Woodstock in 1969 was one of his most memorable. Hendrix died of drug-related complications in 1970, leaving his imprint on the world of rock music and remaining popular to this day.

On November 27, 1942, in _____, Washington, Hendrix was born Johnny Allen Hendrix (later changed by his father to James Marshall). He had a difficult _____, living in the care of relatives or acquaintances at times.

When Hendrix was born, his _____, Lucille, was only 17 years old. She had a rocky relationship with his father, Al, and eventually left the family after the couple had two more sons, Leon and Joseph. Hendrix only saw his mother on rare occasions before her death in 1958.

Music became a haven for Hendrix in many ways. He was a fan of blues and rock and roll and taught himself to play the _____ with the help of his father.

When Hendrix was 16, his father bought him his first _____ guitar, and the following year, his first electric guitar - a right-handed Supro Ozark that he had to play upside down because he was naturally left-handed. Soon after, he started performing with his band, the Rocking Kings. In 1959, he dropped out of high school and worked _____ jobs while pursuing his musical dreams.

In mid-1966, Hendrix met Chas Chandler, bassist for the British rock band the _____, who agreed to become Hendrix's manager. Chandler persuaded Hendrix to travel to London, where he formed the Jimi Hendrix Experience with bassist Noel Redding and drummer Mitch Mitchell.

While performing in England, Hendrix amassed a cult following among the country's rock royalty, with the Beatles, Rolling Stones, Who, and Eric Clapton all praising his work. According to one critic for the British music magazine Melody Maker, he "had great _____ presence" and appeared to be playing "with no hands at all" at times.

According to one journalist in the Berkeley Tribe, "Nobody could get more out of an electric guitar than Jimi Hendrix. He was the ultimate guitarist."

History: The Mayflower

Score: _____

Date: _____

First, read the entire passage. After that, go back and fill in the blanks. You can skip the blanks you're unsure about and finish them later.

ship	sail	voyage	assist	settlers
passengers	illness	load	leaking	Cape

In 1620, a _____ called the Mayflower transported a group of English colonists to North America. These people established New England's first permanent European colony in what is now Plymouth, Massachusetts. Later, they were named the Pilgrims.

The Mayflower was approximately 106 feet long, 25 feet wide, and had a tonnage of 180. The deck of the Mayflower was about 80 feet long, roughly the length of a basketball court. The ship had three masts for holding sails:

The fore-mast (in front)

The main-mast (in the middle)

The mizzen mast (in the back) (back)

On August 4, 1620, the Mayflower and the Speedwell set sail from Southampton, England. They had to come to a halt in Dartmouth, however, because the Speedwell was leaking. They left Dartmouth on August 21, but the Speedwell began _____ again, and they came to a halt in Plymouth, England. They decided to abandon the Speedwell at Plymouth and _____ as many passengers as possible onto the Mayflower. On September 6, 1620, they set sail from Plymouth.

The Mayflower set _____ from Plymouth, England, west across the Atlantic Ocean. The ship's original destination was Virginia, but storms forced it to change course. On November 9, 1620, more than two months after leaving Plymouth, the Mayflower sighted _____ Cod. The Pilgrims decided to stay even though they were north of where they had planned to settle.

It is estimated that around 30 children were on board the Mayflower during the epic _____ to America, but little is known about many of them.

They were children of passengers, some traveled with other adults, and some were servants - but having young people among the _____ was critical to the Plymouth Colony's survival.

It is believed that when the colonists faced their first harsh winter of _____ and death in a new land, the children would _____ the adults by tending to the sick, assisting in the preparation of food, and fetching firewood and water.

While nearly half of the ship's _____ died during the winter of 1620/1621, it is believed that there were fewer deaths among the children, implying that the struggling colony had a better chance of thriving.

Health: The Food Groups

Score: _____

Date: _____

First, read the entire passage. After that, go back and fill in the blanks. You can skip the blanks you're unsure about and finish them later.

produce	consume	yogurt	stored	bones
repair	water	portion	vitamins	fiber

Eating healthy foods is especially important for children because they are still developing. Children's bodies require nutrition to develop strong, healthy _____ and muscles. You will not grow as tall or as strong as you could if you do not get all the _____ and minerals you require while growing.

Healthy food includes a wide variety of fresh foods from the five healthy food groups:

Dairy: Milk, cheese, and _____ are the most critical dairy foods, which are necessary for strong and healthy bones. There aren't many other foods in our diet that have as much calcium as these.

Fruit: Fruit contains vitamins, minerals, dietary fiber, and various phytonutrients (nutrients found naturally in plants) that help your body stay healthy. Fruits and vegetables provide you with energy, antioxidants, and _____. These nutrients help protect you against diseases later in life, such as heart disease, stroke, and some cancers.

Vegetables and legumes/beans: Vegetables should account for a large _____ of your daily food intake and should be encouraged at all meals (including snack times). To keep your body healthy, they supply vitamins, minerals, dietary fiber, and phytonutrients (nutrients found naturally in plants).

Grain (cereal) foods: choose wholegrain and/or high _____ bread, cereals, rice, pasta, noodles, and so on. These foods provide you with the energy you require to grow, develop, and learn. Refined grain products (such as cakes and biscuits) can contain added sugar, fat, and sodium.

Protein from lean meats and poultry, fish, eggs, tofu, nuts and seeds, and legumes/beans is used by our bodies to _____ specialized chemicals such as hemoglobin and adrenalin. Protein also helps to build, maintain, and _____ tissues in our bodies. Protein is the primary component of muscles and organs (such as your heart).

Calories are a unit of measurement for the amount of energy in food. We gain calories when we eat, which gives us the energy to run around and do things. If we _____ more calories than we expend while moving, our bodies will store the excess calories as fat. If we burn more calories than we consume, our bodies will begin to burn the previously _____ fat.

Grammar: Singular and Plural

Score: _____

Date:_____

Nouns can take many different forms. Singular and plural are two of these forms. A singular noun refers to a single person, place, thing, or idea. A plural noun is one that refers to two or more people, places, things, or ideas. How do you pluralize a singular noun? Making a singular noun plural is usually as simple as adding a **s** to the end of the word.
Example: Singular toy | Plural toys

Some nouns, however, do not follow this rule and are referred to as irregular nouns. How do I pluralize a singular irregular noun?

We'll start with **singular nouns** that end in s, ss, ch, sh, x, or z. If a singular noun **ends in s, ss, ch, sh, x, or z**, add **es** at the end.
Example: beach--->beaches

If the singular noun **ends in a vowel**, the letters a, e, I o, and u are usually suffixed with an **s**.
Example: video--->videos

If a singular noun **ends with a consonant + o**, it is common to add an **es** at the end. Except for a, e, I o, and u, consonants are all the letters of the alphabet.
Example: potato--->potatoes

Simply add a **s** to the end of the word if the singular noun **ends in a vowel + y** pattern.
Example: day--->days

Now we'll look at singular nouns that **end in f or fe**. If the singular noun ends in a f or fe, **change it to a v and then add es**.
Example: life--->lives

Consonant + y is another unusual noun. If the singular noun **ends with a consonant + y** pattern, **change the y to I before adding es**.
Example: bunny---> bunnies

Some nouns are spelled the same way in both the singular and plural forms.

It's now time to make some spelling changes. When you switch from the singular to plural form of a noun, the spelling changes. The following are some examples of common words that change spelling when formed into plurals:
Example: child--->childrens

Select the best answer for each question.

1. **Which word is NOT a plural noun?**
    a. books
    b. hat
    c. toys

2. **Which word is a singular noun?**
    a. bikes
    b. cars
    c. pencil

3. **Which word can be both singular and plural?**
    a. deer
    b. bears
    c. mice

4. **Tommy _____ badminton at the court.**
    a. playing
    b. plays
    c. play's

5. **They _____ to eat at fast food restaurants once in a while.**
    a. likes
    b. like
    c. likies

6. **Everybody _____ Janet Jackson.**
    a. know
    b. known
    c. knows

7. He ___ very fast. You have to listen carefully.
   a. spoken
   b. speak
   c. speaks

8. Which one is the singular form of women?
   a. womans
   b. woman
   c. women

9. The plural form of tooth is
   a. tooths
   b. toothes
   c. teeth

10. The singular form of mice is _____.
   a. mouse
   b. mices
   c. mouses

11. The plural form of glass is _____.
   a. glassies
   b. glasses
   c. glassy

12. The plural form of dress is _____.
   a. dressing
   b. dresses
   c. dressy

13. Plural means many.
   a. True
   b. False

14. Singular means 1.
   a. True
   b. False

15. Is this word singular or plural? monsters
   a. plural
   b. singular

16. Find the plural noun in the sentence. They gave her a nice vase full of flowers.
   a. they
   b. flowers
   c. vase

17. Find the plural noun in the sentence. Her baby brother grabbed the crayons out of the box and drew on the wall.
   a. crayons
   b. box
   c. brothers

18. Find the plural noun in the sentence. My friend, Lois, picked enough red strawberries for the whole class.
   a. strawberries
   b. friends
   c. classes

19. What is the correct plural form of the noun wish?
   a. wishes
   b. wishs
   c. wishy

20. What is the correct plural form of the noun flurry?
   a. flurrys
   b. flurryies
   c. flurries

21. What is the correct plural form of the noun box?
   a. boxs
   b. boxses
   c. boxes

22. What is the correct plural form of the noun bee?
   a. beess
   b. beeses
   c. bees

23. What is the correct plural form of the noun candy?
   a. candys
   b. candyies
   c. candies

24. Find the singular noun in the sentence. The boys and girls drew pictures on the sidewalk.
   a. boys
   b. drew
   c. sidewalk

Grammar Review

Common & Proper Noun: A noun is a word that is used to describe a person, animal, place, thing, or idea. **Common nouns** are words that are used to refer to general objects rather than specific ones. All of these items are named with common nouns: lamp, chair, couch, TV, window, painting, pillow, and candle.

A **proper noun** is a unique (not generic) name for a specific person, place, or thing. In English, proper nouns are always capitalized, regardless of where they appear in a sentence.

Common noun: I want to be a **writer**. ✓
Proper noun: Carlyon Jones wrote many books. ✓

Plural Nouns: **Plural nouns** are words that indicate the presence of more than one person, animal, place, thing, or idea.

- bottle – bottles. ✓
- cup – cups. ✓

Collective Nouns: **Collective nouns** are names for a collection or a number of people or things.

 crowd, government, team, family, audience, etc.

Singular Possessive Noun: A **singular possessive noun** indicates that something is owned by someone or something. We add an's to indicate ownership. • *cat's tail*, for example.

Concrete Noun: A **concrete noun** is a real-world physical object, such as a dog, a ball, or an ice cream cone. Another way to put it, a concrete noun is the name of an object which may be perceived by one or more of the five senses. An **abstract noun** is a concept or idea that does not exist in the physical world and cannot be touched, such as freedom, sadness, or permission.

Verb: A verb is defined as a word (such as jump, think, happen, or exist) that expresses an action and is usually one of the main parts of a sentence.

Adjectives are words that describe the qualities or states of being of nouns: enormous, doglike, silly, yellow, fun, fast.

Simple Subject: A **simple subject** is a subject's main word or words. It lacks any modifiers that could be used to describe the subject. To find the simple subject in a sentence, consider who or what is doing the action in the sentence. But keep in mind that a simple subject is very basic, a subject, a verb, and a completed thought.

Tina waited for the train.
"Tina" = subject, "waited" = verb ✓

Prepositions Object: A preposition is a word that appears before a noun to indicate its relationship to another word in the phrase or clause.
As a result, a noun can serve as the object of the preposition. The noun that follows the preposition is known as the object of the preposition.

To find the preposition's object:

1) Locate the preposition.
2) Then, put the preposition in the blank and ask "_____ who or what?"

Jim's house is across the street. (Across what?) street ✓
The show will begin at 7:00. (At what?) 7:00 ✓

Indirect Object: An indirect object is one that is used with a transitive verb to indicate who benefits from or receives something as a result of an action. In the sentence 'She gave him her address,' for example, 'him' is the indirect object.

Direct object: A direct object is a word or phrase that receives the verb's action. The direct object in the sentence: 'The kids eat cake.' is cake; the verb is eat, and the object being eaten is cake.

Direct Address: Nouns of **direct address** are the nouns used to indicate that a speaker is directly addressing a person or group. When addressing a person or thing directly, the name must be separated by a comma (or commas if in the middle of a sentence).

- Tommy, are you leaving so soon? ✓ (As "Tommy" is being addressed directly, his name is offset with a comma.)

1. **His father is the coach of the team.**
   a. his, father, team
   b. his, father, coach
   c. father, coach, team

2. **David is driving to the beach.**
   a. David, driving, beach
   b. David, driving
   c. David, beach

3. **What are the PROPER nouns in the following sentence?   My grandparents live in Florida.**
   a. grandparents, Flordia
   b. Flordia
   c. My, grandparents

4. **What are all the COMMON nouns in the following sentence?   I have two dogs and one cat.**
   a. cat, one
   b. dogs, cat
   c. I, dogs

5. **Which sentence contains only one common noun and one proper noun?**
   a. These potatoes are from Idaho.
   b. Casey is a talented singer and dancer.
   c. I live near the border of Nevada and Utah.

6. **Which sentence contains the correct form of a plural noun?**
   a. The wolves chase a frightened rabbit.
   b. The wolfes chase a frightened rabbit.
   c. The wolfs chase a frightened rabbit.

7. **Which sentence contains one singular noun and one plural noun?**
   a. The musician tunes her instrument.
   b. The conductor welcomes each musician.
   c. The singers walk across the stage.

8. **Identify the collective noun in the following sentence.**
   Derek is the lead singer in a band.
   a. singer
   b. band
   c. lead

9. Which sentence contains the correct form of a singular possessive noun?

    a. The boxs' lid is torn.

    b. The box's lid is torn.

    c. The boxes' lid is torn.

10. Which sentence contains one concrete noun and on abstract noun?

    a. John feels anxiety about meeting new people.

    b. The young boy plays with trains.

    c. The sand feels warm between my toes.

11. Identify the simple subject in the following sentence.   The children are playing tag.

    a. tag

    b. children

    c. The children

12. Identify the simple subject in the following sentence.
  This computer belongs to my father.

    a. computer

    b. This computer

    c. father

13. Which sentence has an object of a preposition?

    a. Several passengers missed the flight.

    b. Seattle is a city in Washington.

    c. The boys are racing remote-controlled cars.

14. Identify the object of preposition in the following sentence.
  The are playing a game of cards.

    a. cards

    b. game

    c. of cards

15. Identify the subject complement in the following sentence.
  Mr. Smith is a talented poet.

    a. poet

    b. talented

    c. Mr. Smith

16. Identify the subject complement in the following sentence.
  Tulips and daisies are my favorite flowers.

    a. my

    b. flowers

    c. favorite

17. Identify the direct object in the following sentence.   Tyler delivers newspapers each morning.

    a. newspapers

    b. morning

    c. each

18. Identify the direct object in the following sentence.   We will paint the bathroom beige.

    a. bathroom

    b. paint

    c. beige

19. Identify the indirect object in the following sentence.   Mr. Jackson gave the students their grades.

    a. grades

    b. students

    c. their

20. Identify the indirect object in the following sentence.   Mrs. Parker bought her husband a new tie.

    a. new tie

    b. husband

    c. tie

21. **In which sentence is paint used as a noun?**
    a. These artists paint the most amazing murals.
    b. We need two cans of brown paint.
    c. Let's paint the bedroom light green.

22. **In which sentence is sign used as a verb?**
    a. I saw it as a sign of good luck.
    b. Joelle is learning sign language.
    c. Did you sign the letter at the bottom?

23. **In which sentence is file used as an adjective?**
    a. This file contains the detective's notes.
    b. Put these papers in a file folder.
    c. I use a file to smooth the edges of my nails.

24. **Identify the direct address in the following sentence.** This is your baseball bat, Kenny.
    a. Kenny
    b. baseball
    c. bat

25. **Identify the direct address in the following sentence.**
    Hector, did you buy more milk?
    a. Hector
    b. you
    c. milk

26. **Objects of the preposition. Lee cried during the movie.**
    a. Lee
    b. movie
    c. cried

27. **Objects of the preposition. The phone is on the table.**
    a. table
    b. phone
    c. none

28. **Direct Objects: Every actor played his part.**
    a. his part
    b. actor
    c. played

29. **Direct Objects: The crowd will cheer the President.**
    a. the President
    b. cheer
    c. crowd

30. **Examples of concrete nouns are:**
    a. flower, music, bear, pie,
    b. love, cars, them, went
    c. me, I, she, they

31. **Direct Address: Well certainly, Mother, I remember what you said.**
    a. you
    b. Mother
    c. certainly

32. **Direct Address: I heard exactly what you said, Pam.**
    a. Pam
    b. none
    c. you

33. **Collective Noun: A choir of singers**
    a. choir
    b. sing
    c. singers

34. **Collective Noun: A litter of puppies**
    a. litter
    b. puppies
    c. puppy

Geography: Lebanon

Lebanon's land was settled thousands of years ago. The city of Byblos is one of the world's oldest continuously inhabited cities. The Phoenician Empire arose from the land of Lebanon around 1500 BC. They were seafaring people with a culture that thrived and spread throughout the Mediterranean. The Phoenicians ruled until around 300 BC, when the Persian Empire led by Cyrus the Great conquered the land. Tyre was the most well-known Phoenician city. In 332 BC, Alexander the Great burned Tyre. Over time, the land of Lebanon would be ruled by several empires, including the Romans, Arabs, and, finally, the Ottoman Empire. When the Ottoman Empire fell apart following World War I, France seized control of Lebanon. Lebanon gained independence from France in 1943. Lebanon has been involved in wars with Israel as well as internal civil wars since its independence.

Lebanon is a small Middle Eastern country bordered by Syria and Israel. People first established villages in Lebanon over 7,000 years ago. The country has been ravaged by wars, the majority of which have been religious in nature. Following Christ's death, a monk named Maron established a monastery in the hills of Lebanon to avoid persecution by Roman officials. He and the other monks spread Christianity throughout Lebanon and much of the Middle East from here. When Muslim Arabs invaded Lebanon, they converted the majority of the population to Islam.

In the 11th century, the Pope dispatched knights from Europe to re-convert the Middle East to Christianity, resulting in more religious wars. In the late twentieth century, Christian and Muslim factions in Lebanon fought a civil war. Today, the country is still plagued by violence due to the civil war in Syria, which occasionally spills over into Lebanon.

The climate in Lebanon is Mediterranean. Summers are hot and dry, while winters are cool and wet. Mountains, hills, coastal plains, and deserts can all be found in the country.

Remember that there may be some question-answer relationship (QAR) questions, so please keep that in mind when answering the questions below.

1. **Lebanon is a country in the _____, on the Mediterranean Sea.**
    a. Middle East
    b. Western Europe
    c. Africa

2. **Lebanon has _____ rivers all of which are non-navigable.**
    a. 16
    b. 18
    c. 17

3. **What is the capital city of Lebanon?**
    a. Tyre
    b. Sidon
    c. Beirut

4. **Lebanon has a moderate _____.**
    a. Mediterranean climate
    b. Continental climate
    c. Temperate climate

5. **When the Ottoman Empire collapsed after World War I, which country took control of Lebanon?**
    a. France
    b. Britain
    c. Russia

6. **When did Lebanon become a sovereign under the authority of the Free French government?**
    a. November 26, 1943
    b. September 1, 1926
    c. May 25, 1926

7. **What is the national symbol in Lebanon?**
    a. Maple tree
    b. Pine tree
    c. Cedar tree

8. **Lebanon is bordered by _____ to the north and east, _____ to the south, and the Mediterranean Sea to the west.**
    a. Israel, France
    b. Japan, Korea
    c. Syria, Israel

9. Lebanon is divided into how many governorates?
   a. 7
   b. 8
   c. 6

10. The Cedar Revolution occurred in 2005, following the assassination of Lebanese Prime Minister _____ in a car bomb explosion.
   a. Fakhr-al-Din II
   b. Rafik Hariri
   c. Jabal Amel

11. The city of _____ is one of the oldest continuously inhabited cities in the world.
   a. Byblos
   b. Baalbek
   c. Beirut

12. Lebanon is divided into how many districts?
   a. 24
   b. 25
   c. 22

13. Lebanon's capital and largest city is _____.
   a. Brunitz
   b. Beirut
   c. Whales

14. Lebanon was conquered by the _____ Empire in the 16th century
   a. Ottoman
   b. Overmann
   c. US troops

15. Lebanon is a _____ country.
   a. strong
   b. developing
   c. newly built

16. Lebanon gained a measure of independence while France was occupied by _____.
   a. China
   b. Maine
   c. Germany

17. Lebanon supported neighboring Arab countries in a war against _____.
   a. Israel
   b. Africa
   c. United States

18. How old is Lebanon?
   a. nearly 200 years of history
   b. nearly 5,000 years of history
   c. nearly 1 million years of history

Biography: Calvin Coolidge

Calvin Coolidge is well-known for cleaning up after his predecessor, President Harding. He's also known for being a man of few words, earning him the moniker "Silent Cal."

Calvin grew up in the small Vermont town of Plymouth. Calvin's father was a storekeeper who instilled in him puritan values such as frugality, hard work, and honesty. Calvin was a quiet but hardworking young man. Calvin attended Amherst College before relocating to Massachusetts to pursue a law degree. He passed the bar exam and became a lawyer in 1897, opening his law firm a year later. Calvin also worked in various city offices over the next few years before meeting and marrying Grace Goodhue, a schoolteacher, in 1905.

Before becoming president, Coolidge held several elected positions. He was a city councilman and a solicitor in his hometown. He later became a state legislator and the mayor of Northampton. He was then elected as Massachusetts' lieutenant governor, and in 1918, he was elected as the state's governor. During the 1919 Boston Police Strike, Coolidge gained national attention as governor of Massachusetts. This was when the Boston police officers formed a union and decided to strike or not show up for work. With no cops on the beat, Boston's streets became dangerous. Coolidge went on the offensive, fired the strikers, and hired a new police force. Coolidge was unexpectedly chosen as Warren Harding's vice-presidential running mate in 1920. They won the election, and Coolidge was appointed as Vice President.

President Harding died on a trip to Alaska in 1923. Harding's administration was riddled with corruption and scandal. Coolidge, fortunately, had not been a part of the corruption and immediately cleaned the house. He fired corrupt and inept officials and replaced them with new, dependable employees.

Calvin Coolidge's quiet but honest demeanor appeared to be exactly what the country needed at the time. The economy thrived as a result of cleaning up the scandals and showing support for businesses. This prosperous era became known as the "Roaring Twenties." Coolidge was elected president for a second term after Harding's term ended. He campaigned with the slogan "Keep Cool with Coolidge." Coolidge, as president, advocated for limited government. He also desired to keep the country somewhat isolated and refused to join the League of Nations, which was formed following World War I. He advocated for tax cuts, reduced government spending, and less assistance to struggling farmers. In 1928, Coolidge decided not to run for president again. Although he was likely to win, he felt he had served his time as president.

In 1928, Coolidge decided not to run for president again. Although he was likely to win, he felt he had served his time as president.

Remember that there may be some question-answer relationship (QAR) questions, so please keep that in mind when answering the questions below.

1. **Calvin Coolidge was the _____ of the United States.**
   a. 30th President
   b. 31st President
   c. 29th President

2. **Calvin Coolidge served as President from _____ to _____ .**
   a. 1923-1929
   b. 1929-1933
   c. 1913-1921

3. **He is also famous for _____ earning him the nickname _____ .**
   a. breaking up large companies, The Trust Buster
   b. bing excellent in academic, schoolmaster
   c. being a man of few words, Silent Cal

4. **Calvin grew up in the small town of _____ .**
   a. Plymouth, Vermont
   b. Staunton, Virginia
   c. New York, New York

5. **Calvin Coolidge signed the _____, which gave full U.S. citizen rights to all Native Americans.**

   a. The Dawes Act

   b. Indian Citizenship Act

   c. Indian Civil Rights Act

6. **Who was the Vice President under Calvin Coolidge's administration?**

   a. Charles Curtis

   b. Thomas Riley Sherman

   c. Charles Gates Dawes

7. **Coolidge gained national recognition during the 1919 _____ when he served as governor.**

   a. Boston Police Strike

   b. Baltimore Police Strike

   c. NYPD Police Strike

8. **Calvin died of a sudden heart attack _____ years after leaving the presidency.**

   a. five

   b. three

   c. four

9. **Calvin Coolidge became President of the United States after his predecessor, _____ died in office.**

   a. Warren Harding

   b. William Taft

   c. Herbert Hoover

10. **The _____ is a nickname for the 1920s in the United States as it was a time of hope, prosperity, and cultural change during President Calvin Coolidge's presidential term.**

    a. Roaring Twenties

    b. Gilded Age

    c. Reconstruction

11. **Which of the following words best describes President Calvin Coolidge's personality?**

    a. quiet

    b. adventurous

    c. talkative

12. **What was Calvin Coolidge's campaign slogan when he ran for President of the United States?**

    a. Keep Cool with Coolidge

    b. Coolidge, For the Future

    c. Peace, Prosperity, and Coolidge

Art: J. M. W. Turner

Joseph Mallord William Turner, also known as William Turner, was an English Romantic painter, printmaker, and watercolorist. He is well-known for his expressive colorizations, imaginative landscapes, and turbulent, often violent sea paintings.

On April 23, 1775, J. M. W. Turner was born above his father's barbershop in London, England. When Joseph was a child, he began to draw pictures. He enjoyed drawing outside scenes, particularly buildings. His father's shop sold some of his drawings.

He began attending the Royal Academy of Art in London when he was fourteen years old. He kept sketching and painting with watercolors. Many of his sketches were published in magazines. While he mostly drew buildings and architecture, he also began to draw some seascapes.

In 1796, Turner completed his first oil painting. Fishermen at Sea was the title. Turner gained a national reputation as a talented artist as a result of the painting's critical acclaim. Many people compared his work to that of other well-known painters.

Turner was captivated by the power of God in natural scenes, particularly the ocean and the sun. He would make numerous sketches in numbered notebooks, which he would then reference when painting in his studio. He frequently included people in his paintings, but they were small and insignificant compared to the power of nature around them.

Turner's work evolved, with less emphasis on detail and more emphasis on the energy of the natural phenomenon he was painting, such as the sea, a storm, a fire, or the sun. The paintings' objects became less recognizable.

The painting Rain, Steam, and Speed is an example of this. Light and mist are used to power the train engine as it moves down the track in this landscape of a locomotive crossing a bridge. The focus is on the color and changing light as the train passes through the landscape.

Many of Turner's later works are reminiscent of the Impressionist style of painting that would emerge in France in the coming years. Turner's work undoubtedly influenced artists like Monet, Degas, and Renoir.

Many art historians regard J. M. W. Turner as the most incredible landscape painter of all time. His artwork had a significant influence on many artists who came after him, including many impressionists.

1. Turner's later works are reminiscent of the _____ style of painting.
   a. Impressionist
   b. Watercolor

2. In 1796, Turner completed his first _____painting.
   a. colored
   b. oil

3. Turner began attending the _____ of Art in London.
   a. Royal State University
   b. Royal Academy

4. Turner was born above his father's _____.
   a. mechanic shop
   b. barbershop

5. J. M. W. Turner was an English Romantic painter, _____, and watercolorist.
   a. teacher
   b. printmaker

6. Turner frequently included _____ in his painting.
   a. animals
   b. people

Spelling Words City

Use the word bank to unscramble the words below.

bubble	community	reject	husband	pineapple	hostile
compass	tomatoes	alarm	salute	perhaps	fugitive
friends	council	fountain	goose	ankle	tutor
difference	center	hammer	jewel	choir	fatal
children	subject				

1. RNIEFDS   _ _ i _ n _ _

2. UGITIFVE   f _ g _ _ _ _ _

3. EPLIPPNAE   _ _ n _ _ _ _ e

4. RSEPAPH   _ _ r _ _ p _

5. COIRH   _ _ o _ _

6. AOTFNUIN   _ o u _ _ _ _

7. EGOSO   _ _ _ s _

8. ERAMMH   h a _ _ _ _

9. LOCNUIC   _ _ u _ _ i _

10. LHOTEIS   _ o _ _ _ _ e

11. AALTF   _ _ _ a _

12. JLEWE   _ _ w _ _

13. CTIMMUNOY   _ _ _ m _ _ _ t _

14. ASCMPOS   _ _ _ _ a _ s

15. LASUTE   _ _ l _ _ e

16. ESTUCJB   _ _ _ j _ c _

17. CLEDHNRI   _ _ _ _ _ r e _

18. RCEEJT   _ e _ e _ _

19. CIDFEFREEN   _ i f _ _ _ _ _ c _

20. NLEAK   _ _ _ l _

21. HANDSUB   _ u s _ _ _ _

22. EECRTN   _ e _ t _ _

23. MOSOTAET   _ o _ a _ _ _ _

24. OURTT   _ _ _ _ r

25. RALMA   _ _ _ r _

26. LEBUBB   b _ _ b _ _

Science: Vertebrates

To begin, all animals are classified as either vertebrates or invertebrates. Invertebrates lack a backbone, whereas vertebrates do. Scientists can't stop there, because each group contains thousands of different animals! As a result, scientists divide vertebrates and invertebrates into increasingly smaller groups. Let's talk about vertebrates and some of their classifications.

Vertebrates range in size from a frog to a blue whale. Because there are at least 59,000 different types of vertebrates on the planet, they are further classified into five major groups: mammals, birds, fish, amphibians, and reptiles. Remember that animals are classified into these groups based on what they have in common. Why is an elephant classified as a mammal while a crocodile is classified as a reptile? Let's go over some of the characteristics of each vertebrate group.

Warm-blooded animals are mammals. This means that their bodies maintain their temperature, which is usually higher than the temperature of the surrounding air. They also have hair or fur; they have lungs to breathe air; that they feed milk to their babies; and that most give birth to live young, rather than laying eggs, as a dog does.

- Birds have feathers, two wings (though not all birds, such as the ostrich and penguin, can fly), are warm-blooded, and lay eggs.
- Fish have fins or scales, live in water, and breathe oxygen through gills.
- Like salamanders and frogs, Amphibians have smooth, moist skin (amphibians must keep their skin wet); lay eggs in water; most breathe through their skin and lungs.
- Reptiles have scales (imagine a scaly lizard), are cold-blooded (their body temperature changes as the temperature around them changes), breathe air. Most reptiles, including the crocodile and snake, lay hard-shelled eggs on land.

Vertebrates play several vital roles in an ecosystem. Many predator species are large vertebrates in ecosystems. Lions, eagles, and sharks are examples of predatory vertebrates. Many prey species in ecosystems are also vertebrates. Mice, rabbits, and frogs are examples of these animals. Many vertebrates serve as scavengers in ecosystems. They are significant because they remove dead animals from the environment. Turkey vultures and hyenas, for example, are both vertebrate scavengers. Furthermore, many vertebrates serve as pollinators in ecosystems. Bats and monkeys, for example, may aid in pollen spread by visiting various trees and plants.

Humans value vertebrates for a variety of reasons. Vertebrates are domesticated animals used by humans. These animals are capable of producing milk, food, and clothing. They can also help with work. Agricultural animals are usually vertebrates. Humans also hunt a variety of wild vertebrate animals for food.

1. Vertebrates range in _____ from a frog to a blue whale.
   a. age
   b. size

2. Fish have fins or scales, live in water, and breathe ___ through gills.
   a. oxygen
   b. water

3. Invertebrates lack a _____, whereas vertebrates _____.
   a. skin, whereas vertebrates do
   b. backbone, whereas vertebrates do

4. Warm-blooded animals are _____.
   a. mammals
   b. producers

5. Some vertebrates serve as _____, they remove dead animals from the environment.
   a. scavengers
   b. invertebrates

6. Lions, eagles, and sharks are examples of _____ vertebrates.
   a. ecofriendly
   b. predatory

7. _____ animals are capable of producing milk, food, and clothing.
   a. Non-producing
   b. Domesticated

8. Many vertebrates serve as _____ in ecosystems, they may aid in pollen spread by visiting various trees and plants.
   a. water lilies
   b. pollinators

Science: Organelles

Do you and your dog have a similar appearance? We are all aware that people and dogs appear to be very different on the outside. However, there are some similarities on the inside. Cells make up all animals, including humans and dogs.

All animal cells appear to be the same. They have a cell membrane that contains cytoplasm, which is a gooey fluid. Organelles float in the cytoplasm. Organelles function as tiny machines that meet the needs of the cell. The term organelle refers to a "miniature organ." This lesson will teach you about the various organelles found in animal cells and what they do.

The nucleus of the cell is the cell's brain. It is in charge of many of the cell's functions. The nucleus is where DNA, the genetic instructions for building your body, is stored. DNA contains vital information! Your nucleus has its membrane to protect this essential information, similar to the membrane that surrounds the entire cell.

Your cells require energy. Energy is produced by mitochondria, which are oval-shaped organelles. Mitochondria convert the nutrients that enter the cell into ATP. Your cells use ATP for energy. Because they are the cell's powerhouses, you might think of these organelles as the mighty mitochondria.

The nutrients must be digested before they can be converted into energy by the mitochondria. Digestion is carried out by a group of organelles known as lysosomes. Digestive enzymes are found in lysosomes. Enzymes can sometimes be released into the cell. Because the enzymes kill the cell, lysosomes are known as "suicide bags."

Use Google or your preferred source to help match each term with a definition.

1		nucleus		responsible for chromosome segregation	A
2		lysosomes		degradation of proteins and cellular waste	B
3		Golgi Apparatus		protein synthesis	C
4		Mitochondria		lipid synthesis	D
5		SER		site of photosynthesis	E
6		RER		stores water in plant cells	F
7		Microtubules		prevents excessive uptake of water, protects the cell (in plants)	G
8		ribosomes		degradation of H2O2	H
9		peroxysomes		powerhouse of the cell	I
10		cell wall		modification of proteins; "post-office" of the cell	J
11		chloroplast		protein synthesis + modifications	K
12		central vacuole		where DNA is stored	L

Science: Invertebrates

Invertebrates can be found almost anywhere. Invertebrates account for at least 95% of all animals on the planet! Do you know what one thing they all have in common? Invertebrates lack a backbone.

Your body is supported by a backbone, which protects your organs and connects your other bones. As a result, you are a vertebrate. On the other hand, invertebrates lack the support of bones, so their bodies are often simpler, softer, and smaller. They are also cold-blooded, which means their body temperature fluctuates in response to changes in the air or water around them.

Invertebrates can be found flying, swimming, crawling, or floating and provide essential services to the environment and humans. Nobody knows how many different types of invertebrates there are, but there are millions!

Just because an invertebrate lacks a spinal column does not mean it does not need to eat. Invertebrates, like all other forms of animal life, must obtain nutrients from their surroundings. Invertebrates have evolved two types of digestion to accomplish this. The use of intracellular digestion is common in the most simple organisms. The food is absorbed into the cell and broken down in the cytoplasm at this point. Extracellular digestion, in which cells break down food through the secretion of enzymes and other techniques, is used by more advanced invertebrates. All vertebrates use extracellular digestion.

Still, all animals, invertebrates or not, need a way to get rid of waste. Most invertebrates, especially the simplest ones, use the process of diffusion to eliminate waste. This is merely the opposite of intracellular digestion. However, more advanced invertebrates have more advanced waste disposal mechanisms. Similar to our kidneys, specialized glands in these animals filter and excrete waste. But there is a happy medium. Even though some invertebrates do not have complete digestive tracts like vertebrates, they do not simply flush out waste through diffusion. Instead, the mouth doubles as an exit.

Scientists have classified invertebrates into numerous groups based on what the animals have in common. Arthropods have segmented bodies, which means that they are divided into sections. Consider an ant!

Arthropods are the most numerous group of invertebrates. They can live on land, as spiders and insects do, or in water, as crayfish and crabs do. Because insects are the most numerous group of arthropods, many of them fly, including mosquitoes, bees, locusts, and ladybugs.

They also have jointed legs or limbs to help them walk, similar to how you have knees for your legs and elbows for your arms. The majority of arthropods have an exoskeleton, tough outer skin, or shell that protects their body. Have you ever wondered why when you squish a bug, it makes that crunching sound? That's right; it's the exoskeleton!

Mollusks are the second most numerous group of invertebrates. They have soft bodies and can be found on land or in water. Shells protect the soft bodies of many mollusks, including snails, oysters, clams, and scallops. However, not all, such as octopus, squid, and cuttlefish, have a shell.

1. Invertebrates lack a _____.
   a. backbone
   b. tailbone

2. Invertebrates are also _____.
   a. cold-blooded
   b. warm-blooded

3. _____ can live on land, as spiders and insects do, or in water, as crayfish and crabs do.
   a. Vertebrates
   b. Arthropods

4. All animals, invertebrates or not, need a way to get rid of _____.
   a. their skin
   b. waste

5. _____ have soft bodies and can be found on land or in water.
   a. Arthropods
   b. Mollusks

6. Just because an invertebrate lacks a _____ column does not mean it does not need to eat.
   a. spinal
   b. tissues

7. Your body is supported by a backbone, which protects your _____ and connects your other bones.
   a. organs
   b. muscles

8. Invertebrates lack the support of bones, so their bodies are often simpler, ___, and smaller.
   a. softer and bigger
   b. softer and smaller

Music: Instruments

Music is a type of art derived from the Greek word for "art of the Muses." The Muses were the goddesses of ancient Greece who inspired the arts such as literature, music, and poetry.

Music has been performed with instruments and through vocal songs since the dawn of time. While it is unknown how or when the first musical instrument was created, most historians point to at least 37,000-year-old flutes made from animal bones. The oldest known written song is 4,000 years old and was written in ancient cuneiform.

Instruments were created in order to produce musical sounds. Any object that produces sound, especially if it was designed for that purpose, can be considered a musical instrument.

P	T	R	O	M	B	O	N	E	X	I	X
O	I	C	L	A	R	I	N	E	T	D	B
R	B	A	B	A	S	S	O	O	N	R	C
E	A	O	N	B	I	Q	Q	P	J	U	U
C	F	Q	E	O	Y	E	Z	I	S	M	Z
O	W	O	O	D	B	L	O	C	K	S	O
R	S	A	X	O	P	H	O	N	E	Z	R
D	K	E	T	R	U	M	P	E	T	O	G
E	Z	A	Y	J	F	L	U	T	E	I	A
R	F	R	E	N	C	H	H	O	R	N	N
F	O	Y	R	X	A	H	S	J	R	I	I
G	U	I	T	A	R	V	I	O	L	I	N

PIANO	FLUTE	BASSOON	CLARINET	TROMBONE
VIOLIN	WOODBLOCK	TRUMPET	OBOE	SAXOPHONE
GUITAR	DRUMS	ORGAN	RECORDER	FRENCH HORN

History: The Vikings

First, read the entire passage. After that, go back and fill in the blanks. You can skip the blanks you're unsure about and finish them later.

sail	settle	North	Christianity	raided
Middle	defeated	shallow	cargo	Denmark

During the _____ Ages, the Vikings lived in Northern Europe. They first settled in the Scandinavian lands that are now Denmark, Sweden, and Norway. During the Middle Ages, the Vikings played a significant role in Northern Europe, particularly during the Viking Age, which lasted from 800 CE to 1066 CE.

In Old Norse, the word Viking means "to raid." The Vikings would board their longships and _____ across the seas to raid villages on Europe's northern coast, including islands like Great Britain. In 787 CE, they first appeared in England to raid villages. When the Vikings _____, they were known to attack defenseless monasteries. This earned them a bad reputation as barbarians, but monasteries were wealthy and undefended Viking targets.

The Vikings eventually began to _____ in areas other than Scandinavia. They colonized parts of Great Britain, Germany, and Iceland in the ninth century. They spread into northeastern Europe, including Russia, in the 10th century. They also established Normandy, which means "Northmen," along the coast of northern France.

By the beginning of the 11th century, the Vikings had reached the pinnacle of their power. Leif Eriksson, son of Erik the Red, was one Viking who made it to _____ America. He established a brief settlement in modern-day Canada. This was thousands of years before Columbus.

The English and King Harold Godwinson _____ the Vikings, led by King Harald Hardrada of Norway, in 1066. The defeat in this battle is sometimes interpreted as the end of the Viking Age. The Vikings stopped expanding their territory at this point, and raids became less frequent.

The arrival of Christianity was a major factor at the end of the Viking age. The Vikings became more and more a part of mainland Europe as Scandinavia was converted to _____ and became a part of Christian Europe. Sweden's, Denmark's, and Norway's identities and borders began to emerge as well.

The Vikings were perhaps best known for their ships. The Vikings built longships for exploration and raiding. Longships were long, narrow vessels built for speed. Oars primarily propelled them but later added a sail to help in windy conditions. Longships had a shallow draft, which allowed them to float in _____ water and land on beaches.

The Vikings also built _____ ships known as Knarr for trading. The Knarr was wider and deeper than the longship, allowing it to transport more cargo.

Five recovered Viking ships can be seen at the Viking Ship Museum in Roskilde, _____. It's also possible to see how the Vikings built their ships. The Vikings used a shipbuilding technique known as clinker building. They used long wood planks that overlapped along the edges.

Fun Facts:

- The Viking is the mascot of the Minnesota Vikings of the National Football League.
- Certain Vikings fought with monstrous two-handed axes. They are capable of easily piercing a metal helmet or shield.

Grammar: Sentence Building

Score: _____

Date: _____

Practice *sentence* building. *Unscramble* the words to form a complete sentence.

1. _____ can build ____ __ _____ ____ _____
   antibiotics. · up · Germs · to · a · resistance

2. _____ _____ a _____ _____ ____ the _____
   in · curve · road. · There · was · sharp

3. Let's _____ __ graph _____ _____ _____
   make · this · a · with · data.

4. __ like ____ _____ _____ _____ _____ potatoes.
   turkey · mashed · to · eat · and · I

5. ____ _____ built a _____ _____ ____ _____
   clay. · of · out · house · sister · My

6. _____ flight _____ very _____ _____ _____
   boring. · The · was · long · and

7. __ heard _____ _____ ____ very _____
   wealthy. · that · man · is · I

8. __ will _____ _____ _____ _____ for _____
   soup · have · I · and · lunch. · crackers

9. There ____ __ _____ behind ____ _____
   my · brook · home. · a · is

10. __ _____ to _____ _____
    I · like · water. · drink

11. How _____ _____ _____ _____ this _____
    sickness? · you · had · have · long

12. ____ _____ _____ books _____ elephants.

many · wrote · about · He

13. ____ _____ _____ ____ normal.

temperature · is · My · body

14. __ have __ _____ _____ sometimes.

weak · a · I · stomach

15. _____ _____ while __ _____ your _____

Stay · still · fix · I · tie.

16. ____ _____ _____ ____ _____ this morning.

started · to · My · ache · head

17. ____ _____ _____ _____ ____ an office.

My · works · big · in · brother

18. _____ _____ cars _____ _____ forward.

train · The · kept · lurching

19. __ can't possibly _____ __ _____

prediction. · a · I · make

20. __ _____ my school _____ _____ _____

I · like · picture · this · year.

21. _____ _____ pizza have _____ ____ _____

the · it? · Will · on · everything

22. ____ _____ ____ _____ dear to _____

My · is · cat · me. · very

23. I _____ a _____ _____ ____ _____

want · not · enemy. · friend, · an

24. _____ _____ guess ____ _____

my · you · Can · weight?

Grammar Overview: Nouns, Verbs, Adjectives

A noun is a word that describes someone, a place, something, or an idea. Names, locations, physical objects, or objects and concepts that do not exist in the physical world, such as a dream or a theory, are examples of nouns. A noun is a single word, such as sister, home, desk, wedding, hope, pizza, or squirrel.

There are numerous ways to use nouns in language, and these various types of nouns are classified. In general, there are ten distinct types of nouns that are used in specific and unique contexts, but let's look at eight of them today.

Common Noun	a non-specific person, place, or thing	baby, mom
Compound Nouns	made up of two nouns	bus driver, sunflower
Collective Noun	group of individuals	team, family
Proper Noun	A specific person, place, or thing	Dr. Morgan, Amazon
Concrete Noun	identified through one of the five senses	air, chirps
Plural Noun	Multiple people, places, or things	bottles, pencils
Singular Noun	One person, place, or thing	chair, desk
Abstract Noun	things that don't exist as physical objects	fear, love

Common Noun: A generic name for a person, place, or thing in a class or group is a common noun. In contrast to proper nouns, common nouns are not capitalized unless they begin a sentence or appear in a title. All nouns fall into one of two categories: common or proper. Proper nouns are distinct from common nouns in that they name something specific. Nouns in common use do not. Unnecessary capitalization of common nouns is a common spelling error. Some words, such as president, seem to beg for a capital letter because we instinctively want to emphasize their significance. However, if it does not name something or someone specific, even this lofty title is a common noun (in this case, a specific president).

Compound Noun: Every compound noun is made up of two or more words that are combined to form a noun. These distinct words do not have to be nouns in and of themselves; all they need to do is communicate a specific person, place, idea, or thing. A compound noun can be a common noun (for example, fish sticks), a proper noun (for example, Pizza Hut), or an abstract noun (lovesickness). They can be hyphenated or not, and they can have a space between words—especially if one of the words has more than one syllable, as in living room. You'll start noticing compound nouns everywhere once you've learned to recognize them. Fire-flies? Compound noun. Sub sandwich? Compound noun. Software developer, mother-in-law, underworld, toothache, garlic knot? They are all compound nouns.

Collective Noun: A collective noun is a word or phrase that refers to a group of people or things as if they were a single entity. There are some exceptions to the rule that collective nouns are treated as singular. Collective nouns such as team, family, class, group, and host use a singular verb when the entity acts as a whole and a plural verb when the individuals who make up the entity act individually.

Collective nouns refer to more than one person or thing in a category. A pride cannot have just one lion, and a single flower does not make a bouquet. As a result, a collective noun always refers to a plurality of some kind.

Example: The group is working on a mural. (Because the mural is painted collectively by the group, the verb is singular.)

Example: The group cannot agree on how to paint the mural. (Because the group members disagree with one another, the verb is plural.)

Proper Noun: A proper noun is a name that is specific (as opposed to generic) to a specific person, place, or thing. In English, proper nouns are always capitalized, regardless of where they appear in a sentence. That is, whether it appears at the beginning, middle, or end of a sentence, it is always written with the first letter in capital letters. In a sentence, a proper noun is used to name a person, place, or organization, such as Jim, Molly, India, Germany, Amazon, Microsoft, and so on.

Concrete Noun: A concrete noun is one that can be identified using at least one of the five senses (taste, touch, sight, hearing, or smell). Objects and substances that we cannot perceive (see, hear, taste, touch, or smell) with our sense organs are NOT concrete nouns. The majority of nouns become concrete nouns because we can feel them (for example, all animals and people) with our sense organs. Concrete nouns can be common nouns, countable nouns, proper nouns, uncountable nouns, collective nouns, and so on. All nouns are classified into two types: concrete nouns and abstract nouns.

Abstract Nouns: An abstract noun is one that cannot be perceived through any of the five senses (i.e., taste, touch, sight, hearing, smelling). In other words, an abstract noun is a noun that exists only in our minds and cannot be recognized by our senses.

Concrete nouns are tangible, whereas <u>abstract nouns</u> are intangible.

Concrete nouns can be experienced with the five senses, whereas <u>abstract nouns</u> cannot.

Singular Noun: Singular nouns are used in sentences to refer to a single person, place, thing, or idea. Singular nouns include things like boy, girl, teacher, boat, goat, hand, and so on.

Plural noun: There are numerous plural noun rules, and because nouns are used so frequently in writing! The correct spelling of plurals is usually determined by what letter the singular noun ends in. Take a look at some examples.

Add s to the end of regular nouns to make them plural.

cat – cats

house – houses

If the singular noun ends in s, ss, sh, ch, x, or z, add es to make it plural.

bus – buses

lunch – lunches

Singular nouns ending in -s or -z may require you to double the -s or -z before adding the -es for pluralization in some cases.

quiz – quizzes

gas –gasses

If the noun ends in f or fe, the f is frequently changed to ve before adding the -s to form the plural form.

calf–calves

wife – wives

Exceptions:

roof – roofs

chef – chefs

When some nouns are pluralized, they do not change at all.

sheep – sheep

species – species

There are additional rules that we did not cover here. Please spend some time studying the following:

If the final letter of a singular noun is -y and the letter preceding the -y is a consonant, the noun ends in -y. puppy – puppies

If the singular noun ends in -y and the letter preceding the -y is a vowel, add an -s. boy – boys

If the singular noun ends in -o, make it plural by adding -es. potato – potatoes Exception: photo – photos

If a singular noun ends in -us, the plural ending is usually -i. cactus – cacti

When a singular noun ends in -is, the plural ending is -es. ellipsis – ellipses

If a singular noun ends in -on, the plural noun ends in -a. criterion – criteria

Verbs

In theory, verbs are easy to understand. A verb is a word that describes an action, an occurrence, or a state of being. Of course, there are many different types of verbs, but remember that a verb should indicate that something is happening because an action is taking place in some way. When first learning about verbs, many students simply refer to them as 'doing words,' because they always indicate that something has been done, is being done, or will be done in the future (depending on the tense that you are writing in).

Verbs, like nouns, are the main part of a sentence or phrase, telling a story about what is going on. In fact, full thoughts cannot be conveyed without a verb, and even the simplest sentences, such as (Kim sings.) Actually, a verb can be a sentence in and of itself, with the subject, in most cases you, implied, as in Sing! and Drive!

The location of the verb in relation to the subject is one clue that can help you identify it. Verbs are almost always followed by a noun or pronoun. The subject is made up of these nouns and pronouns.

1. Jim **eats** his dinner quickly.
2. We **went** to the bank.

Adjectives

Adjectives are descriptive words for nouns. A noun is defined as a person, place, thing, or idea. We want to be as descriptive as possible when we speak or write. Being descriptive allows the reader or listener to understand better what you are attempting to describe. You want your audience to have the best possible understanding of what you're describing.

What image comes to mind when I say, "I saw a cat?" You might see a spotted cat, a small orange cat, or a shaggy gray cat, depending on your experience. I didn't give you enough adjectives to paint a complete picture.

Do you have a better mental image if I say, "I saw a big, wet, sad, shaggy, orange and white cat"? Of course, you do because I used adjectives to clarify things.

Grammar: Nouns, Verbs, Adjectives

Score: _____

Date: _____

DIRECTIONS: SORT the words (below) by their corresponding *part-of-speech*.

color	chickens	kittens	banjo	library	goldfish
grieving	adorable	cough	stand	nasty	powerful
dance	build	cry	break	easy	circle
coach	aggressive	careful	eat	adventurous	think
mysterious	face	sticks	drink	guitar	busy
calm	window	worm	coast	draw	polka dot
eager	handsome	explain			

Nouns (13)	Verbs (13)	Adjectives (13)

*Usage Activity: CHOOSE (12) words from your completed table & WRITE (1) sentence for each form of the words you chose.

Grammar: Concrete & Abstract Noun

Score: _____

Date:_____

In the English language, both concrete and abstract nouns are essential parts of speech. The primary distinction between concrete and abstract nouns is that concrete nouns refer to people, places, or things that take up physical space, whereas abstract nouns refer to intangible ideas that cannot be physically interacted with.

Words like "luck," "disgust," and "empathy" are examples of abstract nouns. While it is possible to see someone being empathetic, empathy is not a visible or tangible entity. The majority of feelings, emotions, and philosophies can be classified as abstract nouns.

1. FIND THE ABSTRACT NOUN ?

    a. KIND

    b. BOOK

2. FIND THE CONCRETE NOUNS

    a. WINDOW

    b. LOVE

3. FIND THE ABTRACT NOUN: THE KING WAS KNOWN FOR HIS JUSTICE

    a. JUSTICE

    b. KING

4. WHAT ARE THE 5 CONCRETE NOUNS

    a. TASTE, SMELL, WALKING, EYEING, TOUCHING

    b. SMELL,TASTE, SIGHT, HEARING,TOUCH

5. WHICH NOUN BELOW IS AN ABSTRACT NOUN?

    a. TRAIN

    b. LOVE

6. IS THE FOLLOWING NOUN CONCRETE OR ABSTRACT? CUPCAKES

    a. ABSTRACT

    b. CONCRETE

7. WHAT IS A CONCRETE NOUN?

    a. A NOUN THAT YOU CAN EXPERIENCE WITH AT LEAST 1 OF YOUR 5 SENSES.

    b. A NOUN THAT YOU CAN'T EXPERIENCE WITH AT LEAST 1 OF YOUR 5 SENSES.

8. WHICH WORD BELOW IS AN ABSTRACT NOUN?

    a. BRAVERY

    b. FRIEND

9. WHICH WORD BELOW IS NOT A CONCRETE NOUN?

    a. HAMBURGER

    b. ANGER

10. IS THE WORD THOUGHTFULNESS A CONCRETE OR ABSTRACT NOUN?

    a. ABSTRACT

    b. CONCRETE

Grammar: Compound Nouns

Score: _____

Date: _____

A compound noun is one that is composed of two or more words. Each word contributes to the meaning of the noun.

Compound nouns can be written three ways:

A single word	Two words	Hyphenated
haircut	rain forest	self-esteem

Instructions: Match the compound noun pairs correctly.

1	☐	Fund	◉	crow	A
2	☐	News	◉	dresser	B
3	☐	Sun	◉	glasses	C
4	☐	Child	◉	paper	D
5	☐	Door	◉	attack	E
6	☐	heart	◉	hood	F
7	☐	tooth	◉	plane	G
8	☐	apple	◉	cut	H
9	☐	full	◉	ring	I
10	☐	hair	◉	paste	J
11	☐	air	◉	sauce	K
12	☐	ear	◉	book	L
13	☐	scare	◉	moon	M
14	☐	post	◉	way	N
15	☐	hair	◉	raiser	O
16	☐	note	◉	office	P

Grammar: Collective Noun

A collective noun is a noun that refers to a group of people, animals, or things. They are described as a single entity. Collective nouns are distinct from singular nouns in that singular nouns describe only one person or object.

Many collective nouns are common nouns, but when they are the name of a company or other organization with more than one person, such as Microsoft, they can also be proper nouns.

Find the collective noun in each sentence.

1. Our class visited the natural history museum on a field trip.

2. The bison herd stampeded across the prairie, leaving a massive dust cloud in its wake.

3. We eagerly awaited the verdict of the jury.

4. This year's basketball team features three players who stand taller than six feet.

5. At Waterloo, Napoleon's army was finally defeated.

6. The plans for a new park have been approved by the town council.

7. He comes from a large family, as the oldest of eleven children.

8. The rock group has been on tour for several months.

9. When Elvis appeared on stage, the entire audience erupted in applause.

10. The San Francisco crowd were their usual individualistic selves.

11. The crew of sailors boarded the ships.

12. A mob destroyed the company's new office.

13. The fleet of ships was waiting at the port.

14. It was difficult for the committee to come to a decision.

Geography: Canada

Canada is the world's second-largest country, covering 10 million square kilometers. Canada's borders are bounded by three oceans: the Pacific Ocean to the west, the Atlantic Ocean to the east, and the Arctic Ocean to the north. The Canada-United States border runs along Canada's southern border.

Queen Victoria, Queen Elizabeth II's great-great-grandmother, chose Ottawa, which is located on the Ottawa River, as the capital in 1857. It is now the fourth largest metropolitan area in Canada. The National Capital Region, which encompasses 4,700 square kilometers around Ottawa, preserves and improves the area's built heritage and natural environment.

Canada is divided into ten provinces and three territories. Each province and territory has a separate capital city. You should be familiar with the capitals of your province or territory, as well as those of Canada.

Below are some of Canada's Territories, Provinces, and Capital Cities. Draw a line through each word you find.

```
R  L  U  G  M  A  N  I  T  O  B  A  N  K  M  E  X  L  S  P
W  K  A  K  B  B  H  A  L  B  E  R  T  A  G  D  K  P  R  R
Q  M  N  Y  N  X  W  I  S  Z  L  X  B  Q  E  K  B  T  X  I
I  Q  A  L  U  I  T  E  G  I  R  T  O  R  O  N  T  O  Y  N
A  B  R  I  T  I  S  H  C  O  L  U  M  B  I  A  E  C  E  C
V  N  N  R  S  Q  H  G  I  W  I  N  N  I  P  E  G  H  L  E
S  O  G  X  Z  G  A  O  N  T  A  R  I  O  F  B  R  A  L  E
T  V  Q  Z  E  D  M  O  N  T  O  N  C  D  F  W  Q  R  O  D
.  A  V  H  B  E  F  R  E  D  E  R  I  C  T  O  N  L  W  W
J  S  V  P  O  Q  U  E  B  E  C  C  I  T  Y  N  W  O  K  A
O  C  Y  J  R  W  S  H  V  C  V  Q  H  W  W  U  L  T  N  R
H  O  E  L  E  E  B  A  A  Z  O  U  Q  G  H  N  V  T  I  D
N  T  W  X  G  A  Q  L  S  T  J  E  F  H  I  A  I  E  F  I
'  I  K  M  I  D  C  I  L  X  L  B  U  V  T  V  C  T  E  S
S  A  C  P  N  C  O  F  T  Z  M  E  U  E  E  U  T  O  N  L
P  Q  Y  F  A  P  L  A  G  P  Y  C  F  M  H  T  O  W  B  A
I  W  S  D  R  Y  W  X  G  W  P  U  E  U  O  G  R  N  M  N
Y  N  E  W  B  R  U  N  S  W  I  C  K  T  R  P  I  C  R  D
R  X  B  T  E  R  V  Y  J  B  H  H  M  K  S  W  A  J  N  Z
G  F  S  A  S  K  A  T  C  H  E  W  A  N  E  Y  U  K  O  N
```

Yukon	Nunavut	Nova Scotia	Prince Edward Island	New Brunswick
Quebec	Ontario	Manitoba	Saskatchewan	Alberta
British Columbia	Victoria	Edmonton	Regina	Winnipeg
Toronto	Quebec City	Fredericton	Charlottetown	Halifax
St. John's	Iqaluit	Yellowknife	Whitehorse	

Science Words You Should Know Quiz

Score: _____

Date: _____

Circle the correct meaning of each word. Need help? Try Google!

1. Bulb
   a. Light producing instrument
   b. Learning by doing

2. Circuit
   a. A representation of data
   b. A path that electricity follows during its flowing

3. Kinetic
   a. An optical instrument
   b. Movement

4. Friction
   a. Resistance due to movement
   b. Making larger

5. Hygrometer
   a. A path that electricity follows during its flowing
   b. Humidity measuring instrument

6. Barometer
   a. The intensity of sound
   b. Pressure measuring instrument

7. Humidity
   a. A quantity expressing water vapor's amount
   b. Movement

8. Pitch
   a. Findings after an investigation
   b. The intensity of sound

9. Neutron
   a. Sub-particle of an atom
   b. Findings after an investigation

10. Proton
   a. Findings after an investigation
   b. A constituent of an atom

11. Dark
   a. Categorization on a common base
   b. Absence of light

12. Practical
   a. Learning by doing
   b. A path that electricity follows during its flowing

13. Classify
   a. Categorization on a common base
   b. Findings after an investigation

14. Analyze
   a. Detail examination
   b. Resistance due to movement

15. Expand
   a. Absence of light
   b. Making larger

16. Graph
   a. A representation of data
   b. A path that electricity follows during its flowing

17. Results
   a. Findings after an investigation
   b. Sub-particle of an atom

18. Microscope
   a. Making larger
   b. An optical instrument

Art: Draw Facial Expressions

Score: _____

Date:_____

Facial expressions are one of the most effective ways for humans to communicate with one another. We learn to distinguish between a happy and an angry expression from a very young age. As we get older, we develop the ability to express our feelings and read other people's thoughts and emotions without using words.

Try looking at photos of yourself or others expressing various emotions and studying them to identify which parts of your face are moving. It is a great way to start learning how to draw facial expressions and understand points of tension. The more intense the emotion, the more areas of the face are involved.

Environmental Health: Water Pollution

First, read the entire passage. After that, go back and fill in the blanks. You can skip the blanks you're unsure about and finish them later.

causes	toxic	wastewater	ill	food
Gulf	naturally	Dead	crops	reduce
Acid	herds	spills	streams	planet

Water pollution occurs when waste, chemicals, or other particles cause a body of water (e.g., rivers, oceans, lakes) to become _____ to the fish and animals that rely on it for survival. Water pollution can also disrupt and hurt nature's water cycle.

Water pollution can occur _____ due to volcanoes, algae blooms, animal waste, and silt from storms and floods.

Human activity contributes significantly to water pollution. Sewage, pesticides, fertilizers from farms, wastewater and chemicals from factories, silt from construction sites, and trash from people littering are some human _____.

Oil _____ have been some of the most well-known examples of water pollution. The Exxon Valdez oil spill occurred when an oil tanker collided with a reef off the coast of Alaska, causing over 11 million gallons of oil to spill into the ocean. Another major oil spill was the Deepwater Horizon oil spill, which occurred when an oil well exploded, causing over 200 million gallons of oil to spill into the _____ of Mexico.

Water pollution can be caused directly by air pollution. When sulfur dioxide particles reach high altitudes in the atmosphere, they can combine with rain to form acid rain. _____ rain can cause lakes to become acidic, killing fish and other animals.

The main issue caused by water pollution is the impact on aquatic life. _____ fish, birds, dolphins, and various other animals frequently wash up on beaches, killed by pollutants in their environment. Pollution also has an impact on the natural _____ chain. Small animals consume contaminants like lead and cadmium.

Clean water is one of the most valuable and essential commodities for life on Earth. Clean water is nearly impossible to obtain for over 1 billion people on the _____. They can become _____ from dirty, polluted water, which is especially difficult for young children. Some bacteria and pathogens in water can make people sick to the point of death.

Water pollution comes from a variety of sources. Here are a few of the main reasons:

Sewage: In many parts of the world, sewage is still flushed directly into _____ and rivers. Sewage can introduce dangerous bacteria that can make humans and animals very sick.

Farm animal waste: Runoff from large _____ of farm animals such as pigs and cows can enter the water supply due to rain and large storms.

Pesticides: Pesticides and herbicides are frequently sprayed on _____ to kill bugs, while herbicides are sprayed to kill weeds. These potent chemicals can enter the water through rainstorm runoff. They can also contaminate rivers and lakes due to unintentional spills.

Construction, floods, and storms: Silt from construction, earthquakes, and storms can _____ water oxygen levels and suffocate fish. Factories - Water is frequently used in factories to process chemicals, keep engines cool, and wash things away. Sometimes used _____ is dumped into rivers or the ocean. It may contain pollutants.

Storytime: Let Thy Hair Down| Part 2

First, read the entire passage. After that, go back and fill in the blanks. You can skip the blanks you're unsure about and finish them later.

cut	years	dark	terrified	long
happily	tower	husband	escaped	separated
beloved	transport	sobbed	scissors	forest

Rapunzel had magnificent _____ hair as fine as spun gold, and when she heard the Witch's voice, she unfastened her long braided locks and wound them around one of the window hooks above. The hair then fell twenty ells down, and the Witch climbed up by it.

After a year or two, the King's Son rode through the forest and passed by the _____. Then he heard a song that was so lovely that he stopped and listened. This was Rapunzel, who spent her time alone, letting her sweet voice ripple outward.

The King's Son wanted to climb up to her and looked for the tower's door, but there was none to be found. He rode home, but the singing had touched him so deeply that he went out into the _____ every day to listen to it.

When he was standing behind a tree, he saw a Witch come by and heard her cry:

"Rapunzel, Rapunzel, let thy hair down."

Rapunzel then let down her hair braids, and the Witch climbed up to her.

"If that's the ladder by which one climbs up, I'll try my luck for a change," he said.

When it got _____ the next day, he went to the tower and cried:

"Rapunzel, Rapunzel, let thy hair down."

The hair instantly fell down, and the King's Son climbed up.

Rapunzel was _____ at first when a man her eyes had never seen before approached her. But the King's Son began to speak to her as if she were a friend, telling her that his heart had been so shaken that he couldn't sleep and that he had been forced to see her.

When he asked Rapunzel if she would take him as her _____ and she saw that he was young and handsome, she thought to herself, "He will love me more than old Dame Gothel does," and she said yes and laid her hand in his.

"I will gladly go away with you, but I don't know how to get down," she added. Bring a strand of silk with you every time you come, and I'll weave a ladder out of it. When that is completed, I will come down, and you will _____ me on your horse."

They agreed that he should come to her every evening until that time because the older woman came by day. The Witch did not comment until Rapunzel said to her, "Tell me, Dame Gothel, how it is that you are so much heavier for me to draw up than the young King's Son-he will be with me in a moment."

"You wicked child!" exclaimed the Witch. "What do you say!" I hear you say. I thought I'd _____ you from the rest of the world, but you've duped me!"

In her rage, she clutched Rapunzel's lovely locks, wrapped them twice around her left hand, grabbed a pair of _____ with her right, and snip, snap, they were cut off, and the lovely braids lay on the ground. And she was so pitiful that she banished Rapunzel to the desert, where she had to live in agony and misery.

However, on the same day that she cast out Rapunzel, the Witch, in the evening, glued the braids of hair she had _____ off to the window hook; and when the King's Son came and cried:

"Rapunzel, Rapunzel, Let down thy hair," she let the hair down.

The King's Son climbed. He did not see his _____ Rapunzel above but rather the Witch, who glared at him with wicked and cruel eyes.

"Aha!" she mocked, "you would fetch your dearest!" However, the lovely bird is no longer singing in the nest. The cat has it and will scratch your eyes out as well. Rapunzel is no longer yours! You'll never see her again!"

The King's Son was overcome with grief and jumped from the tower in sadness. He _____ with his life, but the thorns he landed on punctured his eyes. Then he wandered around the forest completely blind, eating only roots and berries and doing nothing but mourn and weep over the loss of his dearest wife.

So he wandered around in misery for a few _____ before arriving in the desert, where Rapunzel lived in misfortune. He heard a voice and went toward it because it sounded familiar. When he approached, Rapunzel recognized him and _____ on his neck. Two of her tears wetted his eyes, causing them to clear and allowing him to see as before.

He led her to his Kingdom, where he was joyfully received, and they lived _____ and merrily for a long time.

Storytime: Let Thy Hair Down

Score: _____

Date: _____

First, read the entire story. After that, go back and fill in the blanks. You can skip the blanks you're unsure about and finish them later.

small	loved	stronger	agreed	tower
climbed	condition	child	fresh	terrified

Once upon a time, there was a man and a woman who had long wished for a _____ in desperation. Finally, the woman hoped that God was about to grant her wish.

These people had a _____ window in the back of their house to see a beautiful garden. It was brimming with the most lovely flowers and herbs. It was, however, surrounded by a high wall, and no one dared to enter it because it belonged to a Witch, who wielded great power and was feared throughout the world.

One day, the woman was standing by this window, looking down into the garden, when she noticed a bed planted with the most beautiful rampion (rapunzel), and it looked so _____ and green that she wanted so badly for it and sought to eat some.

This desire grew _____ by the day, and because she knew she couldn't get any of it, she looked pale and miserable.

Then her husband became concerned and demanded to know, "What displeases you, dear Wife?

"Ah," she replied, "if I don't get some of the rampions in the garden behind our house to eat, I'll die."

"Rather than letting your wife die, bring her some of the rampions yourself; let it cost you what it will!" thought the man who _____ her.

In the late afternoon, he _____ over the wall into the Witch's garden, grabbed a handful of rampion, and hurriedly handed it to his wife. She immediately made herself a salad out of it and gobbled up it.

She, on the other hand, liked it so much-so much that she craved it three times as much the next day. Her husband had to return to the garden if he was to get any rest. As a result, in the bleakness of the evening, he let himself down once more. But when he got down the wall, he was _____ because he saw the Witch standing before him.

"How dare you come into my garden and steal my rampion like a thief?" she responded angrily. You will pay for it!"

"Ah, let mercy take the place of justice!" he replied. I had no choice but to do it. My wife saw your rampion from the window and craved it so much that she would have died if she hadn't gotten some to eat."

The Witch then softened her rage and said to him, "If the case is as you say, I will allow you to take as much rampion as you want, but there is one _____: you must give me the child that your wife will bring into the world." It will be well cared for, and I will look after it like a mother."

In his terror, the man _____ to everything, and when the woman finally had a little daughter, the Witch appeared immediately, gave the child the name Rapunzel, and took it away with her.

Rapunzel grew up to be the most beautiful child in the world. When she was twelve years old, the Witch locked her in a _____ in the middle of a forest with no stairs or door. But there was a small window at the very top. When the Witch desired to enter, she positioned herself beneath this and cried:

"Rapunzel, Rapunzel, let thy hair down."

Spelling Words Crossword

Complete the crossword by filling in a word that fits each clue. Fill in the correct answers, one letter per square, both across and down, from the given clues. There will be a gray space between multi-word answers.

Tip: Solve the easy clues first, and then go back and answer the more difficult ones.

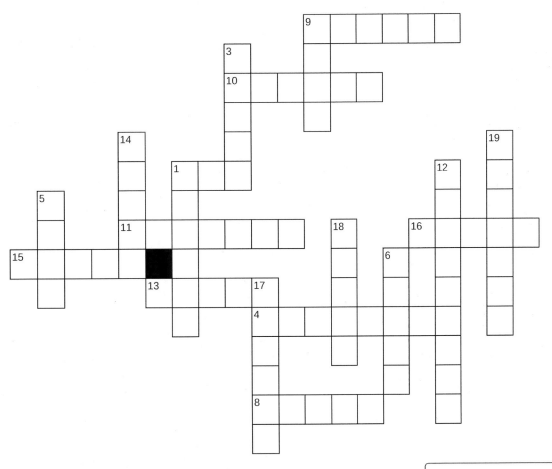

Across

1. behave in a certain manner
4. a strong drive for success
8. hold on tightly
9. mentally quick and resourceful
10. protect against a challenge or attack
11. an impairment of health
13. physically weak
15. an object with a spherical shape
16. hold firmly

Down

1. take in a liquid
3. take into one's family
5. fearless and daring
6. coldness due to a cold environment
9. an organized group of workers
12. having unexpected good luck
14. move smoothly and effortlessly
17. propel with force
18. as far as something can go
19. a child's room for a baby

ABSORB   ADOPT   DISEASE
LIMIT   ACT   CLEVER
AMBITION   NURSERY   FRAIL
BOLD   DEFEND   CHILL
GLIDE   GRASP   FORTUNATE
GLOBE   LAUNCH   CREW
CLING

Spelling Words
Unscramble

Unscramble Word Tip: Try solving the easy words first, and then go back and answer the more difficult ones.

compare	group	pond	taught	laundry	start
grade	wrap	front	stone	pardon	city
shirt	open	am	value	office	hope
highest	close	person	verb	hear	near
travel	pencil				

1. lseoc   c _ _ _ _

2. oesnpr   _ _ _ _ o n

3. npdrao   _ _ _ d _ n

4. ma   a _

5. ntoes   _ _ _ _ e

6. earn   n _ _ _

7. ithrs   _ _ _ r _

8. auevl   _ a _ _ _

9. atelvr   t _ _ v _ _

10. poeh   _ _ p _

11. tciy   _ _ _ y

12. bvre   _ _ _ b

13. aehr   _ e _ _

14. ndpo   p _ _ _

15. tuahgt   t _ _ _ h _

16. adrge   _ _ _ _ e

17. ofrnt   _ _ o _ _

18. trats   s _ _ _ _

19. nydrual   _ a _ _ _ _ y

20. enpo   _ _ e _

21. wapr   _ _ _ p

22. ilencp   _ _ _ _ i l

23. gishteh   _ _ _ h _ s _

24. aempcro   _ o _ _ _ r _

25. orugp   _ r _ _ _

26. oeffic   _ f f _ _ _

Science Spelling Words

Score: _____

Date: _____

Instructions: Match the science words to the correct meaning.

1	☐	Shadow	Having magnetic properties	A
2	☐	Nectar	Study of earth	B
3	☐	Prey	A dark area	C
4	☐	Gas	Unicellular microorganism	D
5	☐	Mixture	Any true information	E
6	☐	Fossil	A coordinating organ of the human body	F
7	☐	Bacteria	A combination of different things	G
8	☐	Brain	A thin tube made up of glass	H
9	☐	Geology	The study of living beings	I
10	☐	Atom	The smallest particle	J
11	☐	Magnetic	Juicy fluid within flowers	K
12	☐	Dissolve	State of matter that can expand freely	L
13	☐	Fact	The remains of plant or animal	M
14	☐	Biology	Bony plates in the fish skin	N
15	☐	Organism	Kill and hunt for food	O
16	☐	Scale	Expression of heaviness	P
17	☐	Test tube	An individual/living being	Q
18	☐	Weigh	Solid form in any liquid	R

GRADE_____

DATE_____

RESEARCH: Martin Cooper

Occupation _____

BORN DATE:_____ Nationality_____

DEATH DATE:_____ Education_____ #Children _____

Childhood and Family Background Facts

Work and Career Facts

Children, Marriage and or Significant Relationships

Friends, Social Life and Other Interesting Facts

Did you enjoy researching this person?

Give a Rating: ☆ ☆ ☆ ☆ ☆

DATE_____   **RESEARCH:** **Nicolaus Copernicus**

Occupation _____

BORN DATE:_____ Nationality_____

DEATH DATE:_____ Education_____ #Children _____

Childhood and Family Background Facts

Work and Career Facts

Children, Marriage and or Significant Relationships

Friends, Social Life and Other Interesting Facts

Did you enjoy researching this person?

Give a Rating: ☆ ☆ ☆ ☆ ☆

GRADE_____

DATE_____   **RESEARCH: Friedrich Clemens Gerke**

Occupation _____

BORN DATE:_____ Nationality_____

DEATH DATE:_____ Education_____ #Children _____

Childhood and Family Background Facts

Work and Career Facts

Children, Marriage and or Significant Relationships

Friends, Social Life and Other Interesting Facts

Did you enjoy researching this person?

Give a Rating: ☆ ☆ ☆ ☆ ☆

Score: _____

History Reading
Comprehension: Walt Disney

Date: _____

First, read the article. After that, go back and fill in the blanks. You can skip the blanks you're unsure about and finish them later. Don't try to do it all at one time. Break it down so that it's "do-able" and not so overwhelming. Take your time. Ask questions. Get help if you need it.

Mickey	Donald	sister	Hollywood	art
Red	Chicago	newspaper	friends	train
four	entertainment	White	Alice	Peter
Club	snacks	vacation	brother	theme

On December 5, 1901, Walter Elias Disney was born in _____, Illinois. His family relocated to a farm outside of Marceline, Missouri, when he was _____ years old, thanks to his parents, Elias and Flora. Walt loved growing up on the farm with his three older brothers (Herbert, Raymond, and Roy) and younger _____ (Ruth). Walt discovered his passion for drawing and art in Marceline.

The Disneys relocated to Kansas City after four years in Marceline. On weekends, Walt continued to draw and attend _____ classes. He even bartered his drawings for free haircuts with a local barber. Walt got a summer job on a train. On the _____, he walked back and forth, selling _____ and newspapers. Walt had a great time on the train and would be fascinated by trains for the rest of his life.

Walt's family relocated to Chicago around the time he started high school. Walt studied at the Chicago Art Institute and worked as a cartoonist for the school _____. Walt decided at the age of sixteen that he wanted to fight in World War I. Due to the fact that he was still too young to join the army, he decided to drop out of school and join the _____ Cross instead. He spent the next year in France driving ambulances for the Red Cross.

Disney returned from the war eager to launch his artistic career. He began his career in an art studio and later moved on to an advertising firm. During this time, he met artist Ubbe Iwerks and became acquainted with animation.

Walt aspired to create his own animated cartoons. He founded his own company, Laugh-O-Gram. He sought the help of some of his _____, including Ubbe Iwerks. They made animated cartoons that were only a few minutes long. Despite the popularity of the cartoons, the business did not make enough money, and Walt was forced to declare bankruptcy.

Disney, on the other hand, was not going to be deterred by a single setback. In 1923, he relocated to _____, California, and founded the Disney Brothers' Studio with his _____ Roy. He enlisted the services of Ubbe Iwerks and a number of other animators once more. They created the well-known character Oswald the Lucky Rabbit. The company was a success. However, Universal Studios acquired the Oswald trademark and hired all of Disney's animators except Ubbe Iwerks.

Walt had to start all over again. This time, he came up with a new character called _____ Mouse. He made the first animated film with sound. Steamboat Willie was the title of the film, which starred Mickey and Minnie Mouse. Walt provided the voices for Steamboat Willie. The movie was a huge success. Disney kept working, creating new characters like _____ Duck, Goofy, and Pluto. With the release of the cartoon Silly Symphonies and the first color animated film, Flowers and Trees, he had even more success.

In 1932, Walt Disney decided to create a full-length animated film called Snow _____. People thought he was insane for attempting to create such a long cartoon. The film was dubbed "Disney's folly." However, Disney was confident that the film would be a success. The film, which was released in 1937, took five years to complete. The film was a huge box office success, becoming the most successful film of 1938.

Disney used the proceeds from Snow White to establish a film studio and produce other animated films such as Pinocchio, Fantasia, Dumbo, Bambi, _____ in Wonderland, and _____ Pan. During WWII, Disney's film production slowed as he worked on training and propaganda films for the United States government. Following the war, Disney began to produce live-action films alongside animated films. Treasure Island was his first major live-action film.

Television was a new technology that was taking off in the 1950s. Disney wished to be a part of the television industry as well. Disney's Wonderful World of Color, the Davy Crockett series, and the Mickey Mouse _____ was among the first Disney television shows to air on network television.

Disney, who is constantly coming up with new ideas, had the idea to build a _____ park featuring rides and entertainment based on his films. In 1955, Disneyland opened its doors. It cost $17 million to construct. Although it wasn't an immediate success, Disney World has since grown into one of the world's most popular _____ destinations. Walt Disney World, a much larger park in Florida, would be built later by Disney. He contributed to the plans but passed away before the park opened in 1971.

Disney died of lung cancer on December 15, 1966. His legacy endures to this day. Every year, millions of people enjoy his films and theme parks. Every year, his company continues to produce fantastic films and _____.

Reading Comprehension
Multiple Choice: Walt Disney

Score: _____

Date:_____

Make sure you go back and read the Disney article through to the very end. If you attempt to complete this assignment solely by scanning for answers, you will almost certainly pick the incorrect answer. Take your time. Ask questions. Get help if you need it. Good Luck!

1. Walter Elias Disney was born in Chicago, ____.
   a. Illinois
   b. Italy

2. Walter's parents names were Elias and Flora.
   a. True
   b. False

3. Walt got a summer job on a _____.
   a. train
   b. boat

4. Walt's younger sister name was ____.
   a. Ruby
   b. Ruth

5. Walt had _____ brothers.
   a. three
   b. two

6. In 1923, walt relocated to Hollywood, _____.
   a. Colorado
   b. California

7. Steamboat ____ was the title of the film, which starred Mickey and Minnie Mouse.
   a. William
   b. Willie

8. Walt spent the next year in France driving _____ for the Red Cross.
   a. taxi cabs
   b. ambulances

9. Walt and his friends created the well-known character Oswald the Lucky _____t.
   a. Dog
   b. Rabbi

10. Walt's first color animated film was____.
    a. Bears and Tigers
    b. Flowers and Trees

11. In ____, Disneyland opened its doors.
    a. 1955
    b. 1995

12. _____ was among the first Disney television shows to air on network television.
    a. Mickey Mouse Club
    b. Mickey and Friends

13. _____ was his first major live-action film.
    a. Treasure Island
    b. Treats Island

14. Walt Disney decided to create a full-length animated film called _____.
    a. Snow White
    b. Robin Hood

Music: The Orchestra
Vocabulary Words

Name: _____

Date: _____

Who wants to attend an orchestral performance? Obviously, you do! Orchestras are fantastic. An orchestra, at its most basic, is a large musical ensemble. Traditional orchestras have sections for woodwind, brass, strings, and percussion instruments.

The orchestra as we know it today originated in the early 1600s. Instruments were added and removed over the next several centuries, and what we now call the modern orchestra began to take shape. Violins became the orchestra's primary string instrument in the 17th century. More woodwind instruments were added over time, and by the 18th century, French horns, trombones, and trumpets were commonplace.

Throughout the 17th century, orchestras were small, with only about 18-20 members, and the composer was often a performer, often on the harpsichord or violin. As a result, there was no real director. In the 18th century, composers like Johann Sebastian Bach and Wolfgang Amadeus Mozart made orchestral music famous and influential, inspiring kings and peasants alike. During this period, concert performance indeed became a respected profession.

Ludwig van Beethoven, a 19th-century composer who standardized the orchestra using pairs of each woodwind and brass instrument, took the next big step. Beethoven composed works that made full use of the entire range of instruments, from high to low, and gave each section more critical roles, rather than letting the strings carry the majority of the melody on their own.

_____

Unscramble the names of the instruments found in the orchestra.

woodwind	cello	xylophone	violin	piano	trumpet
drums	oboe	brass	trombone	flute	clarinet
percussion	conductor	saxophone	harp		

1. tulef   _ _ _ t _

2. involi   v _ _ _ i _

3. eoob   _ _ _ e

4. articlne   _ _ _ _ i n _ _

5. srudm   d _ _ _ _ _

6. ddnwoiwo   w _ _ d _ _ _ _

7. rbass   b _ _ _ _

8. uniocrspse   _ e _ c _ _ _ _ n

9. lceol   _ _ _ _ o

10. ahrp   _ _ _ p

11. erpttum   _ _ u _ _ e _

12. rootmebn   _ _ o m _ _ _ _

13. enlhoxypo   _ _ l _ _ _ _ _ e

14. udcootrnc   c _ _ _ u _ _ _ _

15. oniap   _ _ _ n _

16. heonoasxp   _ _ x _ _ _ o _ _

History: Thomas Edison

First, read the entire passage. After that, go back and fill in the blanks. You can skip the blanks you're unsure about and finish them later.

devices	teacher	dedicated	research	Morse
passed	hearing	invented	light	dream

Thomas Alva Edison was born in Milan, Ohio, on February 11, 1847. He developed _____ loss at a young age. He was a creative and inquisitive child. However, he struggled in school, possibly because he couldn't hear his _____. He was then educated at home by his mother.

Because of his numerous important inventions, Thomas Edison was nicknamed the "wizard." On his own or in collaboration with others, he has designed and built more than 1,000 _____. The phonograph (record player), the lightbulb, and the motion-picture projector are among his most notable inventions.

Although Thomas did not invent the first electric _____ bulb, he did create the first practical electric light bulb that could be manufactured and used in the home. He also _____ other items required to make the light bulb usable in homes, such as safety fuses and on/off switches for light sockets.

As a teenager, Thomas worked as a telegraph operator. Telegraphy was one of the most important communication systems in the country at the time. Thomas was skilled at sending and receiving _____ code messages. He enjoyed tweaking with telegraphic instruments, and he came up with several improvements to make them even better. By early 1869, he had left his telegraphy job to pursue his _____ of becoming a full-time inventor.

Edison worked tirelessly with scientists and other collaborators to complete projects. He established _____ facilities in Menlo Park, California, and West Orange, New Jersey. Finally, Edison established companies that manufactured and sold his successful inventions.

Edison's family was essential to him, even though he spent the majority of his life _____ to his work. He had six children from two marriages. Edison _____ away on October 18, 1931.

History: Christopher Columbus

When Christopher Columbus discovered America, he set in motion centuries of transatlantic colonization. He was an Italian explorer.

Christopher Columbus made four trips across the Atlantic Ocean from Spain in 1492, 1493, 1498, and 1502. He was adamant about finding a direct water route west from Europe to Asia, but he never succeeded. Instead, he discovered the Americas. Though he did not "discover" the so-called New World—millions of people already lived there—his voyages marked the start of centuries of exploration and colonization of North and South America.

With three ships: the Nina, the Pinta, and the Santa Maria, Columbus, and his crew set sail from Spain on August 3, 1492. The ships arrived in the Bahamas on October 12, not in the East Indies, as Columbus had assumed, but on one of the Bahamian islands, most likely San Salvador.

Columbus sailed from island to island in what is now known as the Caribbean for months, looking for the "pearls, precious stones, gold, silver, spices, and other objects and merchandise whatsoever" that he had promised his Spanish patrons, but he didn't find much. In January 1493, he set sail for Spain, leaving several dozen men behind in a makeshift settlement on Hispaniola (present-day Haiti and the Dominican Republic).

During his first voyage, he kept a detailed diary. Christopher Columbus' journal was written between August 3, 1492, and November 6, 1492, and it describes everything from the wildlife he saw, such as dolphins and birds, to the weather and the moods of his crew.

Circle the correctly spelled word.

	A	B	C	D
1.	America	Amerryca	Ameryca	Amerrica
2.	spices	spicesc	spises	spicess
3.	Eurropaen	European	Europaen	Eurropean
4.	coast	coasct	cuast	coasst
5.	abrroad	abruad	abroad	abrruad
6.	sailor	siallor	saillor	sialor
7.	nations	nattions	nascons	natsions
8.	explurers	explorers	expllorers	expllurers
9.	sylver	syllver	sillver	silver
10.	Spayn	Spian	Spyan	Spain
11.	Indains	Indainss	Indianss	Indians
12.	discover	disssover	disscover	dissover
13.	islend	iscland	island	issland

Health Spelling Words:
Healthy Routines

Write the correct word for each sentence.

Reading	overeat	Eating	read	fat
fresh	fruit	health	glass	chair
floss	Breakfast	Staying	daily	Sleep
fiber	enough	burn	Walking	body

1. Creating a healthy _____ routine is simple.

2. _____ hydrated is vital for our health.

3. Exercise has tremendous _____ benefits.

4. Exposure to the sun enables the _____ to produce vitamin D.

5. _____ is one of the most underrated healthy habits you can do.

6. Vegetables are low in calories, yet high in vitamins, minerals, and _____.

7. _____ has benefits to both your physical and mental health.

8. _____ is the only time during the day where our bodies are able to relax, unwind and recover.

9. _____ a variety of good foods.

10. _____ is the most important meal of the day.

11. Drink a _____ of water.

12. Sitting in your _____ all day long isn't good for you.

13. Excess body _____ comes from eating more than we need.

14. Cooking the right amount makes it easier to not _____.

15. Physical activity helps us _____ off the extra calories.

16. Eat _____ instead of eating a candy bar.

17. Make time to _____ every day.

18. Don't forget to _____.

19. Swap sugary desserts for _____ fruit.

20. Get _____ sleep.

Grammar: SUPERLATIVE ADJECTIVES

Score: _____

Date: _____

A superlative adjective is a comparative adjective that describes something as being of the highest degree or extreme. When comparing three or more people or things, we use superlative adjectives. Superlative adjectives typically end in 'est'. Examples of superlative adjectives include the words biggest and fastest.

Unscramble Word Tip: Try solving the easy words first, and then go back and answer the more difficult ones.

prettiest	hottest	crowded	friendliest	biggest	smallest
saddest	best	worst	tallest	shortest	longest
fattest	newest	heaviest	nicest	beautiful	expensive
cheapest	comfortable	youngest	largest		

1. peehtsac   _ h _ a _ _ _ _

2. talresg   _ _ _ _ e s _

3. ntogels   _ o n _ _ _ _

4. wsenet   n e _ _ _ _

5. icetns   n _ _ _ s _

6. tstosreh   _ _ _ r _ _ _ t

7. samlsetl   _ _ _ _ l _ _ t

8. lstteal   _ a _ _ e _ _

9. goysunte   _ _ _ n _ _ s _

10. tggsbie   _ _ _ g _ s _

11. eftastt   _ _ t _ _ _ t

12. ttoesht   h _ _ _ e _ _

13. adstdes   _ _ d _ _ s _

14. filtaubeu   _ _ a _ _ _ _ _ l

15. ctlefarbmoo   _ _ _ _ _ r _ a b _ _

16. ddrwoce   _ _ _ _ _ e d

17. enpsvxeei   e _ _ _ n _ _ _ _

18. esdeirfiltn   _ r _ _ _ _ l _ _ s _

19. hitvseea   h _ _ _ _ _ _ _ t

20. espttriet   _ r _ _ _ i _ _ _

21. bets   _ _ s _

22. wrsot   _ _ _ s _

Grammar:
Contractions

Take a moment to visualize the process of blowing up a balloon. It grows larger and larger. When we let the air out, it shrinks or contracts. To contract means to shrink, reduce or get smaller.

In writing, a contraction is a word that combines two words to form a shorter word. In other words, the contraction makes the two words smaller. A contraction is simply a word that is a shortened form of two words combined.

When the words can and not are combined, the contraction word can't is formed. The apostrophe (as in this symbol: ') is a small punctuation mark that replaces the letters that have been removed. The apostrophe replaces the 'n' and the 'o' of not in can't.

		A	B	C	D
1.	_____	he'd	ha'd	hh'd	hp'd
2.	_____	yoo'rre	yoo're	you'rre	you're
3.	_____	wesn't	wassn't	wascn't	wasn't
4.	_____	sied	mhod	sha'd	she'd
5.	_____	they'll	thay'l	they'l	thay'll
6.	_____	aran't	arran't	aren't	arren't
7.	_____	let's	latt's	lett's	lat's
8.	_____	lad	I's	I'd	wts
9.	_____	she'l	sha'l	she'll	sha'll
10.	_____	wa'e	wa've	wa'va	we've
11.	_____	yoo'd	yood	yuo'd	you'd
12.	_____	ha'l	ha'll	he'l	he'll
13.	_____	I've	I'vw	Ikva	I'va
14.	_____	hesn't	hassn't	hascn't	hasn't
15.	_____	thai'd	thay'd	they'd	thei'd
16.	_____	you'll	yoo'll	you'l	yoo'l
17.	_____	haven'tt	havan't	haven't	havan'tt
18.	_____	wa'll	we'l	wa'l	we'll
19.	_____	yoo've	yoo'e	yuo've	you've
20.	_____	hadn't	hedn't	hedn'tt	hadn'tt
21.	_____	havan'tt	haven'tt	haven't	havan't

Geography Words

Instructions: Match the science words to the correct meaning.

1		Atlas		A coral reef or an island in the shape of a ring.	A
2		Atoll		The study of the planet Earth's physical features.	B
3		Altitude		A stream that flows into a large lake, or a river.	C
4		Border		The half of a sphere. Hint: Northern and Southern___.	D
5		Capital		The measure of the distance from the east or the west of Prime Meridian.	E
6		Country		The measure of elevation above sea level.	F
7		Desert		The 3rd planet of our solar system and the planet in which we all live.	G
8		Earth		A narrow passage of water connecting two water bodies.	H
9		Equator		A political state or a nation. For example, India, Thailand.	I
10		Geography		The measure of the distance from the north or the south of the Equator.	J
11		Glacier		A mass of ice that is slowly moving.	K
12		Hemisphere		A collection of maps of the planet Earth.	L
13		Latitude		A large area covered with sand, where water or vegetation is either very little or not present at all.	M
14		Longitude		An artificial line drawn segregating two geographical areas.	N
15		Meridian		A city exercising primary status and where the government is located.	O
16		Plain		A piece of land on high ground.	P
17		Plateau		A piece of land that is flat.	Q
18		Strait		A line drawn on the center of the earth separating the north and south pole.	R
19		Tributary		An imaginary circle passing through two poles.	S

Art Words

Score: _____

Date: _____

Art truly is a gift to the world. It is what we seek in our human experience. Art gives meaning to our lives and aids in our understanding of the world around us. It is an important part of our culture because it helps us understand our emotions better, increases our self-awareness, and allows us to be open to new ideas and experiences. As a result, art continues to open our minds and hearts and show us what is possible in our world. Art appreciation improves our quality of life and makes us feel good, according to scientific studies. We improve our problem-solving abilities and open our minds to new ideas when we create art.

Instructions: Match the Art words to the correct meaning.

1	☐	Contrast	A closed line.	A
2	☐	Composition	The arrangement of forms in a work of art.	B
3	☐	Cool colors	The area between and around objects.	C
4	☐	Hue	Use of opposites near or beside one another (light and dark, rough and smooth)	D
5	☐	Intensity	The dark values of a color (adding black).	E
6	☐	Texture	Red, orange, yellow.	F
7	☐	Subject matter	The center of interest of an artwork; the part you look at first.	G
8	☐	Tint	Refers to the way things feel or look as though they might feel if they were touched.	H
9	☐	Shade	The topic of interest or the primary theme of an artwork.	I
10	☐	Warm colors	Principle of design concerned with difference or contrast.	J
11	☐	Variety	Brightness of a color.	K
12	☐	Focal point	Light values of a color (adding white)	L
13	☐	Line	The surface quality that can be seen and felt.	M
14	☐	Shape	Mostly green, blue, violet (purple).	N
15	☐	Space	A mark with greater length than width.	O
16	☐	Texture	The name of a color – red blue, yellow, etc.	P

Extra Credit Question: What are the elements of art? List each of them with a description.

DATE_____   **RESEARCH:** Susan B. Anthony

Occupation _____

BORN DATE:_____ Nationality _____

DEATH DATE:_____ Education _____ #Children _____

Childhood and Family Background Facts

Work and Career Facts

Children, Marriage and or Significant Relationships

Friends, Social Life and Other Interesting Facts

Did you enjoy researching this person?

Give a Rating: ☆ ☆ ☆ ☆ ☆

GRADE_____

DATE_____ **RESEARCH:** Juliette Gordon Low

Occupation _____

BORN DATE:_____ Nationality_____

DEATH DATE:_____ Education _____ #Children _____

Childhood and Family Background Facts

Work and Career Facts

Children, Marriage and or Significant Relationships

Friends, Social Life and Other Interesting Facts

Did you enjoy researching this person?

Give a Rating: ☆ ☆ ☆ ☆ ☆

DATE_____   **RESEARCH: Buddha**

Occupation _____

BORN DATE:_____   Nationality_____

DEATH DATE:_____   Education _____   #Children _____

Childhood and Family Background Facts

Work and Career Facts

Children, Marriage and or Significant Relationships

Friends, Social Life and Other Interesting Facts

Did you enjoy researching this person?

Give a Rating: ☆ ☆ ☆ ☆ ☆

Science Vocab Crossword

Complete the crossword by filling in a word that fits each clue. Fill in the correct answers, one letter per square, both across and down, from the given clues. There will be a gray space between multi-word answers.

Tip: Solve the easy clues first, and then go back and answer the more difficult ones.

Across

1. The force that attracts mass
3. Unicellular microorganism
5. A dark area
6. Flow of electron
8. Any true information

Down

2. kill and hunt for food
4. Juicy fluid within flowers
7. Power
8. The remains of plant or animal
9. The smallest particle

GRAVITY   PREY
ATOM   NECTAR
SHADOW   FOSSIL
ENERGY   BACTERIA
ELECTRICITY
FACT

Music: String Family Instruments

Score: _____

Date: _____

Strings vibrate to produce sound in stringed instruments. Stringed instruments come in a wide variety of styles, from guitars to violins to zithers to harps. Stringed instruments vibrate their strings to produce sound. Strings vibrate in different ways depending on the type of instrument being played.

Plucking the strings is one way to make them vibrate. When a guitarist uses their fingers, hands, or a pick to cause the string to vibrate and produce sound, this is how the guitar sounds. The harp, banjo, lute, and sitar are among the other instruments that can be performed in this manner. Picking and strumming are other terms for plucking.

Many stringed instruments are played by stroking a bow over the strings. It's not uncommon for bows to be made from long sticks with a substance woven into them, most commonly horsehair. The movement of the material down the string produces a sound and vibration. Violin, cello, and fiddle are examples of instruments that use a bow as their primary sound source.

The smallest string instrument is the violin and the biggest string instrument is the double bass.

V	H	J	C	B	G	Y	I	G	R	Q	T
M	W	V	Q	A	D	T	C	E	L	L	O
A	K	P	P	N	O	T	S	J	K	W	V
N	Z	V	V	J	U	U	U	J	F	Q	D
D	S	Q	I	O	B	V	H	A	R	P	S
O	F	X	O	U	L	Q	U	B	H	B	O
L	K	Z	L	K	E	H	G	M	J	F	E
I	R	C	A	U	B	V	I	O	L	I	N
N	S	B	P	L	A	Y	J	V	E	B	U
Y	B	O	G	E	S	U	O	I	N	O	O
P	J	B	K	L	S	I	Z	C	M	N	X
A	Q	W	T	E	S	U	A	A	E	N	E

Violin	Viola	Cello	Double Bass
Harp	Banjo	Mandolin	Ukulele

Music: Brass Instruments
List Word Search

Score: _____

Date: _____

You play a brass instrument by blowing into a mouthpiece to change the pitch, or note, of the instrument.

Breath is used by brass musicians to create sound. To play, players buzz their lips against a metal cup-shaped mouthpiece instead of blowing into a reed. Buzzing provides the sound, which is increased by the mouthpiece. In most brass instruments, there are valves attached to the lengthy pipes; the valves resemble buttons in appearance. By applying pressure to the valves, different sections of the pipe can be opened and closed.

M	H	Q	R	L	F	O	C	O	R	N	E	T	L	W	I
Q	E	P	I	C	C	O	L	O	T	R	U	M	P	E	T
Y	T	S	Y	H	U	N	T	I	N	G	H	O	R	N	D
F	S	N	D	T	E	M	F	C	Y	A	S	R	L	J	I
J	E	B	T	R	I	E	L	A	R	F	D	B	S	Z	A
U	R	E	R	U	U	L	U	F	O	B	B	N	T	M	V
L	P	U	O	M	M	L	G	T	M	Q	E	B	N	M	C
P	E	P	M	P	K	O	E	Q	N	P	R	X	J	U	Q
V	N	H	B	E	N	P	L	M	X	Y	B	U	G	L	E
A	T	O	O	T	G	H	H	F	Q	J	Z	D	Z	A	Q
A	E	N	N	B	A	O	O	D	W	R	J	L	K	H	N
N	M	I	E	O	N	N	R	T	U	X	N	Q	O	Z	A
C	V	U	S	W	R	E	N	A	R	J	J	S	O	S	Q
E	V	M	H	J	W	G	C	I	M	B	A	S	S	O	G
K	A	Q	J	R	F	R	E	N	C	H	H	O	R	N	D
X	C	X	Y	H	C	X	C	X	U	K	H	Q	L	I	J

Bugle	Trumpet	Cornet	Piccolo trumpet
Flugelhorn	French horn	Mellophone	Euphonium
Trombone	Cimbasso	Hunting horn	Serpent

History Vocab Words

Score: _____

Date: _____

Complete the crossword by filling in a word that fits each clue. Fill in the correct answers, one letter per square, both across and down, from the given clues. There will be a gray space between multi-word answers.

Tip: Solve the easy clues first, and then go back and answer the more difficult ones.

Across

3. exchange goods without involving money
4. a periodic count of the population
5. all the knowledge and values shared by a society
7. a ruler who is unconstrained by law
9. a period marked by distinctive character

Down

1. how long something has existed
2. a man-made object
5. a period of 100 years
8. of or relating to the home
10. bring in from abroad

ERA   DICTATOR
IMPORT   AGE
CENSUS   ARTIFACT
DOMESTIC
BARTER   CENTURY
CULTURE

Health Spelling Words

Score: _____

Date: _____

Instructions: Match the health term to the correct meaning.

1		acute	in or near an inner area	A
2		infant	feeling discomfort on the skin's surface	B
3		anemia	a device that holds injured body parts in place	C
4		colic	long-lasting or characterized by long-suffering	D
5		brace	acute abdominal pain, especially in infants	E
6		dental	relating to the teeth	F
7		germ	young baby	G
8		disease	a micro-organism, especially one that causes disease	H
9		fever	uniform worn by medical professionals	I
10		cancer	a deficiency of red blood cells	J
11		bedsore	an impairment of health	K
12		chronic	disease caused by the uncontrollable growth of cells	L
13		central	the removal and examination of tissue from a living body	M
14		biopsy	damage to the body	N
15		injury	wounds that develop on a patient's body from lying in one place for too long	O
16		sore	painful	P
17		itchy	ending in a sharp point	Q
18		scrubs	higher than normal body temperature	R

Grammar: Suffix

A suffix is a letter or group of letters attached to the end of a word in order to alter the meaning or function of the word. As with prefixes, the English language comes with tons of suffixes.

Consider the suffix **-ist**; by adding it to a word, you can modify it to refer to someone who performs or practices something. So, **art** becomes **artist**, a skillful performer of a particular art.

Other Examples:

The suffix **-ish** (Blueish) means relating to or resembling something.

The suffix **-ness** (Happiness) indicates a condition or quality. This suffix changes the word from a verb to a noun.

The suffix **-ship** (internship) position held.

The suffix **-less** (restless) means without something.

1. What is a suffix?
   a. A word beginning that changes the meaning of the word
   b. A word ending that changes the meaning of the word

2. What is the suffix in the word "permission"?
   a. -per
   b. -sion

3. What is the suffix in the word careful?
   a. -care
   b. -ful

4. What is the suffix in the word youngest?
   a. -young
   b. -est

5. What is the suffix in the word harmless?
   a. -less
   b. -arm

6. What is the suffix in the word cuter?
   a. -cute
   b. -er

7. What do you think the suffix -less means?
   a. Meaning: More of
   b. Meaning: Without

8. What do you think the suffix -ward, -wards means? (Towards, afterwards, backwards, inward)
   a. Meaning: Direction
   b. Meaning: Driving something

9. What do you think the suffix -ery means? (bakery, pottery, nursery)
   a. Meaning: an occupation or a way to make a living
   b. Meaning: a business or trade, a behavior, a condition

10. What is the suffix in the word breakable?
    a. -able
    b. -break

GRADE_____

DATE_____   **RESEARCH:** Aristotle

Occupation _____

BORN DATE:_____   Nationality_____

DEATH DATE:_____   Education_____   #Children _____

Childhood and Family Background Facts

Work and Career Facts

Children, Marriage and or Significant Relationships

Friends, Social Life and Other Interesting Facts

Did you enjoy researching this person?

Give a Rating: ☆ ☆ ☆ ☆ ☆

GRADE_____

DATE_____

RESEARCH: Francis Beaufort

Occupation _____

BORN DATE:_____ Nationality_____

DEATH DATE:_____ Education _____ #Children _____

Childhood and Family Background Facts

Work and Career Facts

Children, Marriage and or Significant Relationships

Friends, Social Life and Other Interesting Facts

Did you enjoy researching this person?

Give a Rating: ☆ ☆ ☆ ☆ ☆

GRADE_____

DATE_____

RESEARCH: Alan Archibald Campbell-Swinton

Occupation _____

BORN DATE:_____ Nationality_____

DEATH DATE:_____ Education_____ #Children _____

Childhood and Family Background Facts

Work and Career Facts

Children, Marriage and or Significant Relationships

Friends, Social Life and Other Interesting Facts

Did you enjoy researching this person?

Give a Rating: ☆ ☆ ☆ ☆ ☆

Grammar: Prefixes

Score: _____

Date:_____

A prefix is a part of a word or a word contained within another word. It is added to the beginning of another word to give it a new meaning. Additionally, it can refer to a number that is added at the beginning to indicate the position of anything inside a group.

Rules for adding prefix:

- prefix + root word = new word.

Look at the meaning of the prefix added to the meaning of the root word to get the meaning of the new word.

Meanings for prefixes vary depending on which one is used.

Example:

anti- | opposing, against, the opposite| antibiotic

com- | with, jointly, completely | combat

de- | down, away| decrease|

extra- | outside, beyond | extracurricular

1. A prefix comes at the _____ of a word.
   a. beginning
   b. end

2. A prefix changes the meaning of a root word.
   a. True
   b. False

3. What do you think the prefix re- (redo) means _____?
   a. do again
   b. not - or - opposite

4. What do you think the prefix dis- (disadvantage) means _____?
   a. add; multiply
   b. away; removal

5. If you are unable to do something, you are _____.
   a. able to do it again
   b. not able to do it

6. If you dislike green beans, you _____.
   a. really like green beans
   b. do not like green beans

7. If you disobey your parents, you _____.
   a. obey your parents quickly
   b. do not obey your parents

8. My teacher made me ___write name because it was sloppy.
   a. un
   b. re

9. My friends and I ___play our favorite video games over and over again.
   a. re
   b. dis

10. Kids are ___able to drive until they are 16.
    a. un
    b. re

Grammar: Nouns

A noun is a word that names something, such as a person, place, thing, or idea.

Identifying People
It might be the name of any individual, such as Jim, Ree, Tiffany, Jackie, or Tom.

The Naming of Places
It could be the name of any location, such as America, China, beach, North Dakota, or Paris.

Naming Objects or Things
Things such as a car, a hat, a bottle, a table, a cord, and a towel.

Animal Naming
A dog, a rabbit, an elephant, a chicken, and a horse.

Identifying Emotions/Qualities/Ideas
Fear, Joy, Beauty, Strength, and Anger.

1. Find the nouns: Andy likes to eat pie.
   a. eat, pie
   b. Andy, pie

2. Find the noun: The cup fell and broke.
   a. cup
   b. broke

3. A noun is...
   a. A word that describes
   b. A person, place, or thing

4. The word library is a.....
   a. place
   b. thing

5. The word window is a.....
   a. place
   b. thing

6. The word teacher is a.....
   a. thing
   b. person

7. My red bike goes really fast.
   a. bike
   b. red

8. Which answer choice is a noun?
   a. parrot
   b. blue

9. Which answer choice is a noun?
   a. lamp
   b. bright

10. Find the noun: I live in Australia.
   a. I
   b. Australia

11. Find the noun: Jackie is my sister.
   a. my
   b. Jackie

12. What are the nouns in this sentence? Ree lives on an island.
   a. Ree, lives
   b. Ree, island

Grammar: Adjectives

A word that describes an animal, person, thing, or thought is known as an adjective. Adjectives are words that describe how something appears and how it feels to touch, taste, or smell.

Adjectives are an important form of expression in descriptive writing because they provide important details that support the visualization and understanding of a subject. Once more, an adjective can be a color, a word to describe size, or any other word that describes how something looks, feels, tastes, sounds, or smells!

For example:

*"It was a **large** toy truck."*

*"The **red** apple looked delicious."*

*"The **round** table was full."*

Quantitative adjectives - These give the exact or approximate value of a noun.
"There were **six** cats."

Superlative adjectives - These are used to indicate that a noun is of the highest or best quality, and they frequently end in "-est."
"She is the **fastest** soccer player on her team."

1. **They live in a beautiful house.**
   a. beautiful
   b. live

2. **Lisa is wearing a sleeveless shirt today.**
   a. sleeveless
   b. wearing

3. **She wore a colorful dress.**
   a. colorful
   b. wore

4. **This house is much nicer.**
   a. much
   b. nicer

5. **Jim is an adorable baby.**
   a. adorable
   b. baby

6. **Ree's hair is gorgeous.**
   a. hair
   b. gorgeous

7. **This house is bigger than that one.**
   a. bigger
   b. that one

8. **The wooden chair was uncomfortable.**
   a. uncomfortable
   b. wooden

9. **He is a funny little man.**
   a. little man
   b. funny little

10. **Did you have enough food?**
    a. enough
    b. have

11. **Kim bought six apples.**
    a. six
    b. bought

12. **The big dog chased the car.**
    a. chased
    b. big

Grammar:
Abbreviations

An abbreviation is a word that has been shortened. When writing, abbreviations can make it easier and faster to say what you need to say.

There are numerous kinds of abbreviations that can be used. Let us now go over some of the most common ones.

Months

Except for March, April, May, June, and July, the majority of the months are long words. When writing long ones, you might want to use an abbreviation. For example, if you're writing a sticky note to remind a friend to meet you at the ice cream shop at 1:00 p.m. on August 6, you can use the abbreviation 'Aug.' Except for the short months, such as 'May,' each month has an abbreviation.

Because the months of the year begin with capital letters, the abbreviations should, too. Each abbreviation should be followed by a period. What is the abbreviation for the month in which Christmas falls? Dec. Correct! What about this Halloween? Oct. is correct!

Week Days
The words for the days of the week are also quite long! The abbreviations are as follows:

- Mon. – Monday
- Tues. or Tue. – Tuesday
- Wed. – Wednesday
- Thu. or Thurs. – Thursday
- Fri. – Friday
- Sat.- Saturday
- Sun. – Sunday

Addresses

When sending letters or packages via mail, you must include an address. You can use abbreviations in the address so that the true word takes up less space, and an abbreviation is faster.

If you're sending a birthday card to Aunt Kay, who lives on 31st Avenue, you can simply write '31st Ave.' If you want to send a friendly note to your favorite teacher who lives on Rose Street, use the abbreviation 'Rose St.' If you want to send a thank-you note to your best friend who lives in an apartment, write 'Apt. #2' rather than Apartment #2. You can also substitute 'Dr.' for Drive and 'Blvd.' for Boulevard. See? When writing addresses, abbreviations come in handy!

- N- North
- E- East
- S- South
- W- West
- bldg.- building
- st.- Street

States

Finally, when writing the names of states, you can use abbreviations. When mailing something to someone, the most common place to abbreviate a state is on an envelope.

For example, the abbreviation for Virginia is 'VA.' The United States Postal Service assigns an abbreviation to each state so that everyone uses the same abbreviations when mailing a letter or a package.

Instructions: Match the abbreviation to the correct word.

1	Ave.		northeast	A
2	Blvd.		southeast	B
3	Dr.		Boulevard	C
4	Ln.		east	D
5	Rd.		south	E
6	St.		miscellaneous	F
7	E		Mistress	G
8	N		Street	H
9	NE		department	I
10	NW		west	J
11	S		estimated time of arrival	K
12	SE		Road	L
13	SW		north	M
14	W		Mister	N
15	dept.		Avenue	O
16	D.I.Y.		minute or minimum	P
17	est.		Do it yourself	Q
18	E.T.A.		Drive	R
19	min.		established	S
20	misc.		Lane	T
21	Mr.		northwest	U
22	Mrs.		southwest	V

Grammar: Abbreviations

Score: _____

Date: _____

Instructions: Match the abbreviation to the correct word.

1	☐	January		Fri.	A
2	☐	March		Sep. or Sept.	B
3	☐	July		Mon.	C
4	☐	September		Oct.	D
5	☐	November		Aug.	E
6	☐	February		Sun.	F
7	☐	April		Tu., Tue., or Tues.	G
8	☐	June		Wed.	H
9	☐	August		Apr.	I
10	☐	October		Thur., or Thurs	J
11	☐	December		Sat.	K
12	☐	Sunday		Jan.	L
13	☐	Tuesday		Nov.	M
14	☐	Thursday		Dec.	N
15	☐	Saturday		Jun.	O
16	☐	Monday		Feb.	P
17	☐	Wednesday		Jul.	Q
18	☐	Friday		Mar.	R

Grammar & Spelling Building

Score: _____

Date: _____

Write the correct word for each sentence.

teeth	joining	once	lion	ball
old	loved	sing	five	deep
extra	greet	clown	thank	frown
feed	away	coffee	balloons	bang

1. The circus _____ did many silly things.

2. He tried to _____ to make us laugh.

3. We should _____ him for the good memories.

4. We saw a woman _____ really high notes.

5. A loud _____ came from a cannon.

6. The _____ man landed safely.

7. The _____ jumped through a ring of fire.

8. The tiger balanced on a _____.

9. We will pay _____ to see another show.

10. We both _____ the elephants.

11. There was a muscle man who lifted two people at _____.

12. We filled our _____ with helium.

13. My neighbor had no interest in _____ us.

14. Let's _____ the sheep now.

15. Keep brushing your _____ daily.

16. I keep _____ dollars in my pocket.

17. The river was really _____ and wide.

18. Don't scare that deer _____.

19. Let's _____ the new mayor.

20. My grandma makes _____ every morning.

GRADE_____

DATE_____   **RESEARCH: Ken Kutaragi**

Occupation _____

BORN DATE:_____   Nationality_____

DEATH DATE:_____   Education_____   #Children _____

Childhood and Family Background Facts

Work and Career Facts

Children, Marriage and or Significant Relationships

Friends, Social Life and Other Interesting Facts

Did you enjoy researching this person?

Give a Rating: ☆ ☆ ☆ ☆ ☆

GRADE_____

DATE_____

RESEARCH: Charles Macintosh

Occupation _____

BORN DATE:_____ Nationality_____

DEATH DATE:_____ Education_____ #Children _____

Childhood and Family Background Facts

Work and Career Facts

Children, Marriage and or Significant Relationships

Friends, Social Life and Other Interesting Facts

Did you enjoy researching this person?

Give a Rating: ☆ ☆ ☆ ☆ ☆

GRADE_____

DATE_____

RESEARCH: Ilya Ilyich Mechnikov

Occupation _____

BORN DATE:_____ Nationality_____

DEATH DATE:_____ Education _____ #Children _____

Childhood and Family Background Facts

| |
| |
| |
| |
| |
| |

Work and Career Facts

| |

Children, Marriage and or Significant Relationships

| |

Friends, Social Life and Other Interesting Facts

| |

Did you enjoy researching this person?

Give a Rating: ☆ ☆ ☆ ☆ ☆

GRADE_____

DATE_____

RESEARCH: Daniel David Palmer

Occupation _____

BORN DATE:_____ Nationality_____

DEATH DATE:_____ Education_____ #Children _____

Childhood and Family Background Facts

Work and Career Facts

Children, Marriage and or Significant Relationships

Friends, Social Life and Other Interesting Facts

Did you enjoy researching this person?

Give a Rating: ☆ ☆ ☆ ☆ ☆

GRADE_____

DATE_____

RESEARCH: Adolphe Sax

Occupation _____

BORN DATE:_____   Nationality_____

DEATH DATE:_____   Education_____   #Children _____

Childhood and Family Background Facts

Work and Career Facts

Children, Marriage and or Significant Relationships

Friends, Social Life and Other Interesting Facts

Did you enjoy researching this person?

Give a Rating: ☆ ☆ ☆ ☆ ☆

Vehicle Accident Report

It is customary for a law enforcement officer who was on the scene of an accident to create a car accident report. For a variety of reasons, police preserve extensive reports on car accidents in writing. They can use it to begin a criminal investigation into a specific incident. Moreover, if you decide to sue the motorist who caused the accident, you can use the report as physical evidence.

Accident Information

Accident Date: _____ Accident Time: _____ Accident Location: _____

Accident Description:

Violations Issued: _____ Report Number: _____

Your Information

Owner's Name: _____ Owner's Phone #: _____

Owner's Address: _____

Insurance Company: _____ Policy #: _____ Agent: _____

Driver's Name (if different) _____ Relation to Insured: _____

Driver's Address: _____

Phone #: _____ License #: _____ State: _____ DOB: _____

Vehicle Used w/ Permission? ☐ Yes ☐ No Purpose: _____

Damage:

Vehicle Make: _____ Model: _____ Year: _____

Plate #: _____ State: _____ Other Insurance: _____

Injured Parties Information

Pedestrian/Bicyclist ☐ In Your Car ☐ In Another Car ☐ Phone No: _____

If in a car: Make: _____ Model: _____ Year: _____

Insurance: _____ Policy No. _____ Plates: _____

Injury: _____

Pedestrian/Bicyclist ☐ In Your Car ☐ In Another Car ☐ Phone No: _____

If in a car: Make: _____ Model: _____ Year: _____

Insurance: _____ Policy No. _____ Plates: _____

Injury:

Damaged Property

Property: _____

Damage: _____

Owner(s): _____ Phone No. _____

Address: _____

Insurance: _____ Policy No. _____

Witness(es)

Name: _____ Phone No. _____

Address: _____

In Your Car: ☐ In Another Car: ☐ Other: _____

Name: _____ Phone No. _____

Address: _____

In Your Car: ☐ In Another Car: ☐ Other: _____

Dental Health History Form Practice

Dental history reviews the patient's past dental experiences and current dental issues. A look at the dental history can often tell you about past dental problems, previous dental treatment, and how the patient has responded to treatment.

Patient Name: _____ Date: _____

Email Address: _____ Phone No. _____

Address: _____

Medications: _____

_____

Allergies: _____

_____

Pregnant: ☐ Yes ☐ No   Nursing: ☐ Yes ☐ No

Alcohol Use: ☐ Never ☐ Occasionally ☐ Monthly ☐ Weekly ☐ Daily ☐ 4+ per Day

Smoking: ☐ Never ☐ Occasionally ☐ 1 per Day ☐ 1 Pack per Day ☐ 2+ Packs per Day

Illegal Drug Use: ☐ Never ☐ Occasionally ☐ Monthly ☐ Weekly ☐ Daily

Exercise: ☐ Never ☐ Occasionally ☐ Weekly ☐ 2-3 Times per Week ☐ Daily

Dental Symptoms		
Pain in teeth	☐ Yes	☐ No
Teeth sensitivity	☐ Yes	☐ No
Teeth sensitivity to heat	☐ Yes	☐ No
Teeth sensitivity to cold	☐ Yes	☐ No
Teeth sensitivity to sour	☐ Yes	☐ No
Teeth sensitivity to sweet	☐ Yes	☐ No
Bleeding gums	☐ Yes	☐ No
Bleeding gums after flossing	☐ Yes	☐ No
Sensitive gums	☐ Yes	☐ No
Swollen gums	☐ Yes	☐ No
Headaches	☐ Yes	☐ No
Earaches	☐ Yes	☐ No
Jaw aching	☐ Yes	☐ No
Tired jaw	☐ Yes	☐ No
Clicking jaw	☐ Yes	☐ No
Jaw gets stuck	☐ Yes	☐ No
Unable to totally open mouth	☐ Yes	☐ No
TMJ	☐ Yes	☐ No
Clenched jaw	☐ Yes	☐ No
Grinding teeth	☐ Yes	☐ No
Food catches in teeth	☐ Yes	☐ No
Tongue pain	☐ Yes	☐ No
Tongue swelling	☐ Yes	☐ No
	☐ Yes	☐ No
	☐ Yes	☐ No
	☐ Yes	☐ No
	☐ Yes	☐ No
	☐ Yes	☐ No

Dental History		
I gag easily	☐ Yes	☐ No
Dental work makes me nervous	☐ Yes	☐ No
I brush _____ times per day		
I floss _____ times per day		
I use mouthwash _____ times per day		
I chew gum regularly	☐ Yes	☐ No
I chew tobacco regularly	☐ Yes	☐ No
I smoke a pipe regularly	☐ Yes	☐ No
I take pain relievers often	☐ Yes	☐ No
I take muscle relaxants often	☐ Yes	☐ No
I take antidepressants often	☐ Yes	☐ No
I have had trauma to the head	☐ Yes	☐ No
I have had trauma to the face	☐ Yes	☐ No
I have had trauma to the ear	☐ Yes	☐ No
I have had trauma to the mouth	☐ Yes	☐ No
I have had trauma to the throat	☐ Yes	☐ No
I take fluoride supplements	☐ Yes	☐ No
I am dissatisfied with my teeth	☐ Yes	☐ No
I wear dentures	☐ Yes	☐ No
I have braces	☐ Yes	☐ No
I don't like the color of my teeth	☐ Yes	☐ No
I want total dental care	☐ Yes	☐ No
	☐ Yes	☐ No
	☐ Yes	☐ No
	☐ Yes	☐ No
	☐ Yes	☐ No
	☐ Yes	☐ No

Employers who do pre-employment drug tests eliminate the chance of hiring individuals who use illegal drugs or other substances. Substance addiction problems undoubtedly have an adverse effect on an employee's productivity. A drug test can be used both ways. It prevents companies from hiring persons who pose a risk due to drug misuse issues. Simultaneously, employers may offer assistance in rehabilitating current employees facing such difficulties.

Certain state and federal laws mandate business owners to maintain a drug-free work environment. Employers do drug testing to ensure compliance with these rules.

CONSENT TO DRUG TEST

I, _____, am aware that Life Skills & Associates Business is a drug-free workplace and that employment is contingent upon passing a drug test.

I agree that if I am offered and accept a position with the company, I will be subjected to a urine test for the purpose of screening for illegal drug usage.

I acknowledge that I have been told about the scope of the test, which drugs are being looked for, and how samples are taken. I hereby consent to this test.

Additionally, I am aware that these results will become part of my employment record and that positive results may influence my ability to obtain employment.

I give my authorization for the exam results to be shared with Life Skills & Associates Business.

Signature:_____   Date:_____

Witness:_____   Date:_____

Termination of Lease

☒ ☒☒☒☒ ☒☒☒ ☒☒☒☒☒☒ ☒☒☒☒☒☒ ☒☒☒☒☒☒☒☒☒☒ ☒☒☒ ☒☒ ☒ ☒☒☒ ☒☒☒ ☒☒☒☒☒☒☒☒☒☒☒☒☒☒☒ ☒☒ ☒☒☒ ☒☒☒☒ ☒☒☒☒☒☒ ☒☒☒☒☒☒ ☒☒☒☒

☒ ☒☒☒☒☒☒☒☒ ☒ ☒☒ ☒☒☒☒☒☒ ☒☒☒☒ ☒☒☒☒☒ ☒ ☒☒☒☒☒ ☒☒☒☒☒ ☒☒☒☒☒☒☒☒☒☒☒ ☒☒☒ ☒☒☒☒☒ ☒☒☒☒☒☒☒☒☒☒☒☒☒☒☒☒☒☒☒☒☒☒ ☒☒☒ ☒☒☒ ☒ ☒☒☒ ☒☒☒☒☒☒ ☒☒☒☒☒☒ ☒☒☒☒☒☒ ☒☒☒ ☒☒☒☒☒ ☒ ☒☒☒ ☒ ☒☒☒☒☒ ☒☒☒☒☒☒☒☒☒ ☒☒☒☒☒ ☒☒☒ ☒ ☒☒☒☒☒☒☒ ☒ ☒☒☒ ☒☒☒☒ ☒☒☒☒☒ ☒☒☒☒☒ ☒ ☒☒☒ ☒☒☒☒ ☒☒☒☒☒☒ ☒☒☒☒☒ ☒☒☒ ☒☒☒☒☒ ☒ ☒☒☒ ☒ ☒☒☒☒☒ ☒☒☒☒☒☒☒☒ ☒☒☒☒☒ ☒☒☒ ☒☒☒☒ ☒☒☒☒☒☒☒☒☒ ☒☒☒☒ ☒☒☒☒☒ ☒☒☒☒☒ ☒☒ ☒☒☒ ☒☒☒☒☒☒☒☒

☒☒☒ ☒☒☒☒☒☒☒ ☒ ☒☒☒☒☒☒☒☒☒☒☒☒☒ ☒☒☒ ☒☒☒☒☒☒☒☒ ☒☒☒ ☒ ☒☒☒☒ ☒☒☒☒☒☒ ☒☒☒☒☒☒☒☒☒☒ ☒☒☒☒☒☒ ☒☒☒☒☒☒ ☒☒☒☒☒☒ ☒☒☒☒☒☒☒ ☒☒☒☒☒☒☒☒ ☒☒☒ ☒☒☒☒☒☒ ☒☒☒☒☒ ☒☒ ☒☒☒☒☒ ☒☒☒ ☒ ☒☒☒☒☒ ☒☒☒ ☒☒☒☒☒☒☒☒☒☒☒☒☒☒☒☒ ☒☒☒☒☒☒☒☒
☒☒
Instructions: ☒☒☒ ☒☒☒ ☒☒☒ ☒☒☒☒ ☒☒☒☒☒☒ ☒☒☒☒☒☒☒☒ ☒☒ ☒☒ ☒☒☒☒☒☒☒☒ ☒☒☒☒☒☒☒☒☒☒☒☒ ☒☒☒ ☒☒☒☒☒ ☒☒☒☒☒ ☒☒☒☒☒☒☒☒☒☒ ☒☒ **bold**☒

☒☒

☒ ☒☒☒☒**Make sure you address resident by name** ☒☒

☒☒☒☒☒ ☒☒☒☒☒☒☒☒ ☒☒☒☒ ☒☒☒☒☒☒ ☒☒☒☒☒☒☒☒ ☒☒☒**apartment/unit number> at address> as of date/time>]**☒

☒ ☒☒☒☒☒☒☒☒ ☒☒ ☒☒☒ ☒☒☒☒☒ ☒☒☒☒☒☒ ☒☒☒☒☒☒☒ ☒☒☒☒☒☒☒☒ ☒☒☒ ☒☒☒☒☒☒ ☒☒☒☒☒☒☒☒☒ ☒☒☒☒☒ ☒☒☒☒☒☒ ☒☒☒☒☒☒ ☒☒☒ ☒☒☒☒☒ ☒☒☒☒☒☒☒☒☒☒ ☒☒ ☒☒ ☒☒**write reason(s) for termination,**☒☒☒☒☒☒ ☒☒ ☒☒☒☒☒☒☒☒☒☒☒ ☒☒☒☒☒ ☒☒☒☒☒☒☒ ☒ ☒ ☒☒☒☒☒ ☒☒ ☒☒ ☒☒☒☒

☒☒ ☒☒☒ ☒☒☒☒ ☒☒☒☒☒☒ ☒☒☒☒☒☒☒☒☒ ☒ ☒☒☒☒☒☒☒ ☒☒☒ ☒☒☒☒☒ ☒☒☒☒☒☒☒☒☒☒☒☒ ☒☒☒ ☒☒☒ ☒☒☒☒☒☒☒☒☒☒☒☒ ☒ ☒☒☒☒☒☒☒☒ ☒☒☒☒☒ ☒☒☒☒☒ ☒☒ ☒☒☒☒☒☒☒☒☒☒☒ ☒ ☒☒☒☒☒☒ ☒ ☒☒☒☒☒☒☒☒☒☒ ☒ ☒☒ ☒☒ ☒☒☒☒☒☒ ☒ ☒☒☒ ☒☒☒☒ ☒☒☒☒☒☒☒☒☒☒☒☒

☒☒ ☒☒☒☒☒☒☒☒☒☒ ☒ ☒☒ ☒☒☒☒☒☒☒☒☒☒☒☒☒☒ ☒**have/have not**'☒☒☒☒☒☒☒ ☒☒☒ ☒☒☒☒☒☒ ☒☒☒☒**amount**'☒☒☒☒☒☒☒ ☒☒☒☒☒☒☒**** This is where you if the individual receives a refund of their security deposit.****

☒☒☒☒☒ ☒☒☒☒☒☒☒☒ ☒☒ ☒☒☒☒☒ ☒☒☒☒☒ ☒☒☒☒☒ ☒☒☒☒ ☒☒☒☒ ☒☒☒☒☒☒☒☒☒☒☒☒☒☒☒☒☒☒ ☒☒ ☒☒ ☒☒☒ ☒☒☒☒☒☒ ☒☒☒☒☒ ☒☒☒☒☒☒ ☒☒☒☒ ☒☒☒☒☒☒☒☒ ☒☒☒☒☒☒☒☒ ☒☒☒☒

☒☒☒☒☒☒☒☒☒

☒You name or business name goes here☒

Termination of Lease Rewrite Practice

The medical record information release (HIPAA) form lets a patient allow any person or 3rd party to have access to their health records.

AUTHORIZATION FOR RELEASE OF HEALTH INFORMATION

Patient Name _____ **Date of Birth** _____

The above named person must indicate when this authorization is to expire:

☐ When information is received ☐ In one year
☐ In six months ☐ In three years
☐ On date _____

The person named above is or has been a patient of

Name of Person,
Provider, or Facility
Address _____
Phone _____
Fax _____

The person named above hereby authorizes _____ **to**
Name of Person, Provider, or Facility

☐ Request health information from ☐ Send health information to
☐ Discuss health information with ☐ Discuss health information with

The person named above authorizes information to be requested or released by representatives of

Name Of Person,
Provider, Or Facility
Address _____

Phone _____
Fax _____

Scope

☐ All information regarding assessment, diagnosis, and treatment of patient's condition, concern, or disease (specify):
_____

☐ All information regarding care received by patient between the dates of _____ and _____
Starting Date Ending Date

☐ Other information (specify):
_____

Authorization

_____
Printed name of Patient or Authorized Representative

_____ _____ _____ _____
Signature of Patient Date Signature of witness Date
or Authorized Representative

If not signed by the patient, indicate relationship of authorizing person to patient:

☐ Parent or guardian of minor child
☐ Guardian or conservator of conserved patient
☐ Beneficiary or personal Representative of a deceased individual

PRACTICE ONLY

AWESOME BANK

DATE:

PAY TO THE
ORDER OF:

$

DOLLARS

FOR:

00000000 &56   00000000 296   456

AWESOME BANK

DATE:

PAY TO THE
ORDER OF:

$

DOLLARS

FOR:

00000000 &56   00000000 296   456

AWESOME BANK

DATE:

PAY TO THE
ORDER OF:

$

DOLLARS

FOR:

00000000 &56   00000000 296   456

AWESOME BANK

DATE:

PAY TO THE
ORDER OF:

$

DOLLARS

FOR:

00000000 &56   00000000 296   456

Fruit and Vegetables

Name: _____

Date: _____

Unscramble the names of these common fruits and vegetables.

apricot	avocado	kiwi	prune	broccoli	banana
pineapple	carrot	parsley	jalapeno	turnip	tangerine
raisin	asparagus	raspberry	potato	lettuce	garlic
onion	spinach	peach	cantaloupe	cucumber	radish
mango	coconut				

1. PHAEC   _ _ _ c _

2. ABANAN   _ _ n _ n _

3. PTAICOR   _ _ _ i _ _ t

4. IKIW   k _ _ _

5. OMNAG   _ a _ _ _

6. CTNOOCU   _ _ c o _ _ _

7. VOACOAD   _ _ o _ _ d _

8. EUPANTCAOL   c _ _ t _ l _ _ _ _

9. INLEPPEPA   p _ _ _ _ _ _ _ e

10. ENTGNAIER   _ _ _ _ _ r _ n _

11. URENP   p _ _ _ _

12. IIRANS   _ _ _ _ i n

13. BARPSEYRR   _ _ _ _ b _ r _ _

14. CIORBOCL   b _ _ c _ _ _ _

15. CHSPNIA   _ p _ _ _ _ h

16. LPRASYE   _ a r _ _ _ _

17. PRSAASAGU   _ _ p _ _ _ _ u _

18. LCEEUTT   l _ t _ _ _ _

19. AILGRC   _ _ r _ i _

20. ERUCMUCB   _ _ _ _ m _ _ r

21. RACTOR   _ _ _ r o _

22. IRSHDA   _ _ _ i s _

23. OPTATO   _ _ t _ t _

24. LPONEJAA   _ _ _ a _ _ _ o

25. NOINO   _ _ i _ _

26. UIPNTR   _ _ r _ i _

How Tornadoes Form

unstable	clockwise	twisters	waterspout	Supercell
land	presence	tornado	funnel	cloud
width	moisture	common	waters	exceed

A _____ is a violently rotating column of air in contact with and extending between a _____ (often a thunderstorm cloud) and the surface of the earth. Winds in most tornadoes blow at 100 mph or less, but in the most violent, and least frequent tornadoes, wind speeds can _____ 250 mph.

Tornadoes, often nicknamed "_____," typically track along the ground for a few miles or less and are less than 100 yards wide, although rare monsters can remain in contact with the earth for well over 50 miles and exceed one mile in _____.

Several conditions are required for the development of tornadoes and the thunderstorm clouds with which most tornadoes are associated. Abundant low-level _____ is necessary, and a "trigger" (perhaps a cold front or other low-level zones of converging winds) is needed to lift the moist air aloft.

Once the air begins to rise and becomes saturated, it will continue rising to great heights and produce a thunderstorm cloud if the atmosphere is _____. An unstable atmosphere is one in which the temperature decreases rapidly with height. Atmospheric instability can also occur when dry air overlays moist air near the earth's surface.

Tornadoes usually form in areas where winds at all levels of the atmosphere are not only strong, but also turn with height in a _____, or veering, direction.

Tornadoes can appear as a traditional _____ shape, or in a slender rope-like form. Some have a churning, smoky look to them. Others contain "multiple vortices" -- small, individual tornadoes rotating around a common center. Even others may be nearly invisible, with only swirling dust or debris at ground level as the only indication of the tornado's _____.

Tornadic phenomena can take several forms.

_____ Tornadoes
Some of the most violent tornadoes develop from supercell thunderstorms. A supercell thunderstorm is a long-lived thunderstorm that has a continuously rotating updraft of air.

These storms are the most impressive of all thunderstorms and can produce large hail and tornadoes, although less than half of all supercell thunderstorms produce tornadoes.

Supercell thunderstorms and the tornadoes they sometimes produce are most _____ in the central part of the United States.

Waterspout
Resembling a tornado, a _____ is usually less intense and causes far less damage. Rarely more than 50 yards wide, it forms over warm tropical ocean _____, although its funnel is made of fresh water from condensation, not salt water from the ocean. Waterspouts usually dissipate upon reaching _____.

State Capitals 1 - 10

1	Alabama	Montgomery	A
2	Alaska	Little Rock	B
3	Arizona	Denver	C
4	Arkansas	Atlanta	D
5	California	Juneau	E
6	Colorado	Hartford	F
7	Connecticut	Sacramento	G
8	Delaware	Tallahassee	H
9	Florida	Dover	I
10	Georgia	Phoenix	J

Pronouns, Common Nouns, Proper Nouns

teacher	boy	desk	they	mom	table
pen	girl	dad	Spot	it	Monday
Superman	she	cat	us	John	he
Charlie	we	his	computer	I	chair
October	them	car	November	McDonald's	dog
their	him	Friday			

Common Nouns	Proper Nouns	Pronouns

Plural or Possessive

Score: _____

Date: _____

secretaries'	its	libraries	secretary's	nieces
hers	crow's	theirs	witness's	witnesses
niece's	libraries'	country's	nieces'	ours
witnesses'	library's	crows	countries'	countries

1. All the _____ desks are covered with file folders.

2. My young _____ birthday is next month.

3. All the _____ to the crime agreed on what they'd seen.

4. My two _____ bedroom has a window overlooking the park.

5. There were _____ in the trees outside my window.

6. I found a black _____ feather in the woods.

7. It is a _____ duty to tell the truth.

8. I have three nephews and two _____.

9. The _____ job is to help the president with her appointments.

10. There are two _____ in my town.

11. Many _____ sign treaties with one another.

12. My local _____ book sale was full of bargains.

13. A _____ prosperity depends on its economic strength.

14. Our state _____ computer systems are all linked together.

15. Many _____ flags have stripes.

16. My sister has a doll that is _____.

17. My dog has a ball that is _____.

18. My neighbors have a house that is _____.

19. My family has a house that is _____.

20. All of the _____ accounts of the crime were the same.

WEATHER

1 ☐  ● ● A - snowy

2 ☐  ● ● B - sunny

3 ☐ ● ● C - rainy

4 ☐  ● ● D - windy

5 ☐  ● ● E - stormy

6 ☐  ● ● F - partly cloudy

7 ☐ ● ● G - foggy

8 ☐  ● ● H - cloudy

It's Lab Day Scrambler!

Score: _____

Date: _____

Venipuncture	Cholesterol	Prothrombin	Hemostasis	Hemoglobin	Influenza
Infectious	Antecubital	Nitrile gloves	Phlebotomist	Tourniquet	Technologist
Bandage	Capillary	Urinalysis			

1. NPCVUERITEUN   V _ _ _ _ _ _ c _ _ _ e

2. SMAITSHOES   _ _ m _ _ t a _ _ _

3. OQUETTINUR   _ o _ r _ _ _ _ e _

4. TOSEHROCLLE   _ _ o _ e _ _ _ r _ _

5. LBAETIACUNT   _ _ _ e _ _ _ i _ a _

6. YALLRIACP   _ _ _ _ _ _ a _ y

7. SLYARSINIU   _ r _ _ a _ _ _ _ s

8. GANADBE   B _ _ _ _ e

9. ORRTPMOHINB   _ r _ _ _ r _ m _ _ _

10. HNCOOGLESITT   _ _ _ _ n _ l _ g _ _ _

11. LIZEUAFNN   _ _ _ l _ _ n _ _

12. LEIRTIN VSLEGO   N _ t _ _ _ _ _ l _ _ _ s

13. EMLTSTOOBPHI   P _ _ _ _ o _ o _ _ _ _

14. OINESFCIUT   _ n _ e _ _ i _ _ _

15. BEGOOHINLM   _ e _ _ _ l _ b _ _

Vocabulary: Community Services

Directions: Read the words. Sort the words into the community services in which they belong.

insurance	sick	injured	emergency	firefighter	doctor
driver's license	video	adult education	nurse	ticket	EMS worker
Principal	students	teacher	magazines	officer	return
loan	learning	junior high	borrow	newspapers	librarian
medicine	books	pharmacist	911	high school	pharmacy
elementary school					

Hospital (8)	Library (8)	Police/Fire Department (7)	School (8)

Conservation of Mass

Score: _____

Date: _____

Complete the passage below using the box of words provided - you can use each more than once if you need to.

destroyed	measurements	created	oxygen	1789
escaped	increased	exactly	products	decreased
zinc	same	lead		

In _____, Antoine Lavoisier, a French chemist, first proposed the Law of Conservation of Mass. To do this, he had to carry out thousands of experiments, making very careful _____. he found that in any chemical reaction or physical change, the total mass after the reaction was _____ the _____ as the mass before. His law can be summarised as follows:

"Matter cannot be _____, or _____, just changed from one form to another."

If you mix lead nitrate solution with potassium iodide solution a yellow solid is formed called _____ iodide. If you measured the mass of products (the chemicals formed) you would find that it is _____ the _____ as the mass of the reactants (the chemicals that were mixed).

Mass is never _____ or _____ in a chemical reaction - particles cannot just be lost! Sometimes it may look like mass is lost, but in that case it is usually a gas that has been produced and _____ into the air. The same can happen when the chemicals made have a mass more than the mass of the products started with. You may have guessed, that in this case some gas from the air has been added to the _____!

For instance, if you heat zinc in the air you get a white powder. The mass of the white powder is greater than the mass of the _____ you started with. The zinc has combined with _____ from the air to form zinc oxide. The mass of the zinc and the oxygen that reacted would be the same as the mass of the zinc oxide.

Which President?

Match each president to his description

#	President		Description	
1	☐	Zachary Taylor	"I was a U.S. Army General in the Mexican-American War."	A
2	☐	Jimmy Carter	"I was born in Honolulu, Hawaii. I was elected president in 2008."	B
3	☐	John Adams	"I was the only president to have been elected for four terms. I was in office when Japan attacked Pearl Harbor."	C
4	☐	Ronald Reagan	"I was the first television and movie star to become president."	D
5	☐	Andrew Jackson	"I was a lawyer and the 7th president. People called me 'Old Hickory'."	E
6	☐	Barack Obama	"I was born in New York to wealthy parents. I became president in January 2017."	F
7	☐	Franklin D. Roosevelt	"I was the first Vice-President. I signed the Declaration of Independence."	G
8	☐	Donald Trump	"I was a peanut farmer from Georgia."	H

Sustainability - Global Warming - Climate Change

Score: _____

Date: _____

This is a spelling worksheet to check your spelling and then your understanding of keywords to do with sustainability, climate change and global warming,

		A	B	C	D
1.	_____	Ozone Layerr	Ozone Leyerr	Ozone Leyer	Ozone Layer
2.	_____	Sustainability	Sustianability	Susstianability	Susstainability
3.	_____	Deforestation	Defforestation	Defforestasion	Deforestasion
4.	_____	Renewablle Resources	Renewablle Resoorces	Renewable Resources	Renewible Resources
5.	_____	Non Renewable Resources	Non Renewablle Resoorces	Non Renewablle Resources	Non Renewible Resources
6.	_____	Cllimate chanje	Climate change	Climate chanje	Cllimate change
7.	_____	Habitat lous	Habitat los	Habitat loss	Habitat louss
8.	_____	Trropical rian forest	Trropical rain forest	Tropical rian forest	Tropical rain forest
9.	_____	Recicling	Reciclling	Recyclling	Recycling
10.	_____	Carbon dioxide	Carrbon dioxide	Carrbon doixide	Carbon doixide
11.	_____	Mathane	Metthane	Matthane	Methane
12.	_____	Grenhouse gas	Grenhoose gas	Greanhouse gas	Greenhouse gas
13.	_____	Hydrroflurocarbons	Hydroflurocarbons	Hydrophlurocarbons	Hydrrophlurocarbons
14.	_____	Sulphur hexophluoride	Sullphur hexofluoride	Sullphur hexophluoride	Sulphur hexofluoride
15.	_____	Nittrous oxide	Nitrous oxide	Nitroos oxide	Nittroos oxide
16.	_____	Foussil Fuels	Fosil Fuels	Fousil Fuels	Fossil Fuels
17.	_____	Trranspurt	Transpurt	Transport	Trransport
18.	_____	Indusstry	Industry	Indostry	Indusctry
19.	_____	Agrricolture	Agrriculture	Agriculture	Agricolture
20.	_____	Palm Oyl	Palm Oil	Pallm Oil	Pallm Oyl

WEATHER

1 ☐      ●   ●   A - snowy

2 ☐   ●   ●   B - sunny

3 ☐      ●   ●   C - rainy

4 ☐      ●   ●   D - windy

5 ☐      ●   ●   E - stormy

6 ☐   ●   ●   F - partly cloudy

7 ☐   ●   ●   G - foggy

8 ☐   ●   ●   H - cloudy

Holocaust Word Scramble

One of the most heinous events in human history is the Holocaust. It happened during World War II when Hitler was Germany's leader. The Nazis were responsible for the deaths of six million Jews. As many as one million Jewish youngsters were affected. Millions of other people who Hitler despised were also slaughtered. This included Poles, Catholics, Serbs, and individuals with disabilities. It is estimated that the Nazis killed up to 17 million innocent people.

Hitler despised Jews and blamed them for Germany's defeat in World War I. He did not consider Jews to be fully human. Hitler also believed in the Aryan race's superiority. He sought to employ Darwinism and breeding to produce a perfect race of humans. In his book Mein Kampf, Hitler stated that he would banish all Jews from Germany if he were to become the leader. Few doubted he would do it, but as soon as he became Chancellor, he began his anti-Semitic campaign. He passed legislation declaring that Jews had no rights. He then orchestrated attacks on Jewish businesses and residences. Many Jewish homes and businesses were burned down or vandalized on November 9, 1938. The Kristallnacht, or "Night of Broken Glass," was the name given to this event.

Ghettos	Propaganda	Liberation	Captured	Typhus	anti-Semitism
Swastika	Surrender	Starvation	Jews	Gestapo	Executed

1. errnrudse   _ _ _ _ _ _ d _ r

2. askwatsi   _ w _ _ _ i _ _

3. ewsj   _ e _ _

4. ptsuhy   _ _ p _ _ s

5. eaptcdur   _ _ p _ _ r _ _

6. dueceext   _ _ e _ u _ _ _

7. heogstt   _ _ _ _ t _ s

8. stoatanvri   S _ _ r _ _ _ _ o _

9. airtlenbio   L _ _ _ _ a t _ _ _

10. stmeains-itim   _ _ _ _ _ _ _ _ t _ s m

11. noaragpdpa   P _ _ _ a _ a _ _ _

12. gaopset   G e _ _ _ _ _

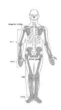

The Lymphatic System
Unscramble

There is a part of the immune system called the lymphatic system. It maintains a healthy balance of body fluids and protects the body from illness. Lymphatic (lim-FAT-ik) veins, tissues, organs, and glands collaborate to drain a watery fluid known as lymph from the body.

When there is a lot of extra lymph (LIMF) fluid in the body, the lymphatic system drains it and sends it back to the body's bloodstream. Lymph contains lymphocytes (LIM-fuh-sites), white blood cells, and chyle (KYE-ul), which is made up of fats and proteins from the intestines.

This is critical because water, proteins, and other substances constantly leak out of microscopic blood capillaries and into the surrounding bodily tissues. This additional fluid would build up in the tissues and cause them to bulge if the lymphatic system did not drain it.

lymphatic	antivirals	cytotoxic	leukocyte	phagocyte	immunology
lymphoma	pathogen	lymphedema	tonsillectomy	thymus	capillaries
spleen					

1. yhmtcalpi   l _ _ p _ _ _ _ _

2. muloinmoyg   i _ m _ _ _ l _ _ _

3. tcgayphoe   _ _ _ _ _ _ y t _

4. mehdeaplmy   _ _ m p _ _ _ e _ _

5. ottcyxoci   c _ _ _ t _ _ _ _

6. tvalriinsa   _ _ t _ v _ _ a _ _

7. nymseltooiltc   _ o _ _ _ _ _ _ _ _ _ m y

8. stumyh   _ _ _ _ u s

9. nlsepe   s _ _ e _ _

10. aomlmhyp   l _ _ _ h _ _ _

11. uekloytec   _ _ u k _ _ _ _ _

12. lecasiriapl   _ _ p i _ _ _ _ i _ _

13. hgetpnao   _ a _ _ o _ _ _

Grammar: Personal Pronouns

1. Pronouns stand-in for the people and _____ .

   a. animals

   b. nothing at all

2. Using pronouns allows a speaker or writer to vary how they refer to a _____ .

   a. adverb

   b. noun

3. The tie is very special. ___ is a magic tie.

   a. He

   b. It

4. Charlie and I went to a pond. _____ saw two frogs.

   a. They

   b. We

5. The turtle is tired. _____ is rest under the tree.

   a. Him

   b. It

6. Tim and I saw the lion in the jungle. _____ were very afraid.

   a. Their

   b. We

7. The rabbit escaped from the trap and ran away. _____ was safe.

   a. They

   b. It

8. The farmer's wife saw a wolf. _____ shouted to the farmer for help.

   a. She

   b. It

9. The boys found a magic chain. _____ gave it to the queen.

   a. They

   b. He

10. _____ 20 years old.

   a. Them

   b. She's

11. _____ house is big.

   a. He

   b. His

12. _____ name's Farah.

   a. Her

   b. She

13. How old is she?

   a. He's seven.

   b. She's seven.

14. What's his name?

   a. His name's Ali.

   b. Her name's Ali.

15. Mia and Omar enjoy listening to Ree's singing. Becomes:

   a. Them enjoy listening to Ree's singing.

   b. They enjoy listening to Ree's singing.

16. Dana kicked the ball. Becomes:

   a. She kicked the ball.

   b. He kicked the ball.

17. The dog is barking. _____ is barking at someone.

   a. He

   b. It

18. My sister likes basketball. _____ plays everyday.

   a. She

   b. He

Proofreading Skills:
Volunteering

There are **10** mistakes in this passage. 3 capitals missing. 4 unnecessary capitals. 3 incorrect homophones.

Your own life can be changed and the lives of others, through volunteer work. ~~to~~ **To** cope with the news that there has been a disaster, you can volunteer to help those in need. Even if you can't contribute financially, you can donate ~~you're~~ **your** time instead.

Volunteering is such an integral part of the American culture that many high schools require their students to participate in community service to graduate.

When you volunteer, you have the freedom to choose what you'd like to do and who or what you think is most deserving of your time. Start with these ideas if you need a little inspiration. We've got just a few examples here.

Encourage the growth and development of young people. Volunteer as a ~~Camp~~ **camp** counselor, a Big Brother or Big Sister, or an after-school sports program. Special Olympics games and events are excellent opportunities to know children with special needs.

Spend the holidays doing good deeds for others. Volunteer at a food bank or distribute toys to children in need on Thanksgiving Day, and you'll be doing your part to help those in need. ~~your~~ **Your** church, temple, mosque, or another place of worship may also require your assistance.

You can visit an animal shelter and play with the ~~Animals.~~ **animals.** Volunteers are critical to the well-being of shelter animals. (You also get a good workout when you walk rescued dogs.)

Become a member of a political campaign. ~~Its~~ **It's** a great way to learn more about the inner workings of politics if ~~your~~ **you're** curious about it. If you are not able ~~To~~ **to** cast a ballot, you can still help elect your preferred candidate.

Help save the planet. Join a river preservation group and lend a hand. Participate in a park cleanup day in your community. Not everyone is cut out for the great outdoors; if you can't see yourself hauling trees up a hill, consider working in the park's office or education center instead.

Take an active role in promoting health-related causes. Many of us know someone afflicted with a medical condition (like cancer, HIV, or diabetes, for example). ~~a~~ **A** charity that helps people with a disease, such as delivering meals, raising money, or providing other assistance, can make you ~~Feel~~ **feel** good about yourself.

Find a way to combine your favorite things if you have more than one. For example, if you're a fan of kids and have a talent for arts and crafts, consider volunteering at a children's hospital.

Weather and Climate

The difference between weather and climate is simply a matter of time. Weather refers to the conditions of the atmosphere over a short period of time, whereas climate refers to how the atmosphere "behaves" over a longer period of time.

When we discuss climate change, we are referring to changes in long-term averages of daily weather. Today's children are constantly told by their parents and grandparents about how the snow was always piled up to their waists as they trudged off to school. Most children today have not experienced those kinds of dreadful snow-packed winters. The recent changes in winter snowfall indicate that the climate has changed since their parents were children.

Weather is essentially the atmosphere's behavior, particularly in terms of its effects on life and human activities. The distinction between weather and climate is that weather refers to short-term (minutes to months) changes in the atmosphere, whereas climate refers to long-term changes. Most people associate weather with temperature, humidity, precipitation, cloudiness, brightness, visibility, wind, and atmospheric pressure, as in high and low pressure.

Weather can change from minute to minute, hour to hour, day to day, and season to season in most places. However, the climate is the average of weather over time and space. A simple way to remember the distinction is that climate is what you expect, such as a very hot summer, whereas weather is what you get, such as a hot day with pop-up thunderstorms.

Use the word bank to unscramble the words!

Pressure	Density	Cloudy	Latitude	Elevation	Weather
Absorb	Humid	Precipitation	Windy	Forecast	Climate
Sunshine	Temperature				

1. IUMHD   Humid

2. UDLOYC   Cloudy

3. FSEATOCR   Forecast

4. UDLTITAE   Latitude

5. IEOCAIIPPTRNT   Precipitation

6. TEEERPAURMT   Temperature

7. RSEREUPS   Pressure

8. LEICATM   Climate

9. SNNIEHUS   Sunshine

10. OBBASR   Absorb

11. VETIEOANL   Elevation

12. EATWRHE   Weather

13. NDWIY   Windy

14. TYNEIDS   Density

Test Your Mathematics
Knowledge

1. To add fractions_____

    a. the denominators must be the same

    b. the denominators can be same or different

    c. the denominators must be different

2. To add decimals, the decimal points must be?

    a. column and carry the first digit(s)

    b. lined up in any order before you add the columns

    c. lined up vertically before you add the columns

3. When adding like terms_____

    a. the like terms must be same and they must be to the different power.

    b. the exponent must be different and they must be to the same power.

    c. the variable(s) must be the same and they must be to the same power.

4. The concept of math regrouping involves_____

    a. regrouping means that $5x + 2$ becomes $50 + 12$

    b. the numbers you are adding come out to five digit numbers and 0

    c. rearranging, or renaming, groups in place value

5. _____ indicates how many times a number, or algebraic expression, should be multiplied by itself.

    a. Denominators

    b. Division-quotient

    c. Exponent

6. _____ is the numerical value of a number without its plus or minus sign.

    a. Absolute value

    b. Average

    c. Supplementary

7. Any number that is less than zero is called_____

    a. Least common multiple

    b. Equation

    c. Negative number

8. $23 = 2 \times 2 \times 2 = 8$, 8 is the

    a. third power of 2

    b. first power of 2

    c. second power of 2

9. -7, 0, 3, and 7.12223 are

    a. all real numbers

    b. all like fractions

    c. all like terms

10. How do you calculate $2 + 3 \times 7$?

    a. $2 + 3 \times 7 = 2 + 21 = 23$

    b. $2 + 7 \times 7 = 2 + 21 = 35$

    c. $2 + 7 \times 3 = 2 + 21 = 23$

11. How do you calculate (2 + 3) x (7 - 3)?

    a. (2 + 2) x (7 - 3) = 5 x 4 = 32

    b. [(2 + 3) x (7 - 3) = 5 x 4 = 20]

    c. (2 + 7) x (2 - 3) = 5 x 4 = 14

12. The Commutative Law of Addition says_____

    a. positive - positive = (add) positive

    b. [that it doesn't matter what order you add up numbers, you will always get the same answer]

    c. parts of a calculation outside brackets always come first

13. The Zero Properties Law of multiplication says_____

    a. [that any number multiplied by 0 equals 0]

    b. mathematical operation where four or more numbers are combined to make a sum

    c. Negative - Positive = Subtract

14. Multiplication is when you_____

    a. numbers that are added together in multiplication problems

    b. [take one number and add it together a number of times]

    c. factor that is shared by two or more numbers

15. When multiplying by 0, the answer is always_____

    a. [0]

    b. [-0]

    c. 1

16. When multiplying by 1, the answer is always the _____

    a. same as the number multiplied by 0

    b. same as the number multiplied by -1

    c. [same as the number multiplied by 1]

17. You can multiply numbers in_____

    a. any order and multiply by 2 and the answer will be the same

    b. [any order you want and the answer will be the same]

    c. any order from greater to less than and the answer will be the same

18. Division is____

    a. set of numbers that are multiplied together to get an answer

    b. [breaking a number up into an equal number of parts]

    c. division is scaling one number by another

19. If you take 20 things and put them into four equal sized groups

    a. there will be 6 things in each group

    b. [there will be 5 things in each group]

    c. there will be 10 things in each group

20. The dividend is_____

    a. the number you are multiplied by

    b. [the number you are dividing up]

    c. the number you are grouping together

21. The divisor is _____

    a. are all multiples of 3

    b. [the number you are dividing by]

    c. common factor of two numbers

22. The quotient is _____

    a. [the answer]

    b. answer to a multiplication operation

    c. any number in the problem

23. When dividing something by 1_____

    a. the answer is the original number

    b. the answer produces a given number when multiplied by itself

    c. the answer is the quotient

24. Dividing by 0_____

    a. the answer will always be more than 0

    b. You will always get 1

    c. You cannot divide a number by 0

25. If the answer to a division problem is not a whole number, the number(s) leftover_____

    a. are called the Order Property

    b. are called the denominators

    c. are called the remainder

26. You can figure out the 'mean' by_____

    a. multiply by the sum of two or more numbers

    b. adding up all the numbers in the data and then dividing by the number of numbers

    c. changing the grouping of numbers that are added together

27. The 'median' is the_____

    a. last number of the data set

    b. middle number of the data set

    c. first number of the data set

28. The 'mode' is the number_____

    a. that appears equal times

    b. that appears the least

    c. that appears the most

29. Range is the_____

    a. difference between the less than equal to number and the highest number.

    b. difference between the highest number and the highest number.

    c. difference between the lowest number and the highest number

30. Please Excuse My Dear Aunt Sally: What it means in the Order of Operations is____

    a. Parentheses, Exponents, Multiplication and Division, and Addition and Subtraction

    b. Parentheses, Equal, Multiplication and Decimal, and Addition and Subtraction

    c. Parentheses, Ellipse, Multiplication and Data, and Addition and Subtraction

31. A ratio is_____

    a. a way to show a relationship or compare two numbers of the same kind

    b. short way of saying that you want to multiply something by itself

    c. he sum of the relationship a times x, a times y, and a times z

32. Variables are things_____

    a. that can change or have different values

    b. when something has an exponent

    c. the simplest form using fractions

33. Always perform the same operation to_____of the equation.

    a. when the sum is less than the operation

    b. both sides

    c. one side only

34. The slope intercept form uses the following equation:

    a. $y = mx + b$

    b. $y = x + ab$

    c. $x = mx + c$

35. The point-slope form uses the following equation:

    a. $y - y1 = m(y - x2)$

    b. $y - y1 = m(x - x1)$

    c. $x - y2 = m(x - x1)$

36. Numbers in an algebraic expression that are not variables are called____

    a. Square

    b. Coefficient

    c. Proportional

37. A coordinate system is _____

    a. a type of cubed square

    b. a coordinate reduced to another proportion plane

    c. a two-dimensional number line

38. Horizontal axis is called_____

    a. h-axis

    b. x-axis

    c. y-axis

39. Vertical axis is called____

    a. v-axis

    b. y-axis

    c. x-axis

40. Equations and inequalities are both mathematical sentences____

    a. has y and x variables as points on a graph

    b. reduced ratios to their simplest form using fractions

    c. formed by relating two expressions to each other

ANSWERS
Adding Fractions

1) $\dfrac{5}{7} + \dfrac{4}{7} = \dfrac{5}{7} + \dfrac{4}{7} = \dfrac{9}{7} = 1\dfrac{2}{7}$

2) $\dfrac{2}{8} + \dfrac{5}{8} = \dfrac{2}{8} + \dfrac{5}{8} = \dfrac{7}{8}$

3) $\dfrac{6}{7} + \dfrac{4}{7} = \dfrac{6}{7} + \dfrac{4}{7} = \dfrac{10}{7} = 1\dfrac{3}{7}$

4) $\dfrac{5}{4} + \dfrac{3}{4} = \dfrac{5}{4} + \dfrac{3}{4} = \dfrac{8}{4} = \dfrac{2}{1} = 2\dfrac{0}{1}$

5) $\dfrac{1}{8} + \dfrac{3}{8} = \dfrac{1}{8} + \dfrac{3}{8} = \dfrac{4}{8} = \dfrac{1}{2}$

6) $\dfrac{2}{6} + \dfrac{5}{6} = \dfrac{2}{6} + \dfrac{5}{6} = \dfrac{7}{6} = 1\dfrac{1}{6}$

7) $\dfrac{2}{6} + \dfrac{2}{6} = \dfrac{2}{6} + \dfrac{2}{6} = \dfrac{4}{6} = \dfrac{2}{3}$

8) $\dfrac{5}{4} + \dfrac{3}{4} = \dfrac{5}{4} + \dfrac{3}{4} = \dfrac{8}{4} = \dfrac{2}{1} = 2\dfrac{0}{1}$

9) $\dfrac{8}{8} + \dfrac{6}{8} = \dfrac{8}{8} + \dfrac{6}{8} = \dfrac{14}{8} = \dfrac{7}{4} = 1\dfrac{3}{4}$

10) $\dfrac{3}{7} + \dfrac{5}{7} = \dfrac{3}{7} + \dfrac{5}{7} = \dfrac{8}{7} = 1\dfrac{1}{7}$

11) $\dfrac{7}{9} + \dfrac{1}{9} = \dfrac{7}{9} + \dfrac{1}{9} = \dfrac{8}{9}$

12) $\dfrac{3}{9} + \dfrac{6}{9} = \dfrac{3}{9} + \dfrac{6}{9} = \dfrac{9}{9} = 1$

13) $\dfrac{2}{7} + \dfrac{4}{7} = \dfrac{2}{7} + \dfrac{4}{7} = \dfrac{6}{7}$

14) $\dfrac{3}{6} + \dfrac{2}{6} = \dfrac{3}{6} + \dfrac{2}{6} = \dfrac{5}{6}$

15) $\dfrac{3}{6} + \dfrac{5}{6} = \dfrac{3}{6} + \dfrac{5}{6} = \dfrac{8}{6} = \dfrac{4}{3} = 1\dfrac{1}{3}$

Greatest Common Factor ANSWERS

1)   15 , 3   <u> 3 </u>

2)   24 , 12   <u> 12 </u>

3)   10 , 4   <u> 2 </u>

4)   40 , 4   <u> 4 </u>

5)   8 , 40   <u> 8 </u>

6)   10 , 4   <u> 2 </u>

7)   12 , 20   <u> 4 </u>

8)   5 , 20   <u> 5 </u>

9)   8 , 2   <u> 2 </u>

10)   24 , 40   <u> 8 </u>

11)   6 , 8   <u> 2 </u>

12)   10 , 3   <u> 1 </u>

13)   8 , 6   <u> 2 </u>

14)   24 , 10   <u> 2 </u>

15)   24 , 12   <u> 12 </u>

16)   40 , 24   <u> 8 </u>

17)   8 , 10   <u> 2 </u>

18)   10 , 20   <u> 10 </u>

19)   2 , 3   <u> 1 </u>

20)   6 , 12   <u> 6 </u>

Prime Factors ANSWERS

1) 38   2 , 19

2) 49   7

3) 35   5 , 7

4) 25   5

5) 15   3 , 5

6) 44   2 , 11

7) 32   2

8) 48   2 , 3

9) 22   2 , 11

10) 21   3 , 7

11) 30   2 , 3 , 5

12) 20   2 , 5

13) 39   3 , 13

14) 14   2 , 7

15) 12   2 , 3

16) 26   2 , 13

17) 46   2 , 23

18) 40   2 , 5

19) 24   2 , 3

20) 10   2 , 5

ANSWERS

Find the Prime Factors of the Numbers

1)
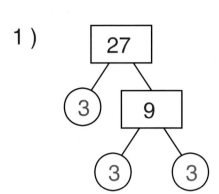

2)
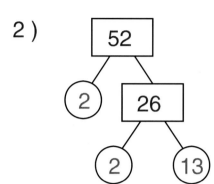

3)
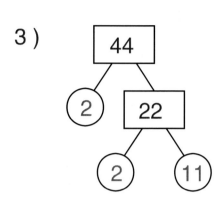

Factors
3 x 3 x 3 = 27

Factors
2 x 2 x 13 = 52

Factors
2 x 2 x 11 = 44

4)
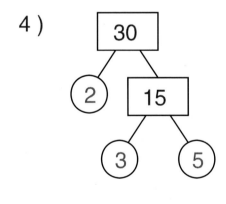

5)
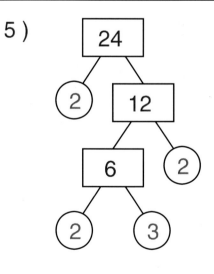

6)
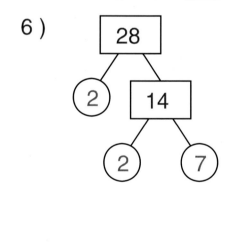

Factors
2 x 3 x 5 = 30

Factors
2 x 2 x 2 x 3 = 24

Factors
2 x 2 x 7 = 28

ANSWERS
Rearranging Digits

1) 399   993

2) 744   744

3) 488   884

4) 616   661

5) 734   743

6) 846   864

7) 844   844

8) 345   543

9) 959   995

10) 559   955

1) 897   789

2) 696   669

3) 825   258

4) 135   135

5) 751   157

6) 149   149

7) 862   268

8) 212   122

9) 557   557

10) 675   567

ANSWERS
Rearranging Digits

1) 1,182   <u>8,211</u>   6) 7,769   <u>9,776</u>

2) 1,549   <u>9,541</u>   7) 7,521   <u>7,521</u>

3) 5,366   <u>6,653</u>   8) 8,146   <u>8,641</u>

4) 3,869   <u>9,863</u>   9) 8,161   <u>8,611</u>

5) 2,853   <u>8,532</u>   10) 7,769   <u>9,776</u>

1) 7,816   <u>1,678</u>   6) 6,636   <u>3,666</u>

2) 3,827   <u>2,378</u>   7) 8,176   <u>1,678</u>

3) 4,946   <u>4,469</u>   8) 9,222   <u>2,229</u>

4) 5,938   <u>3,589</u>   9) 2,172   <u>1,227</u>

5) 1,627   <u>1,267</u>   10) 5,366   <u>3,566</u>

TIME ANSWERS

What time is on the clock? ___6:00___

What time was it 1 hour ago? ___5:00___

What time was it 3 hours and 40 minutes ago? ___2:20___

What time will it be in 4 hours and 20 minutes? ___10:20___

What time is on the clock? ___7:40___

What time was it 2 hours ago? ___5:40___

What time will it be in 3 hours ? ___10:40___

What time will it be in 4 hours and 20 minutes? ___12:00___

What time is on the clock? ___10:20___

What time was it 1 hour ago? ___9:20___

What time was it 3 hours and 20 minutes ago? ___7:00___

What time will it be in 2 hours ? ___12:20___

What time is on the clock? ___10:00___

What time will it be in 3 hours and 20 minutes? ___1:20___

What time was it 2 hours ago? ___8:00___

What time was it 1 hour ago? ___9:00___

ANSWER SHEET
Find the Missing Addends.

1) $59 = 19 + 40$

2) $19 + 17 = 36$

3) $34 + 17 = 51$

4) $14 + 27 = 41$

5) $25 + 28 = 53$

6) $33 = 15 + 18$

7) $57 = 17 + 40$

8) $27 + 15 = 42$

9) $35 + 10 = 45$

10) $65 = 34 + 31$

11) $27 + 26 = 53$

12) $47 = 20 + 27$

13) $43 = 28 + 15$

14) $11 + 13 = 24$

15) $40 = 25 + 15$

16) $22 + 36 = 58$

17) $72 = 33 + 39$

18) $38 = 16 + 22$

19) $16 + 21 = 37$

20) $13 + 37 = 50$

21) $28 + 23 = 51$

22) $28 + 18 = 46$

23) $20 + 32 = 52$

24) $57 = 22 + 35$

25) $37 + 38 = 75$

26) $34 = 15 + 19$

27) $28 = 10 + 18$

28) $66 = 33 + 33$

29) $20 + 33 = 53$

30) $29 = 19 + 10$

What time is on the clock?   9:56

What time will it be in 7 hours and 15 minutes?   5:11

What time was it 3 hours and 45 minutes ago?   6:11

What time will it be in 1 hour and 30 minutes?   11:26

What time is on the clock?   4:27

What time will it be in 7 hours ?   11:27

What time was it 4 hours and 45 minutes ago?   11:42

What time will it be in 6 hours and 15 minutes?   10:42

What time is on the clock?   12:21

What time will it be in 9 hours and 45 minutes?   10:06

What time was it 8 hours ago?   4:21

What time will it be in 1 hour and 30 minutes?   1:51

What time is on the clock?   10:59

What time will it be in 2 hours ?   12:59

What time was it 7 hours and 15 minutes ago?   3:44

What time will it be in 1 hour and 45 minutes?   12:44

Social Studies Vocabulary 8

Choose the best answer to each question.

1. The workplace where people labor long hours for very low pay.

   a. Factory

   b. Sweatshop

2. To make plain or understandable; to give reasons for.

   a. Explain

   b. Interpret

3. What is the meaning of the word "Evaluate"?

   a. to examine and judge the significance, worth or condition of or value of

   b. to observe or inspect carefully or critically

4. The process by which an immigrant becomes a citizen.

   a. Dual Citizenship

   b. Naturalization

5. What is the meaning of the word "Draft"?

   a. selection of people who would be forced to serve in the military

   b. a person who enlists in military service by free will

6. A conference between the highest-ranking officials of different nations.

   a. Diplomatic Conference

   b. Summit Meeting

7. Select the correct meaning of the word "Identify".

   a. to recognize by or divide into classes

   b. to establish the essential character of

8. A person who flees his or her homeland to seek safety elsewhere.

   a. Immigrant

   b. Refugee

9. To make clear or obvious by using the examples or comparisons.

   a. Illustrate

   b. Demonstrate

10. To investigate closely; to examine critically

   a. Scrutinize

   b. Analyze

11. Select the correct meaning of the word "Laissez Fair".

   a. literally means "hands off"; business principle advocating an economy free of governmental business regulations

   b. an economic system whereby monetary goods are owned by individuals or companies.

12. The theory that Earth's atmosphere is warming up as a result of air pollution, causing ecological problems.

   a. Global Warming

   b. Climate Change

Social Studies Vocabulary IV

Choose the best answer to each question.

1. Political movement of the late 1800's favoring greater government regulation of business, graduated income tax and greater political involvement by the people
   a. Socialism
   b. Populism

2. To arrange in a systematic way.
   a. Manage
   b. Organize

3. Protests in which people sit in a particular place or business and refuse to leave.
   a. Strike
   b. Sit-In

4. An index based on the amount of goods, services, education, and leisure time that a people have.
   a. Standard of Living
   b. Quality of Life

5. Combination of businesses joining together to limit competition within an industry.
   a. Trust
   b. Monopolies

6. The factors that cause people to leave an area. (e.x. famine, war, political upheaval).
   a. Push factors
   b. Pull factors

7. The factors that attract people to a new area (e.x. jobs, freedom, family).
   a. Pull factors
   b. Push factors

8. What is the meaning of the word "Stock"?
   a. a legal entity that holds and manages assets on behalf of another individual or entity
   b. a share in a business

9. What is the meaning of the word "Suburb"?
   a. a community located within commuting distance of a city
   b. a community that's in a city or town

10. What is the meaning of the word "Recession"?
   a. a short term mild depression in which business slows and some workers lose their jobs
   b. an increase in the price of products and services over time in an economy

11. The movement of population from farms to city.
   a. Industrialization
   b. Urbanization

12. A belief that one's own ethnic group is superior to others.
   a. Ethnocentrism
   b. Ethnorelativism

Social Studies Vocabulary II

Choose the best answer to each question.

1	G	Solar Energy	→	power source derived from the sun.
2	L	Naturalization	→	The process by which an immigrant becomes a citizen.
3	K	Restate	→	to say again in a slightly different way.
4	J	Totalitarian State	→	a country where a single party controls the government and every aspect of the loves of people.
5	H	Inflation	→	sharp rise in prices and decrease in the value of money.
6	B	Environmentalist	→	person who works to reduce pollution and protect the natural environment.
7	D	Greenbacks	→	paper money issued by the federal government during the Civil War.
8	F	Assembly Line	→	manufacturing process, developed by Henry Ford in the 1920's, whereby factory workers engage in specific and repetitive tasks.
9	I	Détente	→	easing of tensions between nations.
10	E	Affirmative Action	→	program in areas such as employment and education to provide more opportunities for members of groups that faced discrimination in the past.
11	C	Civil Disobedience	→	nonviolent opposition to a government policy or law by refusing to comply with it.
12	A	Popular Sovereignty	→	an idea that supreme governing power belongs to the voters.

Social Studies Vocabulary XV

Choose the best answer to each question.

1	I	Primary source	⟶	firsthand information about people or events.
2	L	Rural	⟶	country or farmland.
3	B	Bicameral Legislature	⟶	Two house law-making body.
4	F	Act	⟶	law
5	K	Suffrage	⟶	vote
6	J	Tariff	⟶	tax
7	D	Senate	⟶	group of elected officials that make laws (each state has two).
8	C	Federal	⟶	Central government
9	E	Haudenosaunee	⟶	Native American word to describe the Iroquois people.
10	M	Import	⟶	trade product brought into a country.
11	G	Civilization	⟶	highly developed level of cultural and technological development.
12	A	Exports	⟶	products made in one country and going to another.
13	H	Expansion	⟶	to make a country larger.

Shakespeare: Romeo and Juliet

Across

1. an enemy or opponent
2. something surrendered or subject to surrender as punishment for a crime, an offense, an error, or a breach of contract
3. loathsome; disgusting
7. to expel or banish a person from his or her country
8. to feel sorry for; regret
12. a small container, as of glass, for holding liquids
15. long and tiresome

Down

3. boldly courageous; brave; stout-hearted
5. to express disapproval of; scold; reproach
6. a musician, singer, or poet
9. an expression of grief or sorrow
10. to flood or to overwhelm
11. a malicious, false, or defamatory statement or report
13. infliction of injury, harm, humiliation, or the like, on a person by another who has been harmed by that person; violent revenge
14. to read through with thoroughness or care

VALIANT LAMENT SLANDER
MINSTREL PERUSE
TEDIOUS CHIDE EXILE
VILE FORFEIT INUNDATE
REPENT ADVERSARY VIAL
VENGEANCE

Science Vocabulary 6

Choose the best answer to each question.

1	G	Precipitation	⇢	Process of water falling from clouds to earth in the form of rain, sleet, show, or hail
2	D	Inner Core	⇢	Inner most layer composed of solid iron and nickel. Stays solid due to the pressure of the layers above it.
3	B	Continental Drift	⇢	The movement of the Earth's continents relative to each other by appearing to drift across the ocean bed
4	A	Crust	⇢	Earth's solid, rocky surface.
5	H	Asthenosphere	⇢	Solid layer of the mantle beneath lithosphere; made of mantle rock that flows very slowly allowing tectonic plates to move on top of it.
6	C	Condensation	⇢	Process of water vapor changing to liquid water
7	J	Mantle	⇢	The layer of Earth beneath the crust.
8	F	Core	⇢	Made up of mostly molten (melted) iron and nickel.
9	I	Plate Tectonics	⇢	Scientific theory that describes the large-scale motions of Earth's lithosphere.
10	E	Water Cycle	⇢	Continuous movement of water from the air to the earth and back again.

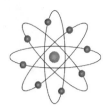

Science Vocabulary 5

Choose the best answer to each question.

1. Energy that all objects have that increases as the object's temperature increases.

    a. Thermal Energy

    b. Potential Energy

2. Energy carried by electric current.

    a. Electrical Energy

    b. Radiant Energy

3. Transfer of heat by the flow of material. Heat rises and cool air sinks.

    a. Conduction

    b. Convection

4. What is the meaning of the word "Radiant Energy"?

    a. Energy that all objects have that increases as the object's temperature increases.

    b. Energy carried by light.

5. Transfer of energy that occurs when molecules bump into each other.

    a. Convection

    b. Conduction

6. The crust and the rigid part of Earth's mantle. Divided into tectonic plates.

    a. Lithosphere

    b. Asthenosphere

7. What is the meaning of the word "Potential Energy"?

    a. Energy stored in an object due to its position.

    b. Energy stored in chemical bonds.

8. Energy contained in atomic nuclei; splitting uranium nuclei by nuclear fission.

    a. Nuclear Energy

    b. Thermal Energy

9. States that energy can change its form but is never created or destroyed.

    a. Law of Conservation of Mass

    b. Law of Conservation of Energy

10. What is the meaning of the word "Chemical Energy"?

    a. Energy stored in chemical bonds.

    b. Energy stored in an object due to its position.

Science Vocabulary 4

Choose the best answer to each question.

1. Family of elements in the periodic table that have similar physical or chemical properties.
   a. Group
   b. Subgroup

2. Table of elements organized into groups and periods by increasing atomic number.
   a. Periodic Table
   b. Chemical Elements

3. It is the property of many substances that give the ability to do work; many forms of energy (i.e., light, heat, electricity, sound)
   a. Energy
   b. Power

4. Number of protons in the nucleus of an atom of a given element.
   a. Mass Number
   b. Atomic Number

5. The sum of neutrons and protons in the nucleus of an atom.
   a. Mass Number
   b. Atomic Number

6. Force of attraction between all objects in the universe.
   a. Gravity
   b. Friction

7. What is the meaning of the word "Isotope"?
   a. Atoms of the same element that have different numbers of neutrons.
   b. An atom or molecule with a positive or negative charge.

8. What is the meaning of the word "Period"?
   a. Vertical row of elements in the periodic table.
   b. Horizontal row of elements in the periodic table.

9. What is the meaning of the word "Tides"?
   a. Rise and fall of ocean water levels.
   b. Ae formed because of the winds blowing over the surface of the ocean.

10. What is the meaning of the word "Kinetic Energy"?
    a. Energy an object has due to its motion.
    b. A form of energy that has the potential to do work but is not actively doing work or applying any force on any other objects.

Science: Titanium (Ti) Element

Titanium is the first element in the periodic table's fourth column. It is a transition metal. Titanium atoms contain 22 protons and 22 electrons.

Titanium is a complex, light, silvery metal under normal conditions. It can be brittle at room temperature, but it becomes more bendable and pliable as the temperature rises.

Titanium's high strength-to-weight ratio is one of its most desirable properties. This means it is both extremely strong and lightweight. Titanium is double the strength of aluminum but only 60% heavier. It is also as strong as steel but weighs a fraction of the weight.

Compared to other metals, titanium is relatively non-reactive and highly resistant to corrosion caused by different metals and chemicals such as acids and oxygen. As a result, it has relatively low thermal and electrical conductivity.

Titanium is not found in nature as a pure element but rather as a compound found in the Earth's crust as a component of many minerals. According to the International Atomic Energy Agency, it is the ninth most prevalent element in the Earth's crust. Rutile and ilmenite are the two most essential minerals for titanium mining. Australia, South Africa, and Canada are the top producers of these ores.

Titanium is mostly used in the form of titanium dioxide (TiO2). Tio2 is a white powder used in various industrial applications such as white paint, white paper, white polymers, and white cement.

Metals like iron, aluminum, and manganese are combined with titanium to create strong and lightweight alloys that can be utilized in spacecraft, naval vessels, missiles, and armor plating. Due to its corrosion resistance, it is particularly well-suited for seawater applications.

The biocompatibility of titanium is another valuable property of the metal. This indicates that the human body will not reject it. Together with its strength, durability, and lightweight, titanium is a good material for medical applications. It is utilized in various applications, including hip and dental implants. Titanium is also utilized in the manufacture of jewelry, such as rings and watches.

Reverend William Gregor recognized titanium as a new element for the first time in 1791. As a hobby, the English clergyman was fascinated by minerals. He coined the term menachanite for the element. M.H. Kalproth, a German chemist, eventually altered the name to titanium. M. A. Hunter, an American scientist, was the first to create pure titanium in 1910.

Titanium is named after the Greek gods Titans.

Titanium has five stable isotopes: titanium-46, titanium-47, titanium-48, titanium-49, and titanium-50. The isotope titanium-48 accounts for the vast bulk of titanium found in nature.

1. Titanium has five stable ____.
    a. isotopes
    b.

2. Titanium is the first element in the periodic table's ____ column.
    a. 4rd
    b. fourth

3. Titanium is a transition ____.
    a. metal
    b.

4. Titanium is mostly used in the form of ____ (TiO2).
    a. titanium dioxide
    b. dioxide oxygen

Proofreading Interpersonal
Skills: Peer Pressure

Tony is mingling with a large group of what he considers to be the school's cool kids. Suddenly, someone in the group begins mocking Tony's friend Rob, who walks with a limp due to a physical ~~dasability.~~ **disability.**

They begin to imitate ~~rob's~~ **Rob's** limping and ~~Call~~ **call** him 'lame cripple' and other derogatory terms. Although Tony disapproves of their behavior, he does not want to risk being excluded from the group, and thus joins them in mocking Rob.

Peer pressure is the influence exerted on us by ~~member's~~ **members** of our social group. It can manifest in a variety of ways and can lead to us engaging in behaviors we would not normally ~~consider~~ **consider,** such as Tony joining in and mocking his friend Rob.

However, peer pressure is not always detrimental. Positive peer pressure can motivate us to make better ~~chioces,~~ **choices,** such as studying harder, staying in school, or seeking a better job. ~~Whan~~ **When** others influence us to make poor ~~Choices,~~ **choices,** such as smoking, using illicit drugs, or bullying, we succumb to negative peer pressure. We all desire to belong to a group and fit in, so ~~Developing~~ **developing** strategies for resisting peer pressure when necessary can be beneficial.

Tony and his friends are engaging in bullying by ~~moking~~ **mocking** Rob. Bullying is defined as persistent, ~~unwanted.~~ **unwanted,** aggressive behavior directed toward another person. It is ~~moust~~ **most** prevalent in school-aged children but can also ~~aphfect~~ **affect** adults. Bullying can take on a variety of forms, including the following:

~~· Verbil~~
· **Verbal** bullying is when someone is called names, threatened, or taunted verbally.
· Bullying is physical in nature - ~~hitting~~ **hitting,** spitting, tripping, or ~~poshing~~ **pushing** someone.
· Social ~~Bullying~~ **bullying** is intentionally excluding ~~Someone~~ **someone** from ~~activities~~ **activities,** spreading rumors, or embarrassing ~~sumeone.~~ **someone.**
· Cyberbullying is the act of verbally or socially bullying someone via the internet, such as through social media sites.

Peer pressure exerts a significant influence on an individual's decision to engage in bullying ~~behavoir.~~ **behavior.** In Tony's case, even though Rob is a friend and ~~tony~~ **Tony** would never consider mocking his disability, his desire to belong to a group outweighs his willingness to defend his ~~friend~~ **friend.**

Peer pressure is a strong force that is exerted on us by our social group members. Peer pressure is classified into two types: negative peer pressure, which results in poor decision-making, and positive peer pressure, which influences us to make the correct choices. Adolescents are particularly susceptible to peer pressure because of their desire to fit ~~in~~ **in.**

Peer pressure can motivate someone to engage in bullying behaviors such as mocking someone, threatening to harm them, taunting them online, or excluding them from an activity. Each year, bullying ~~affect's~~ **affects** an astounding 3.2 million school-aged children. ~~Severil~~ **Several** strategies for avoiding peer pressure bullying include the following:

- ~~consider~~ **Consider** your actions by surrounding yourself with good company.
- Acquiring the ability to say no to someone you trust.

Speak up - bullying is never acceptable and is taken ~~extramely~~ **extremely** ~~seroiusly~~ **seriously** in schools and the workplace. If someone is attempting to convince you to bully another person, speaking with a trusted adult such as a teacher, coach, counselor, or coworker can frequently help put ~~thing's~~ **things** into perspective and highlight the issue.

Julius Caesar Roman Dictator

1. **Caesar made changes to the Roman ____.**
   a. history
   b. calendar

2. **Julius Caesar parents were the most powerful people in politics.**
   a. True
   b. False

3. **Julius Caesar became a public speaker and advocated for the ____.**
   a. government
   b. law

4. **Julius was chosen to run Spain in ____ BC**
   a. 62
   b. 32

5. **Caesar worked closely with ____, a former military officer, and ____, one of the wealthiest men in Rome**
   a. Crassus, Poindexter
   b. Pompey, Crassus

6. **Caesar changed the debt laws in ___.**
   a. Rome
   b. Egypt

7. **____ came up with a plan to kill Caesar on the Ides of March.**
   a. Marcus Brutus
   b. Mark Buccaning

8. **What wars helped to form the Roman Empire?**
   a. civil wars
   b. World War II

Jackie Robinson: The First African-American Player In MLB

On January 31, 1919, in Cairo, Georgia, Jack **Roosevelt** Robinson was born. There were five children in the family, and the youngest one was him. After Jackie was born, Jackie's father left the family, and he never returned. His mother, Millie, took care of him and his three brothers and one sister when they were young.

The family moved to **Pasadena** , California, about a year after Jackie was born. Jackie was awed by his older brothers' prowess in sports as a child. Meanwhile, his brother Mack rose to prominence as a track star and Olympic silver medalist in the 200-meter dash.

Jackie was an avid sports **enthusiast** . Like his older brother, he competed in track and field and other sports like football, baseball, and tennis. Football and baseball were two of his favorite sports to play. Throughout high school, Jackie was subjected to racism daily. Even though white teammates surrounded him, he felt like a second-class citizen off the field.

After high school, Jackie went to UCLA, where he excelled in track, baseball, **football** , and basketball. To his credit, he was the first player at UCLA to receive all four varsity letters in the same season. The long jump was another event where he excelled at the NCAA level.

With the outbreak of World War II, Robinson's football career was over before it began. He was called up for **military** service. Jackie made friends with the legendary boxing champion Joe Lewis at basic training. Robinson was accepted into officer training school thanks to Joe's assistance.

After completing his officer training, Jackie was assigned to the 761st Tank Battalion at Fort Hood, **Texas** . Only black soldiers were assigned to this battalion because they could not serve alongside white soldiers. When Jackie refused to move to the back of an army bus one day, he got into trouble. In 1944, he was discharged with an **honorable** discharge after nearly being expelled from the military.

Robinson began his professional baseball career with the Kansas City Monarchs soon after he was discharged from the military. The Negro Baseball **League** was home to the Monarchs. Black players were still not allowed to play in Major League Baseball at this time. Jackie performed well on the field. He was an outstanding shortstop, hitting .387 on average.

While playing for the Monarchs, Branch Rickey, the Dodgers' **general** manager, approached Jackie. Branch hoped that the Dodgers could win the pennant by signing an African-American player. Branch warned Robinson that he would encounter racial **prejudice** when he first joined the Dodgers. Branch was looking for a person who could take insults without reacting. This famous exchange between Jackie and Branch occurred during their first conversation:

Jackie: "Are you looking for a Negro who is afraid to fight back, Mr. Rickey?"
Jackie: "Are you looking for a Negro who is afraid to fight back, Mr. Rickey?" Robinson, I'm looking for a baseball player who has the guts not to fight back."

For the Montreal Royals, Jackie first played in the minor leagues. He was constantly confronted with racism. Because of Jackie, the opposing team would occasionally fail to show up for games. Then there were the times when people would verbally abuse or throw objects at him. In the midst of all this, Jackie remained calm and focused on the game. He had a .349 batting average and was named the league's most valuable player.

Robinson was called up to play for the Brooklyn **Dodgers** at the start of the 1947 baseball season, and he did. On April 15, 1947, he became the first African-American to play in the sport's major leagues. Racially charged taunts were once again directed at Jackie from both fans and fellow players alike. Death threats were made against him. But Jackie had the courage not to fight back. He kept his word to Branch Rickey and dedicated himself solely to the game of baseball. The Dodgers won the pennant that year, and Jackie was named the team's **Rookie** of the Year for his achievements.

Jackie Robinson was one of the best **major** league baseball players for the next ten years. During his lengthy career, his **batting** average stood at .311, and he hit 137 home runs while also stealing 197 bases. Six times he was selected to the All-Star team, and in 1949 he was named the National League MVP.

Because of Jackie Robinson's groundbreaking work, other African-American players could play in the major leagues. He also **paved** the way for racial integration in different facets of American life. He was inducted into the Baseball Hall of Fame in 1962. On October 24, 1972, Robinson suffered a heart attack and died.

Flamingos Bird Facts

Flamingos are the show stoppers of the avian world. Their long legs, bending beaks, and **vivid** orange hue make them a sight to behold. They're a popular attraction at zoos and nature preserves because they are fascinating to see up close.

Phoenicopterus ruber is the scientific name for the American Flamingo. They reach a height of 3 to 5 feet and a weight of 5 to 6 pounds at maturity. Males tend to be larger than **females** in general. Feathers of the common flamingo are typically pinkish red. Additionally, their pink feet and pink and white bill, which has a black tip, distinguish them.

Central and South America and the Caribbean are home to the American Flamingo. It can also be found in the Bahamas and Cuba, and the Yucatan Peninsula of Mexico's Caribbean coast. As far as Brazil, there are some that can be found on the northern **coast**. In addition, the Galapagos Islands have a population.

Lagoons and low-lying **mudflats** or lakes are the preferred environments for the Flamingos. They like seeking food by wading across the water. They form enormous flocks, sometimes numbering in the tens of thousands.

Flamingos come in a variety of colors, including pink and orange. Carotenoids are responsible for the orange hue of several foods, such as carrots. Carrots would turn your skin and eyes orange if you just ate them. Flamingoes appear pink or orange because they eat **algae** and small shellfish rich in carotenoids. They would lose their vibrant hue if they switched to a different **diet**.

Is it possible for flamingoes to fly? Yes. Flamingos can fly, even though we usually associate them with **wading** in the water. Before they can take off, they have to run to build up their speed. They often fly in big groups.

Scientists don't know why Flamingos stand on one leg, but they have a few ideas. There is a rumor that it is to keep one leg warm. Because it's cold outside, they can keep one leg near their body to keep it warm. Another **theory** is that they are drying out one leg at a time. A third idea argues that it aids them in deceiving their **prey**, as one leg resembles a plant more than two.

It doesn't matter the reason; these **top-heavy** birds can stand on one leg for long periods. They even sleep with one leg balanced on the ground!

Financial: Money, Stocks, and Bonds

Three important __conditions__ must be met in order for something to qualify as a financial asset. It has to be:

Something you can have
Something monetary in nature
A contractual claim provides the basis for that monetary value

That last condition may be difficult to grasp at first, but it will become clear in a few minutes.

As a result, financial assets differ from physical assets such as land or __gold__ . You can touch and feel the actual physical asset with land and gold, but you can only touch and feel something (usually a piece of paper) that represents the asset of value with financial assets.

Money is a government-defined official medium of __exchange__ that consists of cash and __coins__ . Money, currency, cash, and legal tender all refer to the same thing. They are all symbols of a central bank's commitment to keeping money's value as stable as possible. Money is a financial asset because its value is derived from the faith and credit of the government that issued it, not from the paper or metal on which it is printed.

Money is obviously a __valuable__ financial asset. We would all have to __barter__ with one another without a common medium of exchange, trading whatever goods and services we have for something else we need, or trade what we have for something else we could then trade with someone else who has what we need. Consider how complicated that can become!

Stock is another crucial financial asset in the US __economy__ . Stock, like money, is simply a piece of paper that represents something of value. The something of value' represented by stock is a stake in a company. Stock is also known as 'equity' because you have a stake in its profits when you own stock in a company.

Consider little Jane's lemonade stand as the most basic example. Jane only has $4 to begin her business, but she requires $10. Jane's parents give her $3 in exchange for 30% of her business, a friend gives her $1 for 10%, and her brother gives her $2 in exchange for 20%. Jane, her parents, a friend, and her brother are now all __shareholders__ in her company.

That example, as simple as it is, accurately describes stock. The complexities arise when we attempt to assign a __monetary__ value to that stock. A variety of factors determines a stock's value. One share of stock in one company does not equal one share of stock in another. The number of shares issued by each company, as well as the size and profitability of each company, will affect the value of your share. Anything that has an impact on a business, good or bad, will affect the stock price.

These are the most basic and fundamental factors that can influence the value of a share of stock. Individual stock prices are affected by macroeconomic trends as well. Thousands of books have been written in an attempt to discover the __golden__ rule that determines the exact value of a share of stock.

The value of a stock can fluctuate from minute to minute and even second to second. The New York Stock Exchange and __NASDAQ__ were the world's two largest stock exchanges in 2014. (both located in the United States).

Bonds are the final financial asset we'll look at. Bonds are, in essence, loans. When an organization, such as a company, a city or state, or even the federal government, requires funds, bonds can be __issued__ . Bonds come in various forms, but they are all debt instruments in which the bondholder is repaid their __principal__ investment, plus interest, at some future maturity date.

The only way a bondholder's money is lost is if the entity that issued the bond declares __bankruptcy__ . Bonds are generally safer investments than stocks because they are a legal __obligation__ to repay debt, whereas stocks represent ownership, which can make or lose money.

Boston Tea Party

Was it a big, boisterous tea party? Not at all. There was tea in the mix, but no one was drinking it. It was a __protest__ by the American Colonists against the British government that resulted in the Boston Tea Party. They boarded three trade ships in Boston __Harbor__ and threw the ships' __cargo__ of tea into the ocean to show their anger at the government. Into the water, they threw 342 chests of tea. Some of the colonists dressed up as Mohawk __Indians__, but they fooled no one. The British knew who had thrown away the tea.

First, it might seem like a silly idea to throw tea into the ocean dressed as Mohawks. But the people who lived in colonial America knew why they did this. Among the British, tea was a __favorite__ drink. People who worked for the East India Trading company made a lot of money from it. They were told they could only buy tea from this one company in the colonies. This was a British company. They were also informed that the tea would be taxed at a __hefty__ rate. The Tea Act was the name given to the tax that was levied on the sale of tea.

People in the colonies didn't think this was fair because they weren't represented in British __Parliament__ and didn't say how taxes were done. They asked that the tea be returned to Great Britain since they refused to pay taxes on it. As a result, they decided to toss the tea into the ocean as a form of protest against Britain's excessive taxes.

Historians wouldn't know for sure if the protest was planned or not. People in the town had met earlier that day to talk about the tea taxes and fight them. Samuel Adams was in charge of the meeting, which was significant. Samuel Adams was a key revolutionary __leader__ in Boston. Many people liked him because he could use public __displeasure__ with Parliament's power to tax the colonies to do good things for the country. The tea was destroyed, but no one is sure if Samuel Adams planned to do this. Instead, a group of people did it on their own because they were angry. In the future, Samuel Adams said that it was people defending their rights, not a group of people who were mad at each other. Although Adams did not participate in the Boston Tea Party, he was undoubtedly one of its planners.

It was, in fact, a lot of tea. The 342 containers had 90,000 __pounds__ of tea in them! In today's money, that would be equivalent to around one million dollars in tea.

Single Quadrant Ordered Pairs

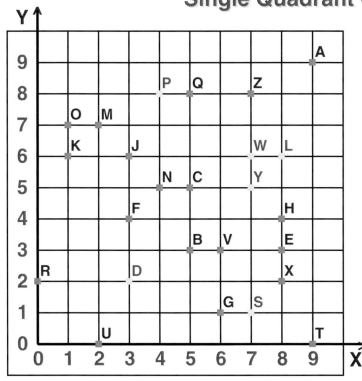

Tell what point is located at each ordered pair.

1) (8,3) __E__   6) (1,6) __K__

2) (9,9) __A__   7) (4,5) __N__

3) (8,2) __X__   8) (0,2) __R__

4) (6,3) __V__   9) (9,0) __T__

5) (6,1) __G__   10) (5,8) __Q__

Write the ordered pair for each given point.

11) **B** _(5,3)_   14) **Z** _(7,8)_   17) **O** _(1,7)_

12) **M** _(2,7)_   15) **J** _(3,6)_   18) **U** _(2,0)_

13) **C** _(5,5)_   16) **H** _(8,4)_   19) **F** _(3,4)_

Plot the following points on the coorinate grid.

20) **W** (7,6)   22) **L** (8,6)   24) **Y** (7,5)

21) **S** (7,1)   23) **D** (3,2)   25) **P** (4,8)

ANSWERS

What is the Fraction of the Shaded Area ?

1) $\dfrac{3}{4}$

2) $\dfrac{1}{3}$

3) $\dfrac{3}{5}$

4) $\dfrac{6}{8}$

5) $\dfrac{2}{5}$

6) $\dfrac{3}{5}$

7) $\dfrac{7}{8}$

8) $\dfrac{2}{3}$

9) $\dfrac{3}{8}$

10) $\dfrac{2}{5}$

Shade the Figure with the Indicated Fraction.

11) $\dfrac{1}{2}$

12) $\dfrac{1}{4}$

13) $\dfrac{1}{5}$

14) $\dfrac{5}{8}$

15) $\dfrac{2}{8}$

16) $\dfrac{4}{8}$

17) $\dfrac{4}{5}$

18) $\dfrac{1}{8}$

19) $\dfrac{2}{4}$

20) $\dfrac{4}{5}$

ANSWERS

Visually Adding Simple Fractions

1) $\dfrac{3}{11}$ + $\dfrac{4}{11}$ = $\dfrac{7}{11}$

2) $\dfrac{1}{10}$ + $\dfrac{6}{10}$ = $\dfrac{7}{10}$

3) $\dfrac{4}{11}$ + $\dfrac{5}{11}$ = $\dfrac{9}{11}$

4) $\dfrac{3}{12}$ + $\dfrac{6}{12}$ = $\dfrac{9}{12}$

5) $\dfrac{1}{4}$ + $\dfrac{2}{4}$ = $\dfrac{3}{4}$

ARTS Vocabulary Terms 3

Choose the best answer to each question.

1	A, E	India ink	⟶	A waterproof ink made from lampblack.
2	A, E	Impressionism	⟶	A movement in the 19th century which bridged the "realist" tradition with the modern movements of the 20th century. The focus was on light and atmosphere.
3	J	Kiln	⟶	A large "oven" used for firing clay work.
4	H	Linear perspective	⟶	Creating the illusion of depth on a picture plane with the use of lines and a vanishing point.
5	D	Marquette	⟶	French word for "small model". Used particularly by sculptors as a "sketch" of their work.
6	L	Medium	⟶	The process or material used in a work of art.
7	F	Monochrome	⟶	Light and dark tones of a singular color.
8	B	Mural	⟶	A painting either on a wall or on a surface to be attached to a wall.
9	K	Newsprint	⟶	Newspaper stock used for sketching, preliminary drawings and printing.
10	G	Oil pastel	⟶	Oil based crayons.
11	I	Palette	⟶	The surface used to dispense and mix paint on.
12	C	Pattern	⟶	Design, motif or symbol repeated over and over.

ARTS Vocabulary Terms 2

Choose the best answer to each question.

1	D	Computer art	⇢	Art made with the use of a computer program.
2	B	Diptych	⇢	Painting, usually an altarpiece, made up of hinged panels.
3	H	Earth colors	⇢	Pigments made using earth (dirt) that contain metal oxides mixed with a binder such as glue
4	K	Eye-level	⇢	The artists' view of where the perceived line or perspective came from.
5	A	Environmental art	⇢	Art made on a grand scale, involving the creation of a man-made environment such as architecture, sculpture, light or landscape.
6	I	Facade	⇢	The front or face of a building.
7	C	Figurative	⇢	Artwork based on the human form.
8	L	Foreshortening	⇢	A rule in perspective to create the illusion of coming forward or receding into space
9	E	Gilding	⇢	Applying gold leaf to a painting or other surface.
10	G	Greenware	⇢	Dried clay forms that have not been fired.
11	J	Gum Arabic	⇢	A binder used in watercolors made from the gum of an acacia tree.
12	F	Horizon line	⇢	The horizontal line that distinguishes the sky from the earth, or the ground from the wall. The eye-level of the artists view. Also, where the vanishing point lies in a perspective drawing.

ARTS Vocabulary Terms 1

Choose the best answer to each question.

1	G	The arrangement of the parts of a work of art.	→	Composition
2	F	Coarse cloth or heavy fabric that must be stretched and primed to use for painting, particularly for oil paintings.	→	Canvas
3	C	The use of found objects or three-dimensional objects to create a work of art.	→	Assemblage
4	D	Colors next to each other on the color wheel.	→	Analogous colors
5	I	An arrangement of shapes adhered to a background.	→	Collage
6	K	The organization of colors on a wheel. Used to help understand color schemes.	→	Color wheel
7	A	The "glue" the holds pigment together and makes it stick to a surface.	→	Binder
8	L	Originally the study of beautiful things; currently refers to the study or understanding of anything that is visually pleasing or "works" within the boundaries of the principles of art.	→	Aesthetics
9	H	A print made from a collage of assorted pasted materials such as papers, cardboards, string etc.	→	Collagraph
10	J	The art principle which refers to the arrangement of elements in an art work. Can be either formal symmetrical, informal asymmetrical or radial.	→	Balance
11	B	Italian word for "light-shade". The use and balance of light and shade in a painting, and in particular the use of strong .contrast.	→	Chiaroscuro
12	E	Clay objects that have been fired one time. (unglazed).	→	Bisque

Alice & The Rabbit-Hole

ALICE was growing tired of sitting beside her _sister_ on the bank and having nothing to do: she had peeped into the book her sister was reading once or twice, but it was lacking _pictures_ or words; "and what use is a book," Alice argued, "without pictures or conversations?"

Thus, she was wondering in her mind (as best she could, given how sleepy and foolish she felt due to the heat) whether the pleasure of creating a cute daisy chain was worth the difficulty of getting up and gathering the daisies when a white _Rabbit_ with pink eyes darted nearby her.

There was nothing _remarkable_ about that; nor did Alice consider it strange to hear the Rabbit exclaim to itself, "Oh no! Oh no! I will arrive too late!" (On reflection, she should have been surprised, but at the time, it seemed perfectly natural). Still, when the Rabbit actually removed a watch from its waistcoat-pocket, examined it, and then hurried on, Alice jumped to her _feet_, for it flashed across her mind that she had never seen a rabbit with either a waistcoat-pocket or a watch to remove from it, and burning with curiosity, she ran across the field after it. Alice saw the Rabbit go down a hole under the hedge. Alice followed it down in a _hurry_, never once thinking how she would get out again.

The rabbit-hole continued straight ahead like a _tunnel_ for some distance and then suddenly dipped down, so quickly that Alice had no time to think about stopping herself before falling into what appeared to be a very deep well.

Either the well was really deep, or she dropped very slowly, as she had plenty of time to look around her and ponder on what might happen next. She first attempted to glance down and see what she was approaching, but it was too _dark_ to see anything; then, she discovered the sides of the well were lined with cupboards and bookcases; here and there, she observed maps and images hung on hooks. She removed a _jar_ from one of the shelves as she passed; it was labeled "ORANGE MARMALADE," but it was empty; she did not want to drop the jar for fear of killing someone beneath, so she managed to stuff it into one of the cupboards as she passed it.

"Perfect!" Alice exclaimed to herself. "After such a tumble, I shall have no worries about falling downstairs! How _courageous_ they will all believe I am at home!

Addition Worksheet

53125	893724	7754653	40034
58540	759775	8766279	70732
79810	403688	7714657	43161
+ 11737	+ 200969	+ 4524724	+ 41196
203212	2258156	28760313	195123

192189	2241377	84097	413796
965026	7928905	19687	877734
531938	5984195	69704	997766
+ 385320	+ 8264879	+ 21157	+ 742703
2074473	24419356	194645	3031999

7059169	86799	636053	6947438
5369228	28259	120921	8770263
9985601	90783	897238	9488267
+ 8707044	+ 14295	+ 447023	+ 9910513
31121042	220136	2101235	35116481

35283	189936	7019570	24476
17919	753760	1010287	75122
61158	617906	5621292	61687
+ 49632	+ 863520	+ 5479675	+ 55646
163992	2425122	19130824	216931

A Community Garden Letter
Questions

1. Who sent this letter?

    a. Andrew Fitzgerald

    b. Jill Kindle

    c. Dawn Clover

2. Who is the letter for?

    a. Jill Kindle

    b. Dawn Clover

    c. Andrew Fitzgerald

3. How much is the 10 x 12 plot per year?

    a. $90.00

    b. $45.00

    c. $55.00

4. What is Dawn Clover's phone number?

    a. 693-555-9006

    b. 963-555-9669

    c. 693-555-9009

5. What job does Jill Kindle have?

    a. Community Garden Person

    b. Director of Community Gardens

    c. Garden Coordinator

6. What town or city is this community garden in?

    a. Gibbons

    b. Billings

    c. Riverstide

7. Where is the Greendale Community Garden?

    a. 678 Warren Drive

    b. 780 Billings St.

    c. 789 Gibbons St.

8. How many plots are available?

    a. 2

    b. 10

    c. 12

9. The water costs extra.

    a. True

    b. False

10. When was this letter written?

    a. June 5, 2018

    b. June 5, 2019

    c. June 9, 2015

Science: Protists

Protists are organisms that are classified under the biological kingdom protista. These are neither plants, animals, bacteria, or fungi, but rather __unclassifiable__ organisms. Protists are a large group of organisms with a wide variety of characteristics. They are essentially all species that do not fit into any of the other categories.

Protists as a group share very few characteristics. They are eukaryotic microorganisms with eukaryote __cell__ structures that are pretty basic. Apart from that, they are defined as any organism that is not a plant, an animal, a bacteria, or a fungus.

Protists can be classified according to their mode of movement.

Cilia - Certain protists move with __tiny__ hair called cilia. These tiny hairs can flap in unison to assist the creature in moving through water or another liquid.

Other protists have a lengthy __tail__ known as flagella. This tail can move back and forth, aiding in the organism's propulsion.

Pseudopodia - When a protist extends a portion of its cell body in order to __scoot__ or ooze. Amoebas move in this manner.

Different protists collect __energy__ in a variety of methods. Certain individuals consume food and digest it internally. Others digest their food through the secretion of enzymes. Then they __consume__ the partially digested meal. Other protists, like plants, utilize photosynthesis. They absorb sunlight and convert it to glucose.

Algae is a main form of protist. Algae are photosynthesis-capable protists. Algae are closely related to plants. They contain chlorophyll and utilize __oxygen__ and solar energy to generate food. However, they are not called plants because they lack specialized organs and tissues such as leaves, roots, and stems. Algae are frequently classified according on their __color__, which ranges from red to brown to green.

Slime __molds__ are distinct from fungus molds. Slime molds are classified into two types: cellular and plasmodial. Slime molds of Plasmodium are formed from a single big cell. They are also referred to as __acellular__. Even though these organisms are composed of only one cell, they can grow quite __enormous__, up to several feet in width. Additionally, they can contain several nuclei inside a single cell. Cellular slime molds are little single-celled protists that can form a single organism when combined. When combined, various __cellular__ slime molds will perform specific activities.

__Amoebas__ are single-celled organisms that move with the assistance of pseudopods. Amoebas have no structure and consume their food by engulfing it with their bodies. Amoebas __reproduce__ by dividing in two during a process called mitosis.

Science: Black Hole

Black holes are one of the universe's most mysterious and powerful forces. A black hole is a region of space where gravity has become so strong that nothing, not even light, can escape. A black hole's mass is so compact or dense that the force of gravity is so strong that even light cannot escape.

Black holes are entirely invisible. Because black holes do not reflect light, we cannot see them. Scientists can detect black holes by observing light and objects in their vicinity. Strange things happen in the vicinity of black holes due to quantum physics and space-time. Even though they are authentic, they are a popular subject for science fiction stories.

When giant stars explode at the end of their lives, black holes form, this type of explosion is known as a supernova. If a star has enough mass, it will collapse in on itself and shrink to a tiny size. Because of its small size and massive mass, the gravity will be so strong that it will absorb light and turn into a black hole. As they continue to absorb light and mass around them, black holes can grow enormously large. They can absorb other stars as well. Many scientists believe that supermassive black holes exist at the centers of galaxies.

An event horizon is a special boundary that exists around a black hole. At this point, everything, including light, must gravitate toward the black hole. Once you've crossed the event horizon, there's no turning back!

In the 18th century, two scientists, John Michell and Pierre-Simon Laplace, proposed the concept of a black hole. The term "black hole" was coined in 1967 by physicist John Archibald Wheeler.

1. Black holes are _____.
   a. can be seen with telescope
   b. [invisible]
   c. partial visible

2. Black holes are one of the most mysterious forces in the _____.
   a. near the moon
   b. under the stars
   c. [universe]

3. A black hole is where _____ has become so strong that nothing around it can escape.
   a. black dust
   b. [gravity]
   c. the sun

4. We can't actually see black holes because they don't _____.
   a. need sun
   b. [reflect light]
   c. have oxygen

5. Black holes are formed when _____ explode at the end of their lifecycle.
   a. [giant stars]
   b. planets
   c. Mars

6. Black holes can grow incredibly huge as they continue to absorb_____.
   a. stars
   b. other planets
   c. [light]

Science Multiple Choice
Quiz: Noble Gases

Select the best answer for each question.

1. The noble gases are located to the far right of the periodic table and make up the _____.
   a. 16th column
   b. 18th column
   c. 17th column

2. Noble gases are _____, meaning each molecule is a single atom and almost never react with other elements.
   a. diatomic
   b. polyatomic
   c. monoatomic

3. The six noble gases are:
   a. Chlorine, bromine, iodine, astatine, tennessine
   b. Helium, hydrogen, radon, lithium, krypton, neon
   c. helium, neon, argon, krypton, xenon, and radon.

4. Helium is the second most abundant element in the universe after _____.
   a. radon
   b. hydrogen
   c. argon

5. Xenon gets its name from the _____ word "xenos" which means "stranger or foreigner."
   a. Greek
   b. Latin
   c. Spanish

6. _____ has the lowest melting and boiling points of any substance.
   a. Neon
   b. Radon
   c. Helium

7. All of the noble gases except for _____ have stable isotopes.
   a. radon
   b. argon
   c. neon

8. This element is non-flammable and it is much safer to use in balloons than hydrogen.
   a. Krypton
   b. Helium
   c. Xenon

9. Many of the noble gases were either discovered or isolated by _____ chemist _____.
   a. Scottish, Sir William Ramsay
   b. Russian, Dmitri Mendeleev
   c. German, Robert Bunsen

10. Krypton gets its name from the _____ word "kryptos" meaning "_____".
   a. Greek; "sweet"
   b. Greek; "the hidden one."
   c. Greek; "lazy"

11. _____, mixed with nitrogen, is used as a filler gas for incandescent light bulbs.
   a. Carbon monoxide
   b. Hydrogen
   c. Argon

12. _____, a highly radioactive element and is only available in minute amounts, is utilized in radiotherapy.
   a. Radon
   b. Carbon
   c. Uranium

Science Multiple Choice
Quiz: Alkali Metals

Select the best answer for each question.

1. **The elements of the alkali metals include _____, _____, _____, _____, _____, and _____.**

   a. magnesium, calcium, radium, beryllium, silicon,and lithium

   b. lithium, sodium, potassium, rubidium, cesium, and francium

   c. radium, beryllium, lithium, sodium, calcium, and francium

2. **The alkali metals are all in the _____ of the periodic table except for hydrogen.**

   a. 1st column

   b. 2nd column

   c. 16th column

3. **Alkali Metals have a _____ when compared to other metals.**

   a. high density

   b. low density

   c. light density

4. **The word "alkali" comes from the _____ word meaning "ashes."**

   a. German

   b. Arabic

   c. Greek

5. **_____ is the most important alkali metal.**

   a. lithium

   b. sodium

   c. potassium

6. **Alkali metals are generally stored in _____.**

   a. oil

   b. soil

   c. water

7. **All alkali metals have _____ atomic numbers.**

   a. even

   b. odd

   c. prime

8. **Potassium's atomic number is ____ and its symbol is ____.**

   a. 19 and P

   b. 19 and K

   c. 11 and Na

9. **Alkali metals are the _____in group one of the periodic systems.**

   a. non metals

   b. chemical elements

   c. late transition metals

10. **_____ is the lightest known metal.**

    a. Sodium

    b. Lithium

    c. francium

Organisms Multiple Choice
Quiz: Domestic Pig

Select the best answer for each question.

1. Domestic pigs are often _____ but small pigs kept as pets (pot-bellied pigs) are often other colors.
   a. white
   b. black
   c. pink

2. The dental formula of adult pigs is 3.1.4.3/3.1.4.3, giving a total of _____ teeth.
   a. 36
   b. 44
   c. 50

3. Pigs are_____ in the genus Sus
   a. reptiles
   b. amphibians
   c. mammals

4. _____ of piglet fatalities are due to the mother attacking, or unintentionally crushing, the newborn pre-weaned animals.
   a. 60%
   b. 50%
   c. 30%

5. The ancestor of the domestic pig is the _____, which is one of the most numerous and widespread large mammals.
   a. wild boar
   b. babirusa
   c. warthog

6. Pigs are _____, which means that they consume both plants and animals.
   a. omnivores
   b. herbivores
   c. carnivores

7. Pigs need a _____, _____ under a roof to sleep, and they should not be crowded.
   a. warm, muddy area
   b. warm, clean area
   c. cold, clean area

8. Piglets weigh about _____ at birth, and usually double their weight in one week.
   a. 1.5 kilograms
   b. 2.2 kilograms
   c. 1.1 kilograms

9. Pigs often roll in _____ to protect themselves from sunlight.
   a. water
   b. mud
   c. grass

10. Pigs are among the smartest of all domesticated animals and are even smarter than _____.
    a. dogs
    b. cats
    c. birds

Math: Linear Equation

What exactly is a linear equation?

First, consider the word equation. An equation is a mathematical statement containing the equals sign. Of course, linear means "in a straight line."

A linear equation is an equation with degree 1 -, which means that the highest exponent on all variables in the equation is 1. It turns out that if you plot the solutions to a linear equation in a coordinate system, they form a straight line.

A linear equation resembles an equation (there must be an equals sign) with variables that all have an exponent of one (in other words, no variable is raised to a higher power, and no variable is under a square root sign).

These equations are linear: y=2x+9 or 5x=6+3y

1. Which of the following is a solution to both y - 3x = 6 and y - 6x = 3?

   a. (6,9)

   b. (3,6)

   c. (1,9)

2. Different plans are available from two cellphone carriers. AT&K charges a monthly flat rate of $100 plus $10 for each gigabyte of data used. Verikon Communications does not have a flat rate, but instead charges $40 for each gigabyte of data used. Let c represent your total cost and d represent the data used. What is the equation system that represents these two plans?

   a. V = 100 + 10d and A = 40d

   b. A = 100d and V = 40d

   c. c = 100 + 10d and c = 40d

3. Solve the following system of equations 3x + y = 1 and -x + 2y = 2

   a. (2, 1)

   b. (3, 1)

   c. (0, 1)

4. What is the slope of a line with a graph that moves one place to the right by going up three places on a coordinate plane?

   a. -3

   b. 3

   c. 2

5. Find the slope of the line 2x - y = 6.

   a. 6

   b. 2

   c. -2

6. Which of the following linear equations has a y-intercept of 3 and a graph that slopes upward from left to right?

   a. -4x + 2y - 6 = 0

   b. -4x + 2y + 6 = 0

   c. 4x + y + 3 = 0

7. What are the x and y-intercepts of 3x + 4y = 12?

   a. (0, 12) and (3, 0)

   b. (4, 0) and (0, 3)

   c. (12, 4) and (4, 3)

8. Which linear equation has the solutions (1, 3) and (3, 9)?

   a. x = 1y

   b. y = 9x + 2

   c. y = 3x

Math: Inequalities

Mathematics isn't always about "equals"; sometimes all we know is that something is greater or less than another. An inequality is a mathematical equation that uses greater or less than symbols and is useful in situations where there are multiple solutions.

For example: Alexis and Billy compete in a race, and Billy wins!

What exactly do we know?

We don't know how fast they ran, but we do know Billy outpaced Alexis:

Billy was quicker than Alexis. That can be written down as follows: b > a

(Where "b" represents Billy's speed, ">" represents "greater than," and "a" represents Alex's speed.)

Do you require any other assistance? Try looking for instructional videos on Pre-Calculus Functions on YouTube.

---

1. A truck is driving across a bridge that has a weight limit of 50,000 pounds. The front of the truck weighs 19,800 pounds when empty, and the back of the truck weighs 12,500 pounds. How much cargo (C), in pounds, can the truck carry and still cross the bridge?

    a. C ≤ 10000

    b. C ≤ 17700

    c. C ≤ 7700

2. Monica wants to buy a phone, and the cheapest one she's found so far is $15. Monica has $4.25 set aside for a cell phone. How many hours (H) will Monica have to work to afford a mobile phone if she earns $2.15 per hour?

    a. H ≥ 3.75

    b. H ≥ 5.50

    c. H ≥ 5

3. Solve the inequality 4x + 8 > 5x +9

    a. x < 8

    b. x > 2

    c. x < -1

4. Solve the following inequality - 4|2 - x| - 4 < -28

    a. x > 8 or x < -4

    b. x < 8 or x > -4

    c. x > 4 or x < 28

5. Which of the following best describes the appearance of these two inequalities when graphed together? 2y - 9 ≥ 4x and 4 < x + y

    a. both boundary lines will be solid or dotted

    b. both boundary lines will be dotted

    c. one boundary line will be solid and one will be dotted

6. Which compound inequality has the solution x < -8 ?

    a. x + 2 > 16 OR x + 6 < 8

    b. 6 - 2x > 22 OR 3x + 14 < -10

    c. 4x + 2 > 7 AND 2 - 6x > -1

7. If 2x - 8 ≥ 2, then

    a. x ≤ 4

    b. x ≥ 5

    c. x ≤ 8

8. Which of the following is an example of an inequality?

    a. 70 - 2(15) = 88

    b. 60 + 2x < 120

    c. 70 + 3x = 80

Math: Domain and Range

The collection of all input values on which a function is defined is known as the domain. If a value is entered into the function, the function will remain defined regardless of what value is entered. A function's range is defined as the set of all possible output values for the function. It can also be thought of as the collection of all possible values that the function will accept as input.

1. Which of the following describes a collection of a function's outputs?
   a. Domain
   b. Inputs
   c. Range

2. What is the range of the function: $g(x) = |x| + 1$
   a. $R = \{1 \geq x\}$
   b. $R = \{x \geq 1\}$
   c. $R = \{y \geq 1\}$

3. A set of ordered pairs is called what?
   a. the domain
   b. a function
   c. a relation

4. What is the domain of a relation?
   a. the set of all y-values
   b. the set of all y + x values
   c. the set of all x-values

5. Which is the set of all y-values or the outputs?
   a. Domain
   b. Function
   c. Range

6. For the function {(0,1), (1,-3), (2,-4), (-4,1)}, write the domain and range.
   a. D:{0, 1, 2, -4} R:{1, -3, -4}
   b. D: {1, -3, -4,} R: {0, 1, 2, -4}
   c. D:{0, 1, 2, 3, 4} R:{1, -3, -4}

7. Identify the range of the following function when given the domain { 2, 3, 10}: $y = 4x - 12$
   a. -10, 0, 28
   b. -4, 0, 28
   c. 4, 5, 20

8. Which set of ordered pairs is not a function?
   a. (-9, 4), (-6, 3), (-2, 8), (0, 21)
   b. (1, 2), (3, 5), (6, 9), (7, 11)
   c. (2, 3), (4, 9), (3, 8), (4, 15)

9. What variable does Domain represent?
   a. Range
   b. X
   c. output

10. Which is the set of all y-values or the outputs?
    a. Range
    b. Domain
    c. Relation

Language:
Technology

Match the English and German words. Use Google translate.

1	C	mouse	⇢	Maus
2	F	touch	⇢	berühren
3	H	screen	⇢	Bildschirm
4	L	Wi-Fi	⇢	WLAN
5	A	message	⇢	Nachricht
6	E	game	⇢	Spiel
7	O	website	⇢	Webseite
8	B	mobile	⇢	Handy
9	K	smart	⇢	klug, intelligent
10	G	computer	⇢	Rechner
11	I	desktop	⇢	Schreibtischplatte
12	D	lap	⇢	Schoß
13	M	net	⇢	Netz
14	N	app(lication)	⇢	App, Anwendung
15	J	keyboard	⇢	Tastatur

Language: Spanish

Use Google to help translate.

1. You would answer: ¡Muy bien! to which of the following questions in Spanish?

    a. 'Cómo te llamas?

    b. 'De dónde eres?

    c. 'Cómo estás?

2. What does Soy de Virginia means?

    a. I am from Virginia

    b. My name is Virginia

    c. I am Virginia

3. Buenas tardes is a Spanish greeting for which time of the day?

    a. Good night

    b. Good morning

    c. Afternoon

4. You would answer: Me llamo Antonio to which of the following questions in Spanish?

    a. 'A quién llamas?

    b. 'Cómo te llamas?

    c. 'Cuándo llamas?

5. You would answer: Soy de Carolina to which of the following questions in Spanish?

    a. 'De dónde eres?

    b. 'Dónde vas?

    c. 'Cómo te llamas?

6. How would you say 'Good morning' to a store clerk?

    a. Buenos días

    b. Hola

    c. My llamo

7. 'Soy de California.

    a. 'She from California.

    b. 'I am from California.

    c. 'I live in California.

8. Which of the following persons would you address by using the pronoun 'Tú'?

    a. a teacher

    b. Your aunt

    c. Your sibling

9. What would be the best greeting for the nighttime?

    a. Buenas tardes

    b. Soy

    c. Buenas noches

10. Which of the following is NOT a way to tell someone your name?

    a. Soy de...

    b. Me llamo...

    c. Mi nombre es...

11. Which two words mean 'you?'

    a. Tú and Usted

    b. Yo and Cómo

    c. Usted and Nónde

12. Buenos días, señor. ?

    a. Good night sir. ?

    b. Good morning sir. ?

    c. Good afternoon sir. ?

13. Cómo se llama ud.?'

    a. What's your name.?'

    b. What time is it.?'

    c. Where are you?

14. Where it is?'

    a. Me rónde es?'

    b. De dónde es?'

    c. Re dónde see?'

History: Age of Discovery

Tip: After you've answered the easy ones, go back and work on the harder ones.

valuable	Navigator	Middle	Discovery	Columbus
voyage	Africa	tobacco	sugar	sailed

Early in the 14th century, the Age of __Discovery__ (also known as the Age of Exploration) began. It lasted until the mid-1600s. European nations began to explore the globe during this time period. A large part of the Far East and the Americas were found as well as new routes to India and the __Middle__ East. The Renaissance occurred at the same time as the Age of Exploration.

The process of preparing for an expedition can be costly and time-consuming. Many ships __sailed__ away and never came back. So what was it about exploration that piqued the interest of Europeans? Answering this question is as easy as saying "money." Despite the fact that some explorers went on expeditions to acquire notoriety or to have an exciting experience, the primary goal of an organization was to make money.

New trade routes discovered by expeditions brought quite a lot of money for their countries. Many traditional routes to India and China were closed after the Ottoman Empire took Constantinople in 1453. Spices and silk were brought in via these trading routes, making them extremely __valuable__. New explorers were seeking oceangoing routes to India and the Far East. Gold and silver were discovered by some journeys, including the Spanish ones to the Americas, which made them wealthy. They also found fresh territory to create colonies and cultivate crops like __sugar__, cotton, and __tobacco__.

Henry the __Navigator__, a Portuguese explorer, kicked off the Age of Exploration in the country. Henry dispatched a fleet of ships to map and investigate the continent's western coast. They explored a large portion of west __Africa__ for the Portuguese after traveling further south than any previous European expedition had. Portuguese explorer Bartolomeu Dias discovered the southern tip of Africa and into the Indian Ocean in 1488

The Spanish urgently needed a trade route to Asia. The famed European explorer, Christopher __Columbus__, believed he might reach China by sailing west over the Atlantic Ocean. He turned to the Spanish for funding after failing to secure it from the Portuguese. Isabella and Ferdinand, the monarchs of Spain, agreed to foot the bill for Columbus' __voyage__. Columbus made his voyage to the New World in 1492 and discovered the Americas.

Financial: Money, Stocks and Bonds

Three important **conditions** must be met in order for something to qualify as a financial asset. It has to be:

Something you can have
Something monetary in nature
A contractual claim provides the basis for that monetary value

That last condition may be difficult to grasp at first, but it will become clear in a few minutes.

As a result, financial assets differ from physical assets such as land or gold. You can touch and feel the actual physical asset with land and **gold**, but you can only touch and feel something (usually a piece of **paper**) that represents the asset of value with financial assets.

Money is a government-defined official medium of exchange that consists of cash and **coins**. Money, **currency**, cash, and legal tender all refer to the same thing. They are all symbols of a central bank's commitment to keeping money's value as stable as possible. Money is a financial asset because its value is derived from the faith and credit of the government that issued it, not from the paper or metal on which it is printed.

Money is obviously a valuable financial **asset**. We would all have to **barter** with one another without a common medium of exchange, trading whatever goods and services we have for something else we need, or **trade** what we have for something else we could then trade with someone else who has what we need. Consider how complicated that can become!

Stock is another crucial financial asset in the US **economy**. Stock, like money, is simply a piece of paper that represents something of value. The something of value' represented by stock is a **stake** in a company. Stock is also known as 'equity' because you have a stake in its profits when you own stock in a company.

Consider little Jane's lemonade stand as the most basic example. Jane only has $4 to begin her business, but she requires $10. Jane's parents give her $3 in exchange for 30% of her business, a friend gives her $1 for 10%, and her brother gives her $2 in exchange for 20%. Jane, her parents, a friend, and her brother are now all **shareholders** in her company.

That example, as simple as it is, accurately describes stock. The complexities arise when we attempt to assign a **monetary** value to that stock. A variety of factors determines a stock's value. One share of stock in one company does not equal one share of stock in another. The number of shares issued by each company, as well as the size and profitability of each company, will affect the value of your share. Anything that has an impact on a business, good or bad, will affect the stock price.

These are the most basic and fundamental factors that can influence the value of a share of stock. Individual stock prices are affected by macroeconomic trends as well. Thousands of books have been written in an attempt to discover the golden rule that determines the exact value of a share of stock.

The value of a stock can fluctuate from minute to minute and even second to second. The New York Stock Exchange and **NASDAQ** were the world's two largest stock exchanges in 2014. (both located in the United States).

Bonds are the final financial asset we'll look at. Bonds are, in essence, loans. When an organization, such as a company, a city or state, or even the federal government, requires funds, bonds can be issued. Bonds come in various forms, but they are all debt instruments in which the bondholder is repaid their **principal** investment, plus interest, at some future maturity date.

The only way a bondholder's money is lost is if the entity that issued the bond declares **bankruptcy**. Bonds are generally safer investments than stocks because they are a legal **obligation** to repay debt, whereas stocks represent ownership, which can make or lose money.

Art: Pablo Picasso

depressed	suicide	features	Carlos	newspapers
blue	historians	circuses	collaborated	sand
painter	Madrid	prestigious	Spanish	French

Pablo Picasso was born on October 25, 1881, in Spain and grew up there. His father was a **painter** who also taught art. Pablo has always enjoyed drawing since he was a child. According to legend, his first word was "piz," which is **Spanish** for "pencil." Pablo quickly demonstrated that he had little interest in school but was an extremely talented artist. Pablo enrolled in a **prestigious** art school in Barcelona when he was fourteen years old. He transferred to another school in **Madrid** a few years later. Pablo, on the other hand, was dissatisfied with the traditional art school teachings. He didn't want to paint in the manner of people from hundreds of years ago. He wished to invent something new.

Pablo's close friend **Carlos** Casagemas committed **suicide** in 1901. Pablo became **depressed**. He began painting in Paris around the same time. For the next four years, the color **blue** dominated his paintings. Many of the subjects appeared depressed and solemn. He depicted people with elongated **features** and faces in his paintings. Poor People on the Seashore and The Old Guitarist are two of his paintings from this time.

Pablo eventually recovered from his depression. He also had feelings for a **French** model. He began to use warmer colors such as pinks, reds, oranges, and beiges in his paintings. The Rose Period is a term used by art **historians** to describe this period in Pablo's life. He also started painting happier scenes like **circuses**. The Peasants and Mother and Child are two of his paintings from this time period.

Picasso began experimenting with a new painting style in 1907. He **collaborated** with another artist, Georges Braque. By 1909, they had developed a completely new painting style known as Cubism. Cubism analyzes and divides subjects into different sections. The sections are then reassembled and painted from various perspectives and angles.

Picasso began combining Cubism and collage in 1912. He would use **sand** or plaster in his paint to give it texture in this area. He would also add dimension to his paintings by using materials such as colored paper, **newspapers**, and wallpaper. Three Musicians and the Portrait of Ambroise Vollard are two of Picasso's Cubism paintings.

Although Picasso continued to experiment with Cubism, he went through a period of painting more classical-style paintings around 1921. He was influenced by Renaissance painters such as Raphael. He created strong characters that appeared three-dimensional, almost like statues. The Pipes of Pan and Woman in White are two of his works in this style.

Pablo became interested in the Surrealist movement around 1924. Surrealist paintings were never meant to make sense. They frequently resemble something out of a nightmare or a dream. Although Picasso did not join the movement, he did incorporate some of its ideas into his paintings. This period was dubbed "Monster Period" by some. Guernica and The Red Armchair are two examples of surrealism's influence on Picasso's art.

Pablo Picasso is widely regarded as the greatest artist of the twentieth century. Many consider him to be one of the greatest artists in all of history. He painted in a variety of styles and made numerous unique contributions to the world of art. He painted several self-portraits near the end of his life. Self-Portrait Facing Death, a self-portrait done with crayons on paper, was one of his final works of art. He died a year later, on April 8, 1973, at the age of 91.

Geography Multiple Choice
Quiz: Antarctic

Select the best answer for each question.

1. _____ is the fifth-largest continent in terms of total area.
   a. Antarctic
   b. Artic
   c. Antarctica

2. _____ is composed of older, igneous and metamorphic rocks.
   a. Lesser Antarctica
   b. Greater Antarctica
   c. Antarctica

3. Antarctica is:
   a. Nearly all exposed land with some glaciers
   b. About half ice and half exposed land
   c. Mainly ice, with a few areas of exposed land

4. Antarctica has the world's largest?
   a. Mountains
   b. Ice
   c. Desert

5. In 1983, the coldest temperature ever recorded in Antarctica is?
   a. -108.5°F
   b. -118.0°F
   c. -128.6°F

6. The Antarctic region has an important role in _____.
   a. global climate processes
   b. Earth's heat balance
   c. Earth's atmosphere

7. The _____ is one of the driest _____ in the world.
   a. Antarctic desert and deserts
   b. Antarctic continent and deserts
   c. Antarctic archipelago and continent

8. One of the apex, or top, predators in Antarctica is the?
   a. penguin
   b. sperm whales
   c. leopard seal

9. _____ study climate patterns, including the "ozone hole" that hovers over the Antarctic.
   a. Climatologists
   b. Meteorologists
   c. Geographers

10. _____ is the largest single piece of ice on Earth.
    a. Antarctic Ice Sheet
    b. Glacial Ice
    c. Ross Ice Shelf

11. _____, is part of the "Ring of Fire," a tectonically active area around the Pacific Ocean.
    a. Antarctica
    b. Greater Antarctica
    c. Lesser Antarctica

12. _____ in the Antarctic is hard to measure as it always falls as snow.
    a. Evaporation
    b. Condensation
    c. Precipitation

Biology: Excretory System

chloride	pressure	bladder	filtering	bloodstream
molecules	concentrate	urine	muscular	detoxifies
kidneys	substances	glomeruli	reabsorbing	converts

Toxins are present in all animals' bodies and must be eliminated. The human liver __detoxifies__ and modifies dangerous __substances__ so that they can be quickly and easily removed from the body. For example, ammonia is very toxic, so the liver __converts__ it to urea, which is far less toxic and easily removed from the body.

The __kidneys__ are the organs responsible for __filtering__ waste products from the blood and regulating blood composition and pressure. The outer layer of the kidneys contains structures known as __glomeruli__, which are ball-like structures made up of very porous capillaries. Large amounts of water and small molecules, including urea, are forced out through the pores by the blood __pressure__ in these capillaries, but blood cells and larger __molecules__ that are too large to fit through the pores remain in the __bloodstream__.

The glomeruli are surrounded by the ends of the renal tubules, which are long, looping tubes in the kidney that collect blood filtrate and __concentrate__ it into the urine. The filtrate travels through the tubules, __reabsorbing__ nutrients, water, and sodium __chloride__ from the renal tubules and returning them to the blood. Waste products are concentrated in the tubules and become urine as water and nutrients are reabsorbed. Urine is stored in the __bladder__ after the kidneys have concentrated it. Most people can control when they empty their bladder by controlling a __muscular__ valve at the exit point. When this valve is opened and the bladder muscles contract, __urine__ enters the urethra, where it travels before exiting the body.

1. George Washington was born on _____.
   a. 02-22-1732
   b. February 24, 1732

2. The United States Constitution is the law of the ____.
   a. land
   b. world

3. George's _____ had deteriorated.
   a. teeth
   b. feet

4. George Washington can be seen on a _____.
   a. one-dollar bill
   b. five-dollar bill

5. George's father died when he was 20 years old.
   a. True
   b. False

6. George was a plantation owner.
   a. True
   b. False

7. George married the widow _____.
   a. Martha Custis
   b. Mary Curtis

8. In his will, Washington freed his _____.
   a. children
   b. slaves

9. George served in the _____ legislature.
   a. Virginia
   b. Maryland

10. George Washington was elected as the _____ President of the USA.
   a. forth
   b. first

11. A widow is someone whose husband has died.
   a. True
   b. False

12. George died on December 14, 1699.
   a. True
   b. False

13. George grew up in _____.
   a. Washington DC
   b. Colonial Virginia

14. The capital of the United States is named after George.
   a. True
   b. False

15. A plantation is a town that is tended by a large number of officials.
   a. True
   b. False

16. Washington caught a ____ just a few years after leaving the presidency.
   a. cold
   b. flight

Health: Immune System

white	defends	cell-mediated	cells	Immune
external	Macrophages	signals	foreign	invading

Your immune system **defends** you against harmful intruders. **Immune** responses occur when your body's immune system detects threats. Learn about antibody-mediated and cell-mediated immunity.

Your immune system, which detects and eliminates **foreign** invaders, provides this tremendous service. An immunological reaction occurs when your body's immune system detects **external** intruders. Your immune system is a great asset that selflessly protects you from antigens, or foreign intruders.

Immunity by Cells

Antibody-mediated immunity is one of your immune system's two arms. The other arm is **cell-mediated** immunity, which helps the body get rid of undesired cells like infected, cancerous, or transplanted cells. **Macrophages** consume antigens in this sort of immunity. If you split down macrophages, you can remember it easily. Big indicates macro- and phages means 'eaters.' So macrophages are voracious consumers of antigens. The macrophage then chews up the antigen and displays the fragments on its surface.

When helper T cells encounter macrophages, they give out **signals** that activate other **white** blood **cells** , such as cytotoxic or killer T cells. These killer T cells multiply fast, forming an army ready to battle and eliminate the **invading** cell that prompted the immune response.

Health: Check Your Symptoms

1. **I've got a pain in my head.**
   a. Stiff neck
   b. headache

2. **I was out in the sun too long.**
   a. Sunburn
   b. Fever

3. **I've got a small itchy lump or bump.**
   a. Rash
   b. Insect bite

4. **I might be having a heart attack.**
   a. Cramps
   b. Chest pain

5. **I've lost my voice.**
   a. Laryngitis
   b. Sore throat

6. **I need to blow my nose a lot.**
   a. Runny nose
   b. Blood Nose

7. **I have an allergy. I have a**
   a. Rash
   b. Insect bite

8. **My shoe rubbed my heel. I have a**
   a. Rash
   b. Blister

9. **The doctor gave me antibiotics. I have a/an**
   a. Infection
   b. Cold

10. **I think I want to vomit. I am**
    a. Nauseous
    b. Bloated

11. **My arm is not broken. It is**
    a. Scratched
    b. Sprained

12. **My arm touched the hot stove. It is**
    a. Burned
    b. Bleeding

13. **I have an upset stomach. I might**
    a. Cough
    b. Vomit

14. **The doctor put plaster on my arm. It is**
    a. Sprained
    b. Broken

15. **If you cut your finger it will**
    a. Burn
    b. Bleed

16. **I hit my hip on a desk. It will**
    a. Burn
    b. Bruise

17. **When you have hay-fever you will**
    a. Sneeze
    b. Wheeze

18. **A sharp knife will**
    a. Scratch
    b. Cut

Spelling: How Do You Spell It?
Part II

	A	B	C	D
1.	compllain	complian	**complain**	compllian
2.	negattyve	negatyve	**negative**	negattive
3.	**importance**	importence	imporrtance	imporrtence
4.	encourragement	**encouragement**	encourragenment	encouragenment
5.	shallves	**shelves**	shellves	shalves
6.	**mixture**	mixttore	mixtore	mixtture
7.	honorrable	**honorable**	honorible	honorrible
8.	lagall	legall	lagal	**legal**
9.	manar	mannar	**manner**	maner
10.	encycllopedia	**encyclopedia**	encycllopedai	encyclopedai
11.	repllacement	replacenment	repllacenment	**replacement**
12.	medycie	medycine	**medicine**	medicie
13.	experriance	**experience**	experiance	experrience
14.	**hunger**	hunjer	hungerr	hunjerr
15.	sallote	sallute	salote	**salute**
16.	horrizon	hurizon	hurrizon	**horizon**
17.	sestion	**session**	setion	sesion
18.	shorrten	shurten	**shorten**	shurrten
19.	fuacett	faucett	fuacet	**faucet**
20.	haadache	haadace	haedache	**headache**
21.	**further**	furrther	forrther	forther
22.	injurry	injory	**injury**	injorry
23.	disstance	distence	**distance**	disstence
24.	rattio	**ratio**	rattoi	ratoi
25.	independense	**independence**	independance	independanse

Spelling: How Do You Spell It?
Part I

	A	B	C	D
1.	**grade**	grrada	grrade	grada
2.	**elementary**	elenmentary	ellenmentary	ellementary
3.	**marks**	marrcks	marrks	marcks
4.	repurt	reporrt	**report**	repurrt
5.	schedolle	**schedule**	schedole	schedulle
6.	timetible	**timetable**	timettable	timettible
7.	**highlight**	highllight	hyghllight	hyghlight
8.	foell	foel	fuell	**fuel**
9.	instrucsion	insstruction	**instruction**	insstrucsion
10.	senttence	sentance	senttance	**sentence**
11.	**vaccination**	vacination	vaccinasion	vacinasion
12.	**proof**	prwf	prouf	proph
13.	mandatury	mandattury	**mandatory**	mandattory
14.	**final**	fynall	finall	fynal
15.	envellope	**envelope**	envellupe	envelupe
16.	equattor	eqauttor	eqautor	**equator**
17.	bllanks	**blanks**	blancks	bllancks
18.	honorible	honorrable	**honorable**	honorrible
19.	scaince	sceince	**science**	sciance
20.	mussic	mosic	muscic	**music**
21.	**history**	hisstory	hisctory	histury
22.	lissten	liscten	lysten	**listen**
23.	entrence	enttrance	enttrence	**entrance**
24.	especialy	especailly	especaily	**especially**
25.	mariage	maraige	marraige	**marriage**

Reading Comprehension: Law Enforcement Dogs

Police dogs are dogs that assist cops in solving crimes. In recent years, they have grown to be an essential part of law enforcement. With their unique abilities and bravery, police dogs have saved many lives. They are often regarded as an important and irreplaceable part of many police departments because they are loyal, watchful, and protective of their police officer counterparts.

Today, police dogs are trained in specific areas. They could be considered experts in their field. Some of the particular police dog roles are as follows:

Tracking: Tracking police dogs use their keen sense of smell to locate criminal suspects or missing people. Tracking dogs are trained for years and can track down even the most elusive criminal. Without police tracking dogs, many suspects would be able to elude capture.

Substance Detectors: Like tracking dogs, these police dogs use their sense of smell to assist officers. Substance dogs are trained to detect a specific substance. Some dogs are trained to detect bombs or explosives. These brave dogs are trained not only to detect explosives but also to respond (very carefully!) and safely alert their officer partner to the explosive location. Other dogs may be drawn to illegal drugs. By quickly determining whether an illegal substance is nearby, these dogs save officers from searching through luggage, a car, or other areas by hand.

Public Order - These police dogs assist officers in keeping the peace. They may pursue a criminal suspect and hold them until an officer arrives, or they may guard an area (such as a jail or prison) to prevent suspects from fleeing.

Cadaver Dogs: Although it may sound disgusting, these police dogs are trained to locate dead bodies. This is a critical function in a police department, and these dogs perform admirably.

A police dog is not just any dog. Police dogs require very special and specialized training. There are numerous breeds of dogs that have been trained for police work. What breed they are often determined by the type of work they will do. German Shepherds and Belgian Malinois are two of the most popular breeds today, but other dogs such as Bloodhounds (good for tracking) and Beagles (good for drug detection) are also used. Police dogs, regardless of breed, are typically trained to do their job from the time they are puppies.

Typically, police dogs are regarded as heroes. They frequently go to live with their human partner police officer. They've known this person for years and have grown to consider them family, which works out well for both the officer and the dog.

1. Tracking police dogs use their _____ to locate criminal suspects or missing people.
   a. keen sense of training
   b. keen sense of taste
   c. keen sense of smell

2. Some substance dogs are trained to detect _____.
   a. runaway children
   b. bombs or explosives
   c. metal and iron

3. Police dogs are trained in ___ areas.
   a. many
   b. a few
   c. specific

4. Police dogs are dogs that assist cops in solving _____.
   a. littering
   b. homelessness
   c. crimes

5. Substance dogs are trained to detect a specific _____.
   a. substance
   b. person
   c. other police dogs

6. What type of police dog is trained pursue a criminal suspect and hold them until an officer arrives?
   a. Crime Fighting dog
   b. Tracking dog
   c. Public Order dog

7. These police dogs are trained to locate dead bodies
   a. Law and Order dogs
   b. Cadaver dogs
   c. Deadly Substance dogs

8. What are the two most popular police dogs used today?
   a. German Shepherds and Belgian Malinois
   b. Bloodhounds and German Shepherds
   c. Belgian Malinois and Rottweiler

Geography: Mountain Range

1. A _____ includes geological features that are in the same region as a mountain range.
   a. mountain passes
   b. mountain chain
   c. mountain system

2. _____ are smaller mountain ranges that can be found within larger mountain ranges.
   a. Hill ranges
   b. Subranges
   c. Micro ranges

3. The world's tallest mountain ranges form when pieces of the Earth's crust, known as _____, collide.
   a. core
   b. mantle
   c. plates

4. The tallest mountain range in the world is the _____ and the longest is the ____.
   a. Himalayas, Andes
   b. Andes, Mt. Vinson
   c. Mt. Everest, Manaslu

5. Mountain ranges usually include highlands or _____.
   a. mountain passes and valleys
   b. valleys and rifts
   c. mountain peaks and edges

6. The Andes Mountains are the world's longest mountain range, stretching approximately _____.
   a. 4,300 miles
   b. 5,000 miles
   c. 2,000 miles

7. _____ is a scientific theory that explains how major landforms are created as a result of Earth's subterranean movements.
   a. Erosion
   b. Plate tectonics
   c. Sedimentation

8. The Himalayas run 1,491 miles across much of _____.
   a. Central Europe
   b. South America
   c. Central Asia

9. What is the highest peak in the Rocky Mountain Range that is 14,440 feet tall?
   a. Mt. Everest
   b. Mt. Elbert
   c. Mt. Mayon

10. The majority of geologically young mountain ranges on Earth's land surface are found in either the _____ or the _____.
    a. Alpide belt, Oceanic Ridge belt
    b. Pacific Ring of Fire, Alpide Belt
    c. Oceanic Ridge belt, Circum-Pacific Seismic Belt

11. The _____ runs somewhat parallel to the Rockies, but further west in the United States.
    a. Sierra Nevada Mountain Range
    b. Appalachian
    c. Himalayas

12. Mountains often serve as _____ that define the natural borders of countries.
    a. enclosure
    b. geographic features
    c. barriers

English: Tenses

Verbs are classified into three tenses: past, present, and future. The term "past" refers to events that have already occurred (e.g., earlier in the day, yesterday, last week, three years ago). The present tense is used to describe what is happening right now or what is ongoing. The future tense refers to events that have yet to occur (e.g., later, tomorrow, next week, next year, three years from now).

borrowed	went	eat	play	go	giving
read	give	gave	will eat	yelled	seeing
will have	had	reading	will go	do	will borrow
playing	doing	yelling	did	will yell	will do
will give	fight	borrow	yell	will fight	will play
borrowing	played	fighting	read	have	will see
going	see	will read	fought	eating	ate
saw	having				

Simple Present (11)	Present Progressive (IS/ARE +) (11)	Past (11)	Future (11)
play	playing	played	will play
go	going	went	will go
read	reading	read	will read
borrow	borrowing	borrowed	will borrow
eat	eating	ate	will eat
have	having	had	will have
see	seeing	saw	will see
fight	fighting	fought	will fight
do	doing	did	will do
give	giving	gave	will give
yell	yelling	yelled	will yell

English: Personal Pronouns

Personal pronouns are words that are used to replace the subject or object of a sentence to make it easier for readers to understand.

To give a brief, personal pronouns are:

1. Replace nouns and other pronouns to make sentences easier to read and understand.

2. A sentence's subject or object can be either. For example, 'I' is the first-person subject pronoun, whereas 'me' is the first-person object pronoun.

3. It is possible to use the singular or plural form.

4. They must agree on gender and number with the words they are substituting.

1. Which of the following sentences has a plural subject pronoun and a plural object pronoun?

   a. She wants to live as long as she can, as long as she have someone by her side.

   b. While Tom believe everything will be fine, many don't agree with him.

   c. Whether we lived or died, it didn't matter to us either way.

2. Which of the following words would make the following sentence grammatically correct? '6th graders should check with their teachers before you leave the classroom.'

   a. Replace 'their' with 'they'

   b. Replace 'you' with 'they'

   c. Replace '6th graders' with 'they'

3. The pronoun 'my' is a . . .

   a. 1st person possessive pronoun

   b. 3rd person nominative pronoun

   c. 2nd person possessive pronoun

4. Which of the following correctly identifies the subjective and objective pronouns in the sentence here? 'Run away from the dinosaurs with the giant feet?' she asked. 'You don't have to tell me twice.'

   a. she - subject pronoun; you - subject pronoun; me - object pronoun

   b. she - object pronoun; you - object pronoun; me - object pronoun

   c. she - object pronoun; you - subject pronoun; me - object pronoun

5. The pronoun 'your' is a . . .

   a. 2nd person possessive pronoun

   b. 1st person possessive pronoun

   c. 2nd person objective pronoun

6. Which pronouns are found in the following sentence? 'I kept telling her that we would go back for John, but I knew we had left him behind. '

   a. I, we, knew, we, him

   b. I, her, we, I, we, him

   c. I, we, I, we, him

7. Kevin likes playing basketball. _____ is a very good player.

   a. Him

   b. He

   c. Their

8. The pronoun 'its' is a . . .

   a. 3rd person possessive pronoun

   b. 2nd person possessive pronoun

   c. 3rd person objective pronoun

9. The pronoun 'their' is a . . .

   a. 2nd person possessive pronoun

   b. 3rd person objective pronoun

   c. 3rd person possessive pronoun

10. Kimmy is a very good cook. _____ can cook any kind of food.

   a. She

   b. Hey

   c. Their

English: Nouns, Verbs, Adjectives, Adverbs

A noun is defined as a person, place, thing, or idea that has been used for thousands of years in all spoken languages.

An action verb is a word that shows action. 'What did they do in the sentence?' is one way to find the action verb. Action verbs are necessary for descriptive and informative writing.

Adjectives are descriptive words for nouns. We use them to provide our audience with a more complete and detailed picture of the noun we are describing. What words would you use to describe yourself? Would you describe yourself as intelligent or amusing? Is your room cluttered or neat? When describing something, adjectives are used.

An adverb is a word that modifies another word, such as a verb, adjective, or adverb. Adverbs improve the precision and interest of writing. Adverbs answer these questions:

- When?
- Where?
- In what manner?
- To what extent?

1. Which of the following is NOT a noun?
   - a. place
   - b. person
   - c. action

2. A verb is a(n) _____.
   - a. action
   - b. word that describes a noun
   - c. person, place, thing, or idea

3. True or False: An adjective describes a verb.
   - a. True
   - b. False

4. Adverbs describe or modify _____.
   - a. adverbs
   - b. adjectives
   - c. verbs

5. What is the adverb in the sentence? Peter neatly wrote a shopping list.
   - a. Peter
   - b. wrote
   - c. neatly

6. Which sentence shows the proper use of an adverb?
   - a. Jim quick walked.
   - b. Jim walked quickly.
   - c. Jim walked quick.

7. Which of the following words is a common noun identifying a person?
   - a. Dr. Jones
   - b. doctor
   - c. Mr. Jones

8. Which of the following nouns is a proper noun?
   - a. Cat
   - b. Central Park
   - c. Fireman

9. Which sentence part contains an action verb?
   - a. baseball or soccer
   - b. eat an ice cream cone
   - c. to the top of the hill and back

10. Adjectives are words that describe what?
   - a. nouns
   - b. other adjectives
   - c. verbs

11. Which adjective would best describe a cat?
   - a. sharp
   - b. furry
   - c. cold

12. Which sentence gives the clearest picture using adjectives?
   - a. The tall, fast lady runs.
   - b. The lady runs fast.
   - c. The sleek, slender, funny little lady runs.

More **Spelling Words**

Fill in the blanks with the correct spelling word.

drank	personal	equipment	I've	heavy
Arkansas	spaghetti	direction	moral	twenty
exist	choose	Wednesday	growls	Japanese
junior	wouldn't	empty		

1. You will make __twenty__ dollars per day.

2. My dog __growls__ at everyone.

3. We sat outside and __drank__ tea.

4. We have a __moral__ obligation to do the right thing.

5. There is an __empty__ lot for sale.

6. The painting is much too __heavy__ to carry by myself.

7. She said we could have lunch on __Wednesday__.

8. My favorite food is __spaghetti__.

9. My uncle has a cabin in __Arkansas__.

10. I didn't even know that they still __exist__.

11. There's no need to get __personal__.

12. My best friend is __Japanese__.

13. She is a __junior__ partner in the law firm.

14. Our __equipment__ is old and broken.

15. A palindrome can be read in either __direction__ like the word mom.

16. I just can't __choose__ between these shoes.

17. He __wouldn't__ tell the secret to anyone.

18. __I've__ always loved to walk on the beach.

More Spelling Words IV

Fill in the blanks with the correct spelling word.

reminded	yesterday	frozen	district	frilly
excellent	terrible	surface	scoop	Florida
present	extent	professors	numb	arrived
mistletoe	graduation			

1. The ground is still **frozen** .

2. We are planning a **graduation** party.

3. Your blue dress is so **frilly** .

4. I will **scoop** out some beans into this bag.

5. The flower was near dead when it **arrived** .

6. The ideas that Kevin had were **excellent** .

7. This **district** will vote at the main office.

8. My hand was almost **numb** .

9. The picture **reminded** me of how much fun we had.

10. The **extent** of the damage was unknown.

11. We will buy the teacher a **present** .

12. The **surface** was smooth and cold.

13. I told you about the test **yesterday** .

14. This program was created by **professors** .

15. My haircut looks **terrible** .

16. My mom will hang **mistletoe** over the door.

17. **Florida** is a peninsula.

Spelling Words Lesson

Write and circle the correct spelling for each word.

	A	B	C	D
1.	grravity	grraviti	graviti	**gravity**
2.	jewelri	jewellri	jewellry	**jewelry**
3.	obstroct	**obstruct**	obsctruct	obsstruct
4.	trompet	trrumpet	**trumpet**	trrompet
5.	imigrant	imygrant	immygrant	**immigrant**
6.	**oxygen**	oxygfn	oxyjen	oxyjtn
7.	sensse	sence	**sense**	sensce
8.	judje	juqje	**judge**	judne
9.	altitode	alltitude	alltitode	**altitude**
10.	**December**	Decemberr	Desember	Desemberr
11.	**tolerable**	tolerible	tollerible	tollerable
12.	acttive	actyve	acttyve	**active**
13.	**aware**	awarre	awarra	awara
14.	trryple	tryple	trriple	**triple**
15.	exselent	excelent	exsellent	**excellent**
16.	adaptible	adapttible	**adaptable**	adapttable
17.	Ausstralia	Ausstralai	Australai	**Australia**
18.	syngle	singlle	**single**	synglle
19.	**launch**	luanch	laonch	loanch
20.	smyled	smilled	**smiled**	smylled
21.	finanse	**finance**	finense	finence
22.	**climb**	cllymb	cllimb	clymb
23.	introducsion	inttroduction	**introduction**	inttroducsion
24.	Japanece	**Japanese**	Japanesse	Japanesce
25.	speciallize	**specialize**	specailize	specaillize
26.	gulible	**gullible**	gulable	gullably

Spelling Words Lesson IV

	A	B	C	D
1.	enttared	**entered**	enttered	entared
2.	**ignorant**	ignurrant	ignurant	ignorrant
3.	brilaint	**brilliant**	briliant	brillaint
4.	**wonder**	wonderr	wunder	wunderr
5.	horable	horible	horrable	**horrible**
6.	horicane	huricane	horricane	**hurricane**
7.	Aprryl	**April**	Apryl	Aprril
8.	respirasion	**respiration**	resspiration	resspirasion
9.	**information**	infformasion	infformation	informasion
10.	crruel	croel	**cruel**	crroel
11.	**January**	Janaurry	Janaury	Januarry
12.	buttom	botom	**bottom**	butom
13.	**bicycle**	bicicle	bicyclle	biciclle
14.	cumett	comett	**comet**	cumet
15.	recieved	reseived	**received**	recyeved
16.	**students**	sttudents	sttodents	stodents
17.	movenment	movenmentt	movementt	**movement**
18.	cumpay	cumpany	**company**	compay
19.	disclike	disslike	dislicke	**dislike**
20.	**sheepish**	shepysh	shepish	sheapish
21.	**surprise**	surrprise	surprice	surrprice
22.	politicain	polliticain	pollitician	**politician**
23.	**senator**	senattur	senatur	senattor
24.	endoy	**enjoy**	enjyy	enjuy
25.	pattroit	pattriot	**patriot**	patroit
26.	brruise	bruice	**bruise**	brruice
27.	**sleeve**	sleve	seeave	tlave

Science: Temperate Forest Biome

1. _____ are found in Northern Hemisphere regions with moist, warm summers and cold winters, primarily in eastern North America, eastern Asia, and western Europe.

   a. Wild forests

   b. Rainforests

   c. Deciduous forests

2. How many types of forest biomes are there?

   a. 2

   b. 3

   c. 4

3. Temperate forests emerged during the period of global cooling that began at the beginning of the

   _____.

   a. Medieval Era

   b. Paleozoic Era

   c. Cenozoic Era

4. Major temperate forests are located in the following areas, except for:

   a. Japan

   b. Korea

   c. Eastern China

5. What makes a forest a temperate forest?

   a. Temperature, Two seasons, Tropics, and Clay soil.

   b. Temperature, Climate, Wet season, and Loam soil.

   c. Temperature, Four seasons, Lots of rain, and Fertile soil.

6. The three main types of forest biomes are: the rainforest, the temperate forest, and the _____.

   a. Taiga

   b. Broad-leafed

   c. Coniferous

7. Many trees rely on _____ to get through the winter.

   a. temperature

   b. sap

   c. rain

8. Temperate forests are usually classified into two main groups, and these are: _____ and _____.

   a. Indigenous, Evergreen

   b. Deciduous, Evergreen

   c. Coniferous, Deciduous

9. Deciduous is a Latin word that means _____.

   a. "to subside"

   b. "to rise up"

   c. "to fall off"

10. Certain trees in a temperate forest can grow up to how many feet?

   a. 50 feet tall

   b. 90 feet tall

   c. 100 feet tall

11. _____ forests are made up mostly of conifer trees such as cypress, cedar, redwood, fir, juniper, and pine trees.

   a. Coniferous

   b. Broad-leafed

   c. Mixed coniferous and broad-leafed

12. The animals that live in temperate forests have _____ that allow them to _____ in different kinds of weather.

   a. adaptations, survive

   b. conformity, thrive

   c. compatibility, survive

Science: Mallard Duck

First, read the entire passage. After that, go back and fill in the blanks. You can skip the blanks you're unsure about and finish them later.

plants	habitats	female	bodies	quacking
North	hatch	foods	waddle	colors

The Mallard Duck is what most people think of when they think of ducks. The Mallard is a common duck that can be found throughout __North__ America, Europe, and Asia. Central America, Australia, and New Zealand are also home to the Mallard Duck. Anas Platyrhynchos is the scientific name for the Mallard Duck. It belongs to the Dabbling Ducks family. Mallard Ducks enjoy the water and are commonly found near rivers, ponds, and other __bodies__ of water.

Mallard ducks can grow to be about two feet long and weigh about two and a half pounds. The __female__ Mallard Duck has tan feathers all over, whereas the male Mallard Duck has a green head, darker back and chest feathers, and a white body. Some people breed domestic Mallard Ducks in order to get different __colors__ .

Mallards are omnivorous birds. This means that they consume both __plants__ and other animals. They primarily feed on the water's surface, consuming various seeds, small fish, insects, frogs, and fish eggs. They also enjoy some human __foods__ , particularly grain from human crops.

Female Mallard ducks are well-known for their "quack." When you were a kid and learned that ducks make a __quacking__ sound, you were hearing the female Mallard. Females quack to attract other ducks, usually their ducklings. This call is also known as the "hail call" or "decrescendo call." This call can be heard for miles by the ducklings.

Like many other birds, Mallard ducks migrate in flocks from the north to the south for the winter and then back north for the summer. This way, they're always where it's warm, and there's food. These ducks are also adaptable in other ways. They thrive even when humans destroy their natural __habitats__ . This is not to say that we should destroy their habitat, but they have not been endangered due to human interaction thus far.

Ducklings are young Mallards. A mother duck will typically lay 10 to 15 eggs. She cares for the eggs in a nest by herself. The mother duck will lead the ducklings to the water shortly after they __hatch__ from the eggs. They usually do not return to the nest after that. Baby ducklings are ready to go just a few hours after hatching. They can swim, __waddle__ , feed themselves, and find food quickly. For the next few months, their mother will keep an eye on them and protect them. The ducklings will be able to fly and become self-sufficient after about two months.

Science Multiple Choice
Quiz: Tyrannosaurus Rex

Tyrannosaurus Rex, one of the most famous and notable dinosaurs, is a theropod dinosaur. Many Tyrannosaurus fossils have been discovered, allowing scientists to learn more about how big it was, how it hunted, and how it lived.

Tyrannosaurus rex was a land predator dinosaur that was one of the largest. The T-rex could grow to be 43 feet long and weigh up to 7.5 tons. Because of its size and overall fearsome image, the dinosaur is frequently used in movies and films such as Jurassic Park.

Tyrannosaurus rex was a two-legged dinosaur. This means it could walk and run on two legs. These two legs were large and strong enough to support the dinosaur's massive weight. The T-arms, rex's, on the other hand, were relatively small. However, it is believed that the small arms were powerful to hold onto prey.

The Tyrannosaurus' massive skull and large teeth are among its most terrifying features. T-rex skulls as long as 5 feet have been discovered! Other evidence suggests that the Tyrannosaurus had a powerful bite that allowed it to crush other dinosaurs' bones easily when combined with sharp teeth.

The Tyrannosaurus Rex ate meat from other animals and dinosaurs. Still, it is unclear whether it was a predator (hunted and killed its food) or a scavenger (meaning it stole food from other predators). Many scientists believe the dinosaur did both. Much is dependent on how fast the dinosaur was. Some claim that the T-Rex was fast and capable of catching its prey. Others argue that the dinosaur was slow and used its fearsome jaws to frighten other predators and steal their prey.

There are numerous significant Tyrannosaurus specimens in museums around the world. "Sue" at the Field Museum of Natural History in Chicago is one of the largest and most comprehensive. "Stan," another significant T-Rex specimen, can be found at the Black Hills Museum of Natural History Exhibit in Hill City, South Dakota. Also on display at the American Museum of Natural History in New York, paleontologist Barnum Brown's largest Tyrannosaurus find (he discovered five in total). The only known Tyrannosaurus Rex track can be found at Philmont Scout Ranch in New Mexico.

Remember that there may be some **question-answer relationship (QAR)** questions, so please keep that in mind when answering the questions below.

1. The T-rex usually measures up to _____ and weighs as much as _____.
   a. 43 feet, 2 tons
   b. 43 feet, 7.5 tons

2. The Tyrannosaurus rex was a _____ dinosaur.
   a. quadrupedal
   b. bipedal

3. The T-rex is a member of the dinosaur subgroup _____, which includes all the flesh-eating dinosaurs.
   a. Thyreophora
   b. Theropoda

4. The Tyrannosaurus rex lived in North America between 65 and 98 million years ago, during the late _____ period.
   a. Cretaceous
   b. Triassic

5. Where could we find the only documented track of a Tyrannosaurus Rex?
   a. at Philmont Scout Ranch in New Mexico
   b. at the Field Museum of Natural History in Chicago

6. Which of the following is the largest and most complete T-rex specimen that can be found on display at the Field Museum of Natural History in Chicago?
   a. Stan
   b. Sue

7. The Tyrannosaurus had a life span of around _____.
   a. 30 years
   b. 50 years

8. It is one of the most ferocious predators to ever walk the Earth.
   a. Giganotosaurus
   b. Tyrannosaurus rex

9. Tyrannosaurus rex was also adept at finding its prey through its keen sense of _____.
   a. smell
   b. sight

10. Tyrannosaurus rex (rex meaning "_____" in Latin).
    a. king
    b. master

Reading Storytime: The Frog

When wishing was a thing, there was a King whose daughters were all __beautiful__, but the youngest was so stunning that even the sun, which has seen so much, was taken aback whenever it shone in her face.

A large dark forest lay close to the King's __castle__, and a fountain was hidden beneath an old lime tree in the woods. When it was a hot day, the King's Child went out into the forest and sat by the cool fountain, and when she was bored, she took a golden ball, threw it up in the air, and caught it. And the ball was her favorite toy.

Now, one day, the King's Daughter's golden __ball__ fell onto the ground and rolled straight into the water rather than into the little hand she was holding up for it. The King's Daughter pursued it with her eyes, but it vanished, and the well was deep, so deep that the bottom could not be seen. She began to cry, and she screamed louder and louder, and she could not be consoled.

And as she sobbed, someone asked her, "What ails you, King's Daughter?" You weep so much that even a stone would feel sorry for you."

When she turned around to the side from which the voice had come, she saw a __Frog__ sticking its thick, ugly head out of the water. "Ah! "Is it you, old water-splasher?" she asked, "I am weeping for my golden ball, which has fallen into the fountain."

"Be quiet and do not weep," the Frog replied, "I can help you." But what will you give me if I bring up your toy again?"

"Whatever you want, dear Frog," she said, "my clothes, my pearls, and jewels, even the golden crown I'm wearing."

"I don't care for your clothes, pearls, and jewels, or your golden crown," the Frog replied, "but if you will love me and let me be your __companion__ and playfellow, and sit by you at your little table, and eat off your little golden plate, and drink out of your little cup, and sleep in your little bed-if you promise me this, I will go down below and bring your golden ball up again."

"Oh, yes," she said, "I promise you everything you want if you just bring my ball back." "How the silly Frog does talk!" she thought. He lives in the water with the other frogs and croaks and can't be a human's companion!"

But, having received this promise, the Frog plunged his head into the water and sank. He quickly came __swimming__ up with the ball in his mouth, and threw it on the grass. The King's Daughter was thrilled to see her pretty plaything again, and she quickly picked it up and ran away with it.

"Wait, wait," the Frog said. "Bring me along. I can't run as fast as you." But what good did it do him to scream his croak, croak, croak, croak, croak, croak! She ignored it and ran home, quickly forgetting the poor Frog, who was forced to return to his __fountain__.

The next day, as she sat at the table with the King and all the courtiers, eating from her little golden plate, something crept up the marble staircase, splish splash, splish splash. When it reached the top, it knocked on the __door__ and cried out:

"Youngest King's Daughter."
"Please open the door!"

She dashed outside to see who was there, but when she opened the door, the Frog was standing in front of it. Then she hurriedly slammed the door, sat down to __dinner__ again, and was terrified.

"My Child, what are you so afraid of?" said the King, seeing her heart beating furiously. Is there a Giant outside looking to take you away?"

"Ah, no," she replied, "it's a disgusting Frog, not a Giant."

"What exactly does the Frog want from you?"

"Ah, dear Father, my golden ball fell into the water yesterday while I was sitting by the fountain in the forest, playing." Because I __cried__ so much, the Frog brought it out for me again. And because he insisted, I promised him he could be my companion, but I never imagined he'd be able to get out of the water! And now he's here, wanting to come in."

Meanwhile, it knocked a second time and cried:

"Youngest King's Daughter!"
Allow me to enter!
Don't you remember yesterday and everything you said to me, besides the cooling fountain's spray?
Youngest King's Daughter!
"Let me in!"

Music: The Piano

Bartolomeo Cristofori was the first to successfully develop a hammer-action keyboard instrument and hence deserves to be regarded as the creator of the piano.

Cristofori was dissatisfied with musicians' lack of control over the harpsichord's loudness level. Around 1700, he is credited for replacing the plucking mechanism with a hammer and thus creating the modern piano. Initially, the instrument was dubbed "clavicembalo con piano e forte" (literally, a harpsichord that can play soft and loud noises). This was later abbreviated to the now-common term "piano."

The piano possesses the characteristics of both a string and percussion instrument. A hammer strikes a string inside the piano (much like a percussion instrument). The piano's sounds and notes are produced by the vibration of these strings (like a string instrument).

The piano is commonly referred to as a keyboard instrument. This is because it is performed similarly to several other keyboard instruments, including the organ, harpsichord, electronic keyboards, and synthesizers.

The organ was the first keyboard instrument, dating back to the third century. However, the organ did not begin to use keys until much later. The harpsichord was invented in the 14th century and quickly gained popularity throughout Europe. The harpsichord plucked a string and resembled modern pianos in appearance. However, plucking the string did not allow for the playing of various volumes and expressions.

The term piano is derived from the Italian phrase pianoforte, which translates as "loud and soft." This is because you may now adjust the volume of notes played on the keyboard.

The grand piano and the upright piano are the two primary types of pianos.

Grand piano - a grand piano's strings and primary frame are horizontal. This enables longer strings and also aids in the piano's mechanics. However, grand pianos can consume a significant amount of room.

Upright piano - This piano style is more compact, making it ideal for use in a home. The strings and mainframe are arranged vertically.

Additionally, there are electronic pianos. While the keyboard and playing technique is typically identical to a standard piano, the sound is frequently quite different.

1. This piano style is more compact, making it ideal for use in a home.
   a. Upright piano
   b. Downright piano

2. A _____ strings and primary frame are horizontal.
   a. organ piano's
   b. grand piano's

3. The term piano is derived from the _____ phrase pianoforte.
   a. English
   b. Italian

4. The _____ was invented in the 14th century.
   a. pianiochord
   b. harpsichord

5. The piano is commonly referred to as a _____ instrument.
   a. singer
   b. keyboard

6. The organ and harpsichord are keyboard instruments.
   a. organ
   b. guitar

Music: Jimi Hendrix

First, read the entire passage. After that, go back and fill in the blanks. You can skip the blanks you're unsure about and finish them later.

guitar	odd	acoustic	mother	Animals
guitarist	stage	Seattle	rock	childhood

Jimi Hendrix, a __guitarist__ , singer, and songwriter, wowed audiences in the 1960s with his outrageous electric guitar skills and experimental sound.

Jimi Hendrix began playing guitar as a teenager and grew up to become a __rock__ legend known for his innovative electric guitar playing in the 1960s. His performance of "The Star-Spangled Banner" at Woodstock in 1969 was one of his most memorable. Hendrix died of drug-related complications in 1970, leaving his imprint on the world of rock music and remaining popular to this day.

On November 27, 1942, in __Seattle__ , Washington, Hendrix was born Johnny Allen Hendrix (later changed by his father to James Marshall). He had a difficult __childhood__ , living in the care of relatives or acquaintances at times.

When Hendrix was born, his __mother__ , Lucille, was only 17 years old. She had a rocky relationship with his father, Al, and eventually left the family after the couple had two more sons, Leon and Joseph. Hendrix only saw his mother on rare occasions before her death in 1958.

Music became a haven for Hendrix in many ways. He was a fan of blues and rock and roll and taught himself to play the __guitar__ with the help of his father.

When Hendrix was 16, his father bought him his first __acoustic__ guitar, and the following year, his first electric guitar - a right-handed Supro Ozark that he had to play upside down because he was naturally left-handed. Soon after, he started performing with his band, the Rocking Kings. In 1959, he dropped out of high school and worked __odd__ jobs while pursuing his musical dreams.

In mid-1966, Hendrix met Chas Chandler, bassist for the British rock band the __Animals__ , who agreed to become Hendrix's manager. Chandler persuaded Hendrix to travel to London, where he formed the Jimi Hendrix Experience with bassist Noel Redding and drummer Mitch Mitchell.

While performing in England, Hendrix amassed a cult following among the country's rock royalty, with the Beatles, Rolling Stones, Who, and Eric Clapton all praising his work. According to one critic for the British music magazine Melody Maker, he "had great __stage__ presence" and appeared to be playing "with no hands at all" at times.

According to one journalist in the Berkeley Tribe, "Nobody could get more out of an electric guitar than Jimi Hendrix. He was the ultimate guitarist."

History: The Mayflower

First, read the entire passage. After that, go back and fill in the blanks. You can skip the blanks you're unsure about and finish them later.

ship	sail	voyage	assist	settlers
passengers	illness	load	leaking	Cape

In 1620, a __ship__ called the Mayflower transported a group of English colonists to North America. These people established New England's first permanent European colony in what is now Plymouth, Massachusetts. Later, they were named the Pilgrims.

The Mayflower was approximately 106 feet long, 25 feet wide, and had a tonnage of 180. The deck of the Mayflower was about 80 feet long, roughly the length of a basketball court. The ship had three masts for holding sails:

The fore-mast (in front)

The main-mast (in the middle)

The mizzen mast (in the back) (back)

On August 4, 1620, the Mayflower and the Speedwell set sail from Southampton, England. They had to come to a halt in Dartmouth, however, because the Speedwell was leaking. They left Dartmouth on August 21, but the Speedwell began __leaking__ again, and they came to a halt in Plymouth, England. They decided to abandon the Speedwell at Plymouth and __load__ as many passengers as possible onto the Mayflower. On September 6, 1620, they set sail from Plymouth.

The Mayflower set __sail__ from Plymouth, England, west across the Atlantic Ocean. The ship's original destination was Virginia, but storms forced it to change course. On November 9, 1620, more than two months after leaving Plymouth, the Mayflower sighted __Cape__ Cod. The Pilgrims decided to stay even though they were north of where they had planned to settle.

It is estimated that around 30 children were on board the Mayflower during the epic __voyage__ to America, but little is known about many of them.

They were children of passengers, some traveled with other adults, and some were servants - but having young people among the __settlers__ was critical to the Plymouth Colony's survival.

It is believed that when the colonists faced their first harsh winter of __illness__ and death in a new land, the children would __assist__ the adults by tending to the sick, assisting in the preparation of food, and fetching firewood and water.

While nearly half of the ship's __passengers__ died during the winter of 1620/1621, it is believed that there were fewer deaths among the children, implying that the struggling colony had a better chance of thriving.

Health: The Food Groups

Eating healthy foods is especially important for children because they are still developing. Children's bodies require nutrition to develop strong, healthy __bones__ and muscles. You will not grow as tall or as strong as you could if you do not get all the __vitamins__ and minerals you require while growing.

Healthy food includes a wide variety of fresh foods from the five healthy food groups:

Dairy: Milk, cheese, and __yogurt__ are the most critical dairy foods, which are necessary for strong and healthy bones. There aren't many other foods in our diet that have as much calcium as these.

Fruit: Fruit contains vitamins, minerals, dietary fiber, and various phytonutrients (nutrients found naturally in plants) that help your body stay healthy. Fruits and vegetables provide you with energy, vitamins, antioxidants, fiber, and __water__. These nutrients help protect you against diseases later in life, such as heart disease, stroke, and some cancers.

Vegetables and legumes/beans: Vegetables should account for a large __portion__ of your daily food intake and should be encouraged at all meals (including snack times). To keep your body healthy, they supply vitamins, minerals, dietary fiber, and phytonutrients (nutrients found naturally in plants).

Grain (cereal) foods: choose wholegrain and/or high __fiber__ bread, cereals, rice, pasta, noodles, and so on. These foods provide you with the energy you require to grow, develop, and learn. Refined grain products (such as cakes and biscuits) can contain added sugar, fat, and sodium.

Protein from lean meats and poultry, fish, eggs, tofu, nuts and seeds, and legumes/beans is used by our bodies to __produce__ specialized chemicals such as hemoglobin and adrenalin. Protein also helps to build, maintain, and __repair__ tissues in our bodies. Protein is the primary component of muscles and organs (such as your heart).

Calories are a unit of measurement for the amount of energy in food. We gain calories when we eat, which gives us the energy to run around and do things. If we __consume__ more calories than we expend while moving, our bodies will store the excess calories as fat. If we burn more calories than we consume, our bodies will begin to burn the previously __stored__ fat.

Grammar: Singular and Plural

1. Which word is NOT a plural noun?

   a. books

   b. hat

   c. toys

2. Which word is a singular noun?

   a. bikes

   b. cars

   c. pencil

3. Which word can be both singular and plural?

   a. deer

   b. bears

   c. mice

4. Tommy _____ badminton at the court.

   a. playing

   b. plays

   c. play's

5. They _____ to eat at fast food restaurants once in a while.

   a. likes

   b. like

   c. likies

6. Everybody _____ Janet Jackson.

   a. know

   b. known

   c. knows

7. He ___ very fast. You have to listen carefully.

   a. spoken

   b. speak

   c. speaks

8. Which one is the singular form of women?

   a. womans

   b. woman

   c. women

9. The plural form of tooth is

   a. tooths

   b. toothes

   c. teeth

10. The singular form of mice is _____.

   a. mouse

   b. mices

   c. mouses

11. The plural form of glass is _____.

   a. glassies

   b. glasses

   c. glassy

12. The plural form of dress is _____.

   a. dressing

   b. dresses

   c. dressy

13. Plural means many.

   a. True

   b. False

14. Singular means 1.

   a. True

   b. False

15. Is this word singular or plural? monsters

   a. plural

   b. singular

16. Find the plural noun in the sentence. They gave her a nice vase full of flowers.

   a. they

   b. flowers

   c. vase

17. **Find the plural noun in the sentence. Her baby brother grabbed the crayons out of the box and drew on the wall.**

   a. crayons

   b. box

   c. brothers

18. **Find the plural noun in the sentence. My friend, Lois, picked enough red strawberries for the whole class.**

   a. strawberries

   b. friends

   c. classes

19. **What is the correct plural form of the noun wish?**

   a. wishes

   b. wishs

   c. wishy

20. **What is the correct plural form of the noun flurry?**

   a. flurrys

   b. flurryies

   c. flurries

21. **What is the correct plural form of the noun box?**

   a. boxs

   b. boxses

   c. boxes

22. **What is the correct plural form of the noun bee?**

   a. beess

   b. beeses

   c. bees

23. **What is the correct plural form of the noun candy?**

   a. candys

   b. candyies

   c. candies

24. **Find the singular noun in the sentence. The boys and girls drew pictures on the sidewalk.**

   a. boys

   b. drew

   c. sidewalk

Grammar Review

1. **His father is the coach of the team.**
   - a. his, father, team
   - b. his, father, coach
   - c. | father, coach, team |

2. **David is driving to the beach.**
   - a. David, driving, beach
   - b. David, driving
   - c. | David, beach |

3. **What are the PROPER nouns in the following sentence?   My grandparents live in Florida.**
   - a. grandparents, Flordia
   - b. | Flordia |
   - c. My, grandparents

4. **What are all the COMMON nouns in the following sentence?   I have two dogs and one cat.**
   - a. cat, one
   - b. | dogs, cat |
   - c. I, dogs

5. **Which sentence contains only one common noun and one proper noun?**
   - a. | These potatoes are from Idaho. |
   - b. Casey is a talented singer and dancer.
   - c. I live near the border of Nevada and Utah.

6. **Which sentence contains the correct form of a plural noun?**
   - a. | The wolves chase a frightened rabbit. |
   - b. The wolfes chase a frightened rabbit.
   - c. The wolfs chase a frightened rabbit.

7. **Which sentence contains one singular noun and one plural noun?**
   - a. The musician tunes her instrument.
   - b. The conductor welcomes each musician.
   - c. | The singers walk across the stage. |

8. **Identify the collective noun in the following sentence.**
   Derek is the lead singer in a band.
   - a. singer
   - b. | band |
   - c. lead

9. **Which sentence contains the correct form of a singular possessive noun?**
   - a. The boxs' lid is torn.
   - b. | The box's lid is torn. |
   - c. The boxes' lid is torn.

10. **Which sentence contains one concrete noun and on abstract noun?**
    - a. | John feels anxiety about meeting new people. |
    - b. The young boy plays with trains.
    - c. The sand feels warm between my toes.

11. **Identify the simple subject in the following sentence.   The children are playing tag.**
    - a. tag
    - b. | children |
    - c. The children

12. **Identify the simple subject in the following sentence.**
    This computer belongs to my father.
    - a. | computer |
    - b. This computer
    - c. father

13. **Which sentence has an object of a preposition?**

    a. Several passengers missed the flight.

    b. Seattle is a city in Washington.

    c. The boys are racing remote-controlled cars.

14. **Identify the object of preposition in the following sentence.**
    The are playing a game of cards.

    a. cards

    b. game

    c. of cards

15. **Identify the subject complement in the following sentence.**
    Mr. Smith is a talented poet.

    a. poet

    b. talented

    c. Mr. Smith

16. **Identify the subject complement in the following sentence.**
    Tulips and daisies are my favorite flowers.

    a. my

    b. flowers

    c. favorite

17. **Identify the direct object in the following sentence.** **Tyler delivers newspapers each morning.**

    a. newspapers

    b. morning

    c. each

18. **Identify the direct object in the following sentence.** **We will paint the bathroom beige.**

    a. bathroom

    b. paint

    c. beige

19. **Identify the indirect object in the following sentence.** **Mr. Jackson gave the students their grades.**

    a. grades

    b. students

    c. their

20. **Identify the indirect object in the following sentence.** **Mrs. Parker bought her husband a new tie.**

    a. new tie

    b. husband

    c. tie

21. **In which sentence is paint used as a noun?**

    a. These artists paint the most amazing murals.

    b. We need two cans of brown paint.

    c. Let's paint the bedroom light green.

22. **In which sentence is sign used as a verb?**

    a. I saw it as a sign of good luck.

    b. Joelle is learning sign language.

    c. Did you sign the letter at the bottom?

23. **In which sentence is file used as an adjective?**

    a. This file contains the detective's notes.

    b. Put these papers in a file folder.

    c. I use a file to smooth the edges of my nails.

24. **Identify the direct address in the following sentence.** **This is your baseball bat, Kenny.**

    a. Kenny

    b. baseball

    c. bat

25. **Identify the direct address in the following sentence.**
    Hector, did you buy more milk?

    a. Hector

    b. you

    c. milk

26. **Objects of the preposition. Lee cried during the movie.**

    a. Lee

    b. movie

    c. cried

27. **Objects of the preposition. The phone is on the table.**

    a. | table |

    b. phone

    c. none

28. **Direct Objects: Every actor played his part.**

    a. | his part |

    b. actor

    c. played

29. **Direct Objects: The crowd will cheer the President.**

    a. | the President |

    b. cheer

    c. crowd

30. **Examples of concrete nouns are:**

    a. | flower, music, bear, pie, |

    b. love, cars, them, went

    c. me, I, she, they

31. **Direct Address: Well certainly, Mother, I remember what you said.**

    a. you

    b. | Mother |

    c. certainly

32. **Direct Address: I heard exactly what you said, Pam.**

    a. | Pam |

    b. none

    c. you

33. **Collective Noun: A choir of singers**

    a. | choir |

    b. sing

    c. singers

34. **Collective Noun: A litter of puppies**

    a. | litter |

    b. puppies

    c. puppy

Geography: Lebanon

1. Lebanon is a country in the _____, on the Mediterranean Sea.

   a. Middle East

   b. Western Europe

   c. Africa

2. Lebanon has _____ rivers all of which are non-navigable.

   a. 16

   b. 18

   c. 17

3. What is the capital city of Lebanon?

   a. Tyre

   b. Sidon

   c. Beirut

4. Lebanon has a moderate _____.

   a. Mediterranean climate

   b. Continental climate

   c. Temperate climate

5. When the Ottoman Empire collapsed after World War I, which country took control of Lebanon?

   a. France

   b. Britain

   c. Russia

6. When did Lebanon become a sovereign under the authority of the Free French government?

   a. November 26, 1943

   b. September 1, 1926

   c. May 25, 1926

7. What is the national symbol in Lebanon?

   a. Maple tree

   b. Pine tree

   c. Cedar tree

8. Lebanon is bordered by _____ to the north and east, _____ to the south, and the Mediterranean Sea to the west.

   a. Israel, France

   b. Japan, Korea

   c. Syria, Israel

9. Lebanon is divided into how many governorates?

   a. 7

   b. 8

   c. 6

10. The Cedar Revolution occurred in 2005, following the assassination of Lebanese Prime Minister _____ in a car bomb explosion.

   a. Fakhr-al-Din II

   b. Rafik Hariri

   c. Jabal Amel

11. The city of _____ is one of the oldest continuously inhabited cities in the world.

   a. Byblos

   b. Baalbek

   c. Beirut

12. Lebanon is divided into how many districts?

   a. 24

   b. 25

   c. 22

13. Lebanon's capital and largest city is _____.

Beirut

14. Lebanon was conquered by the _____ Empire in the 16th century

Ottoman

15. Lebanon is a _____ country.

developing

16. Lebanon gained a measure of independence while France was occupied by _____.

Germany

17. Lebanon supported neighboring Arab countries in a war against _____.

Israel

18. How old is Lebanon?

nearly 5,000 years of history

Biography: Calvin Coolidge

1. **Calvin Coolidge was the _____ of the United States.**
   - a. 30th President
   - b. 31st President
   - c. 29th President

2. **Calvin Coolidge served as President from _____ to _____.**
   - a. 1923-1929
   - b. 1929-1933
   - c. 1913-1921

3. **He is also famous for _____ earning him the nickname _____.**
   - a. breaking up large companies, The Trust Buster
   - b. bing excellent in academic, schoolmaster
   - c. being a man of few words, Silent Cal

4. **Calvin grew up in the small town of _____.**
   - a. Plymouth, Vermont
   - b. Staunton, Virginia
   - c. New York, New York

5. **Calvin Coolidge signed the _____, which gave full U.S. citizen rights to all Native Americans.**
   - a. The Dawes Act
   - b. Indian Citizenship Act
   - c. Indian Civil Rights Act

6. **Who was the Vice President under Calvin Coolidge's administration?**
   - a. Charles Curtis
   - b. Thomas Riley Sherman
   - c. Charles Gates Dawes

7. **Coolidge gained national recognition during the 1919 _____ when he served as governor.**
   - a. Boston Police Strike
   - b. Baltimore Police Strike
   - c. NYPD Police Strike

8. **Calvin died of a sudden heart attack _____ years after leaving the presidency.**
   - a. five
   - b. three
   - c. four

9. **Calvin Coolidge became President of the United States after his predecessor, _____ died in office.**
   - a. Warren Harding
   - b. William Taft
   - c. Herbert Hoover

10. **The _____ is a nickname for the 1920s in the United States as it was a time of hope, prosperity, and cultural change during President Calvin Coolidge's presidential term.**
    - a. Roaring Twenties
    - b. Gilded Age
    - c. Reconstruction

11. **Which of the following words best describes President Calvin Coolidge's personality?**
    - a. quiet
    - b. adventurous
    - c. talkative

12. **What was Calvin Coolidge's campaign slogan when he ran for President of the United States?**
    - a. Keep Cool with Coolidge
    - b. Coolidge, For the Future
    - c. Peace, Prosperity, and Coolidge

Art: J. M. W. Turner

Joseph Mallord William Turner, also known as William Turner, was an English Romantic painter, printmaker, and watercolorist. He is well-known for his expressive colorizations, imaginative landscapes, and turbulent, often violent sea paintings.

On April 23, 1775, J. M. W. Turner was born above his father's barbershop in London, England. When Joseph was a child, he began to draw pictures. He enjoyed drawing outside scenes, particularly buildings. His father's shop sold some of his drawings.

He began attending the Royal Academy of Art in London when he was fourteen years old. He kept sketching and painting with watercolors. Many of his sketches were published in magazines. While he mostly drew buildings and architecture, he also began to draw some seascapes.

In 1796, Turner completed his first oil painting. Fishermen at Sea was the title. Turner gained a national reputation as a talented artist as a result of the painting's critical acclaim. Many people compared his work to that of other well-known painters.

Turner was captivated by the power of God in natural scenes, particularly the ocean and the sun. He would make numerous sketches in numbered notebooks, which he would then reference when painting in his studio. He frequently included people in his paintings, but they were small and insignificant compared to the power of nature around them.

Turner's work evolved, with less emphasis on detail and more emphasis on the energy of the natural phenomenon he was painting, such as the sea, a storm, a fire, or the sun. The paintings' objects became less recognizable.

The painting Rain, Steam, and Speed is an example of this. Light and mist are used to power the train engine as it moves down the track in this landscape of a locomotive crossing a bridge. The focus is on the color and changing light as the train passes through the landscape.

Many of Turner's later works are reminiscent of the Impressionist style of painting that would emerge in France in the coming years. Turner's work undoubtedly influenced artists like Monet, Degas, and Renoir.

Many art historians regard J. M. W. Turner as the most incredible landscape painter of all time. His artwork had a significant influence on many artists who came after him, including many impressionists.

1. Turner's later works are reminiscent of the _____ style of painting.
   a. Impressionist
   b. Watercolor

2. In 1796, Turner completed his first _____ painting.
   a. colored
   b. oil

3. Turner began attending the _____ of Art in London.
   a. Royal State University
   b. Royal Academy

4. Turner was born above his father's _____.
   a. mechanic shop
   b. barbershop

5. J. M. W. Turner was an English Romantic painter, _____, and watercolorist.
   a. teacher
   b. printmaker

6. Turner frequently included _____ in his painting.
   a. animals
   b. people

Spelling Words City

Use the word bank to unscramble the words below.

bubble	community	reject	husband	pineapple	hostile
compass	tomatoes	alarm	salute	perhaps	fugitive
friends	council	fountain	goose	ankle	tutor
difference	center	hammer	jewel	choir	fatal
children	subject				

1. RNIEFDS   f r i e n d s

2. UGITIFVE   f u g i t i v e

3. EPLIPPNAE   p i n e a p p l e

4. RSEPAPH   p e r h a p s

5. COIRH   c h o i r

6. AOTFNUIN   f o u n t a i n

7. EGOSO   g o o s e

8. ERAMMH   h a m m e r

9. LOCNUIC   c o u n c i l

10. LHOTEIS   h o s t i l e

11. AALTF   f a t a l

12. JLEWE   j e w e l

13. CTIMMUNOY   c o m m u n i t y

14. ASCMPOS   c o m p a s s

15. LASUTE   s a l u t e

16. ESTUCJB   s u b j e c t

17. CLEDHNRI   c h i l d r e n

18. RCEEJT   r e j e c t

19. CIDFEFREEN   d i f f e r e n c e

20. NLEAK   a n k l e

21. HANDSUB   h u s b a n d

22. EECRTN   c e n t e r

23. MOSOTAET   t o m a t o e s

24. OURTT   t u t o r

25. RALMA   a l a r m

26. LEBUBB   b u b b l e

Science: Vertebrates

To begin, all animals are classified as either vertebrates or invertebrates. Invertebrates lack a backbone, whereas vertebrates do. Scientists can't stop there, because each group contains thousands of different animals! As a result, scientists divide vertebrates and invertebrates into increasingly smaller groups. Let's talk about vertebrates and some of their classifications.

Vertebrates range in size from a frog to a blue whale. Because there are at least 59,000 different types of vertebrates on the planet, they are further classified into five major groups: mammals, birds, fish, amphibians, and reptiles. Remember that animals are classified into these groups based on what they have in common. Why is an elephant classified as a mammal while a crocodile is classified as a reptile? Let's go over some of the characteristics of each vertebrate group.

Warm-blooded animals are mammals. This means that their bodies maintain their temperature, which is usually higher than the temperature of the surrounding air. They also have hair or fur; they have lungs to breathe air; that they feed milk to their babies; and that most give birth to live young, rather than laying eggs, as a dog does.

- Birds have feathers, two wings (though not all birds, such as the ostrich and penguin, can fly), are warm-blooded, and lay eggs.
- Fish have fins or scales, live in water, and breathe oxygen through gills.
- Like salamanders and frogs, Amphibians have smooth, moist skin (amphibians must keep their skin wet); lay eggs in water; most breathe through their skin and lungs.
- Reptiles have scales (imagine a scaly lizard), are cold-blooded (their body temperature changes as the temperature around them changes), breathe air. Most reptiles, including the crocodile and snake, lay hard-shelled eggs on land.

Vertebrates play several vital roles in an ecosystem. Many predator species are large vertebrates in ecosystems. Lions, eagles, and sharks are examples of predatory vertebrates. Many prey species in ecosystems are also vertebrates. Mice, rabbits, and frogs are examples of these animals. Many vertebrates serve as scavengers in ecosystems. They are significant because they remove dead animals from the environment. Turkey vultures and hyenas, for example, are both vertebrate scavengers. Furthermore, many vertebrates serve as pollinators in ecosystems. Bats and monkeys, for example, may aid in pollen spread by visiting various trees and plants.

Humans value vertebrates for a variety of reasons. Vertebrates are domesticated animals used by humans. These animals are capable of producing milk, food, and clothing. They can also help with work. Agricultural animals are usually vertebrates. Humans also hunt a variety of wild vertebrate animals for food.

1. Vertebrates range in _____ from a frog to a blue whale.
   a. age
   b. size

2. Fish have fins or scales, live in water, and breathe ___ through gills.
   a. oxygen
   b. water

3. Invertebrates lack a _____, whereas vertebrates _____.
   a. skin, whereas vertebrates do
   b. backbone, whereas vertebrates do

4. Warm-blooded animals are _____.
   a. mammals
   b. producers

5. Some vertebrates serve as _____, they remove dead animals from the environment.
   a. scavengers
   b. invertebrates

6. Lions, eagles, and sharks are examples of _____ vertebrates.
   a. ecofriendly
   b. predatory

7. _____ animals are capable of producing milk, food, and clothing.
   a. Non-producing
   b. Domesticated

8. Many vertebrates serve as _____ in ecosystems, they may aid in pollen spread by visiting various trees and plants.
   a. water lilies
   b. pollinators

Science: Organelles

Do you and your dog have a similar appearance? We are all aware that people and dogs appear to be very different on the outside. However, there are some similarities on the inside. Cells make up all animals, including humans and dogs.

All animal cells appear to be the same. They have a cell membrane that contains cytoplasm, which is a gooey fluid. Organelles float in the cytoplasm. Organelles function as tiny machines that meet the needs of the cell. The term organelle refers to a "miniature organ." This lesson will teach you about the various organelles found in animal cells and what they do.

The nucleus of the cell is the cell's brain. It is in charge of many of the cell's functions. The nucleus is where DNA, the genetic instructions for building your body, is stored. DNA contains vital information! Your nucleus has its membrane to protect this essential information, similar to the membrane that surrounds the entire cell.

Your cells require energy. Energy is produced by mitochondria, which are oval-shaped organelles. Mitochondria convert the nutrients that enter the cell into ATP. Your cells use ATP for energy. Because they are the cell's powerhouses, you might think of these organelles as the mighty mitochondria.

The nutrients must be digested before they can be converted into energy by the mitochondria. Digestion is carried out by a group of organelles known as lysosomes. Digestive enzymes are found in lysosomes. Enzymes can sometimes be released into the cell. Because the enzymes kill the cell, lysosomes are known as "suicide bags."

Use Google or your preferred source to help match each term with a definition.

1	L	nucleus	⇢	where DNA is stored
2	B	lysosomes	⇢	degradation of proteins and cellular waste
3	J	Golgi Apparatus	⇢	modification of proteins; "post-office" of the cell
4	I	Mitochondria	⇢	powerhouse of the cell
5	D	SER	⇢	lipid synthesis
6	K	RER	⇢	protein synthesis + modifications
7	A	Microtubules	⇢	responsible for chromosome segregation
8	C	ribosomes	⇢	protein synthesis
9	H	peroxysomes	⇢	degradation of H_2O_2
10	G	cell wall	⇢	prevents excessive uptake of water, protects the cell (in plants)
11	E	chloroplast	⇢	site of photosynthesis
12	F	central vacuole	⇢	stores water in plant cells

Science:
Invertebrates

Invertebrates can be found almost anywhere. Invertebrates account for at least 95% of all animals on the planet! Do you know what one thing they all have in common? Invertebrates lack a backbone.

Your body is supported by a backbone, which protects your organs and connects your other bones. As a result, you are a vertebrate. On the other hand, invertebrates lack the support of bones, so their bodies are often simpler, softer, and smaller. They are also cold-blooded, which means their body temperature fluctuates in response to changes in the air or water around them.

Invertebrates can be found flying, swimming, crawling, or floating and provide essential services to the environment and humans. Nobody knows how many different types of invertebrates there are, but there are millions!

Just because an invertebrate lacks a spinal column does not mean it does not need to eat. Invertebrates, like all other forms of animal life, must obtain nutrients from their surroundings. Invertebrates have evolved two types of digestion to accomplish this. The use of intracellular digestion is common in the most simple organisms. The food is absorbed into the cell and broken down in the cytoplasm at this point. Extracellular digestion, in which cells break down food through the secretion of enzymes and other techniques, is used by more advanced invertebrates. All vertebrates use extracellular digestion.

Still, all animals, invertebrates or not, need a way to get rid of waste. Most invertebrates, especially the simplest ones, use the process of diffusion to eliminate waste. This is merely the opposite of intracellular digestion. However, more advanced invertebrates have more advanced waste disposal mechanisms. Similar to our kidneys, specialized glands in these animals filter and excrete waste. But there is a happy medium. Even though some invertebrates do not have complete digestive tracts like vertebrates, they do not simply flush out waste through diffusion. Instead, the mouth doubles as an exit.

Scientists have classified invertebrates into numerous groups based on what the animals have in common. Arthropods have segmented bodies, which means that they are divided into sections. Consider an ant!

Arthropods are the most numerous group of invertebrates. They can live on land, as spiders and insects do, or in water, as crayfish and crabs do. Because insects are the most numerous group of arthropods, many of them fly, including mosquitoes, bees, locusts, and ladybugs.

They also have jointed legs or limbs to help them walk, similar to how you have knees for your legs and elbows for your arms. The majority of arthropods have an exoskeleton, tough outer skin, or shell that protects their body. Have you ever wondered why when you squish a bug, it makes that crunching sound? That's right; it's the exoskeleton!

Mollusks are the second most numerous group of invertebrates. They have soft bodies and can be found on land or in water. Shells protect the soft bodies of many mollusks, including snails, oysters, clams, and scallops. However, not all, such as octopus, squid, and cuttlefish, have a shell.

1. Invertebrates lack a _____.
   a. backbone
   b. tailbone

2. Invertebrates are also _____.
   a. cold-blooded
   b. warm-blooded

3. _____ can live on land, as spiders and insects do, or in water, as crayfish and crabs do.
   a. Vertebrates
   b. Arthropods

4. All animals, invertebrates or not, need a way to get rid of _____.
   a. their skin
   b. waste

5. _____ have soft bodies and can be found on land or in water.
   a. Arthropods
   b. Mollusks

6. Just because an invertebrate lacks a _____ column does not mean it does not need to eat.
   a. spinal
   b. tissues

7. Your body is supported by a backbone, which protects your _____ and connects your other bones.
   a. organs
   b. muscles

8. Invertebrates lack the support of bones, so their bodies are often simpler, ___, and smaller.
   a. softer and bigger
   b. softer and smaller

Music: Instruments

P	T	R	O	M	B	O	N	E	X	I	X
O	I	C	L	A	R	I	N	E	T	D	B
R	B	A	B	A	S	S	O	O	N	R	C
E	A	O	N	B	I	Q	Q	P	J	U	U
C	F	Q	E	O	Y	E	Z	I	S	M	Z
O	W	O	O	D	B	L	O	C	K	S	O
R	S	A	X	O	P	H	O	N	E	Z	R
D	K	E	T	R	U	M	P	E	T	O	G
E	Z	A	Y	J	F	L	U	T	E	I	A
R	F	R	E	N	C	H	H	O	R	N	N
F	O	Y	R	X	A	H	S	J	R	I	I
G	U	I	T	A	R	V	I	O	L	I	N

PIANO ↘ FLUTE → BASSOON → CLARINET → TROMBONE → VIOLIN →

WOODBLOCK → TRUMPET → OBOE ↘ SAXOPHONE → GUITAR → DRUMS ↓

ORGAN ↓ RECORDER ↓ FRENCH HORN →

15 words in Wordsearch: 3 vertical, 10 horizontal, 2 diagonal. (0 reversed.)

History: The Vikings

During the **Middle**   Ages, the Vikings lived in Northern Europe. They first settled in the Scandinavian lands that are now Denmark, Sweden, and Norway. During the Middle Ages, the Vikings played a significant role in Northern Europe, particularly during the Viking Age, which lasted from 800 CE to 1066 CE.

In Old Norse, the word Viking means "to raid." The Vikings would board their longships and **sail** across the seas to raid villages on Europe's northern coast, including islands like Great Britain. In 787 CE, they first appeared in England to raid villages. When the Vikings **raided** , they were known to attack defenseless monasteries. This earned them a bad reputation as barbarians, but monasteries were wealthy and undefended Viking targets.

The Vikings eventually began to **settle**   in areas other than Scandinavia. They colonized parts of Great Britain, Germany, and Iceland in the ninth century. They spread into northeastern Europe, including Russia, in the 10th century. They also established Normandy, which means "Northmen," along the coast of northern France.

By the beginning of the 11th century, the Vikings had reached the pinnacle of their power. Leif Eriksson, son of Erik the Red, was one Vikings who made it to **North**   America. He established a brief settlement in modern-day Canada. This was thousands of years before Columbus.

The English and King Harold Godwinson **defeated**   the Vikings, led by King Harald Hardrada of Norway, in 1066. The defeat in this battle is sometimes interpreted as the end of the Viking Age. The Vikings stopped expanding their territory at this point, and raids became less frequent.

The arrival of Christianity was a major factor at the end of the Viking age. The Vikings became more and more a part of mainland Europe as Scandinavia was converted to **Christianity**   and became a part of Christian Europe. Sweden's, Denmark's, and Norway's identities and borders began to emerge as well.

The Vikings were perhaps best known for their ships. The Vikings built longships for exploration and raiding. Longships were long, narrow vessels built for speed. Oars primarily propelled them but later added a sail to help in windy conditions. Longships had a shallow draft, which allowed them to float in **shallow**   water and land on beaches.

The Vikings also built **cargo**   ships known as Knarr for trading. The Knarr was wider and deeper than the longship, allowing it to transport more cargo.

Five recovered Viking ships can be seen at the Viking Ship Museum in Roskilde, **Denmark** . It's also possible to see how the Vikings built their ships. The Vikings used a shipbuilding technique known as clinker building. They used long wood planks that overlapped along the edges.

Grammar: Sentence Building

Practice *sentence* building. *Unscramble* the words to form a complete sentence.

1. Germs can build up a resistance to antibiotics.

   antibiotics.   ·   up   ·   Germs   ·   to   ·   a   ·   resistance

2. There was a sharp curve in the road.

   in   ·   curve   ·   road.   ·   There   ·   was   ·   sharp

3. Let's make a graph with this data.

   make   ·   this   ·   a   ·   with   ·   data.

4. I like to eat turkey and mashed potatoes.

   turkey   ·   mashed   ·   to   ·   eat   ·   and   ·   I

5. My sister built a house out of clay.

   clay.   ·   of   ·   out   ·   house   ·   sister   ·   My

6. The flight was very long and boring.

   boring.   ·   The   ·   was   ·   long   ·   and

7. I heard that man is very wealthy.

   wealthy.   ·   that   ·   man   ·   is   ·   I

8. I will have soup and crackers for lunch.

   soup   ·   have   ·   I   ·   and   ·   lunch.   ·   crackers

9. There is a brook behind my home.

   my   ·   brook   ·   home.   ·   a   ·   is

10. I like to drink water.

    I   ·   like   ·   water.   ·   drink

11. How long have you had this sickness?

    sickness?   ·   you   ·   had   ·   have   ·   long

12. He wrote many books about elephants.

    many   ·   wrote   ·   about   ·   He

13. My body temperature is normal.

temperature · is · My · body

14. I have a weak stomach sometimes.

weak · a · I · stomach

15. Stay still while I fix your tie.

Stay · still · fix · I · tie.

16. My head started to ache this morning.

started · to · My · ache · head

17. My big brother works in an office.

My · works · big · in · brother

18. The train cars kept lurching forward.

train · The · kept · lurching

19. I can't possibly make a prediction.

prediction. · a · I · make

20. I like my school picture this year.

I · like · picture · this · year.

21. Will the pizza have everything on it?

the · it? · Will · on · everything

22. My cat is very dear to me.

My · is · cat · me. · very

23. I want a friend, not an enemy.

want · not · enemy. · friend, · an

24. Can you guess my weight?

my · you · Can · weight?

Grammar: Nouns, Verbs, Adjectives

DIRECTIONS: SORT the words (below) by their corresponding *part-of-speech*.

color	chickens	kittens	banjo	library	goldfish
grieving	adorable	cough	stand	nasty	powerful
dance	build	cry	break	easy	circle
coach	aggressive	careful	eat	adventurous	think
mysterious	face	sticks	drink	guitar	busy
calm	window	worm	coast	draw	polka dot
eager	handsome	explain			

Nouns (13)	Verbs (13)	Adjectives (13)
coast	break	adorable
polka dot	build	busy
sticks	coach	eager
banjo	color	grieving
goldfish	cough	easy
chickens	think	calm
window	cry	handsome
face	dance	careful
library	draw	adventurous
circle	drink	aggressive
guitar	eat	mysterious
kittens	explain	nasty
worm	stand	powerful

*Usage Activity: CHOOSE (12) words from your completed table & WRITE (1) sentence for each form of the words you chose.

[Student worksheet has a 25 line writing exercise here.]

Grammar: Concrete & Abstract Noun

In the English language, both concrete and abstract nouns are essential parts of speech. The primary distinction between concrete and abstract nouns is that concrete nouns refer to people, places, or things that take up physical space, whereas abstract nouns refer to intangible ideas that cannot be physically interacted with.

Words like "luck," "disgust," and "empathy" are examples of abstract nouns. While it is possible to see someone being empathetic, empathy is not a visible or tangible entity. The majority of feelings, emotions, and philosophies can be classified as abstract nouns.

1. FIND THE ABSTRACT NOUN ?

    a. KIND

    b. BOOK

2. FIND THE CONCRETE NOUNS

    a. WINDOW

    b. LOVE

3. FIND THE ABTRACT NOUN: THE KING WAS KNOWN FOR HIS JUSTICE

    a. JUSTICE

    b. KING

4. WHAT ARE THE 5 CONCRETE NOUNS

    a. TASTE, SMELL, WALKING, EYEING, TOUCHING

    b. SMELL,TASTE, SIGHT, HEARING,TOUCH

5. WHICH NOUN BELOW IS AN ABSTRACT NOUN?

    a. TRAIN

    b. LOVE

6. IS THE FOLLOWING NOUN CONCRETE OR ABSTRACT? CUPCAKES

    a. ABSTRACT

    b. CONCRETE

7. WHAT IS A CONCRETE NOUN?

    a. A NOUN THAT YOU CAN EXPERIENCE WITH AT LEAST 1 OF YOUR 5 SENSES.

    b. A NOUN THAT YOU CAN'T EXPERIENCE WITH AT LEAST 1 OF YOUR 5 SENSES.

8. WHICH WORD BELOW IS AN ABSTRACT NOUN?

    a. BRAVERY

    b. FRIEND

9. WHICH WORD BELOW IS NOT A CONCRETE NOUN?

    a. HAMBURGER

    b. ANGER

10. IS THE WORD THOUGHTFULNESS A CONCRETE OR ABSTRACT NOUN?

    a. ABSTRACT

    b. CONCRETE

Grammar: Compound Nouns

A compound noun is one that is composed of two or more words. Each word contributes to the meaning of the noun.

Compound nouns can be written three ways:

A single word	Two words	Hyphenated
haircut	rain forest	self-esteem

Instructions: Match the compound noun pairs correctly.

1	O	Fund	⇢	raiser
2	D	News	⇢	paper
3	C	Sun	⇢	glasses
4	F	Child	⇢	hood
5	N	Door	⇢	way
6	E	heart	⇢	attack
7	J	tooth	⇢	paste
8	K	apple	⇢	sauce
9	M	full	⇢	moon
10	H, B	hair	⇢	cut
11	G	air	⇢	plane
12	I	ear	⇢	ring
13	A	scare	⇢	crow
14	P	post	⇢	office
15	B, H	hair	⇢	dresser
16	L	note	⇢	book

Grammar: Collective Noun

A collective noun is a noun that refers to a group of people, animals, or things. They are described as a single entity. Collective nouns are distinct from singular nouns in that singular nouns describe only one person or object.

Many collective nouns are common nouns, but when they are the name of a company or other organization with more than one person, such as Microsoft, they can also be proper nouns.

Find the collective noun in each sentence.

1. Our class visited the natural history museum on a field trip.

   class

2. The bison herd stampeded across the prairie, leaving a massive dust cloud in its wake.

   herd

3. We eagerly awaited the verdict of the jury.

   jury

4. This year's basketball team features three players who stand taller than six feet.

   team

5. At Waterloo, Napoleon's army was finally defeated.

   army

6. The plans for a new park have been approved by the town council.

   council

7. He comes from a large family, as the oldest of eleven children.

   family

8. The rock group has been on tour for several months.

   group

9. When Elvis appeared on stage, the entire audience erupted in applause.

   audience

10. The San Francisco crowd were their usual individualistic selves.

    crowd

11. The crew of sailors boarded the ships.

    crew

12. A mob destroyed the company's new office.

    mob

13. The fleet of ships was waiting at the port.

    fleet

14. It was difficult for the committee to come to a decision.

    committee

Geography: Canada

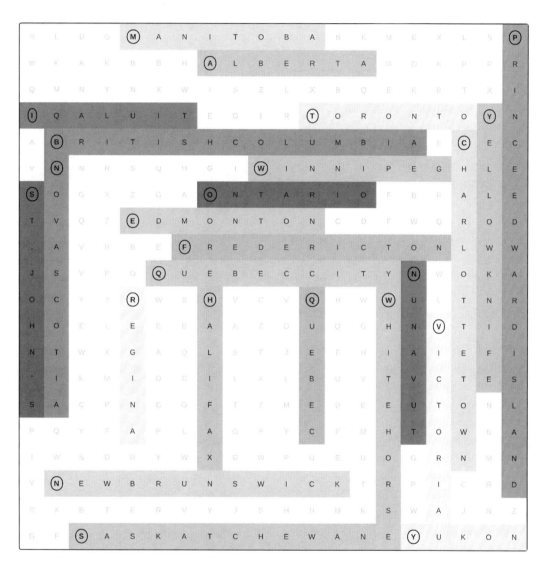

Yukon → | Nunavut ↓ | Nova Scotia ↓ | Prince Edward Island ↓ | New Brunswick → | Quebec ↓ | Ontario → | Manitoba →

Saskatchewan → | Alberta → | British Columbia → | Victoria ↓ | Edmonton → | Regina ↓ | Winnipeg → | Toronto →

Quebec City → | Fredericton → | Charlottetown ↓ | Halifax ↓ | St. John's ↓ | Iqaluit → | Yellowknife ↓ | Whitehorse ↓

24 words in Wordsearch: 11 vertical, 13 horizontal, 0 diagonal. (0 reversed.)

Science Words You Should Know Quiz

Circle the correct meaning of each word. Need help? Try Google!

1. Bulb
   a. Light producing instrument
   b. Learning by doing

2. Circuit
   a. A representation of data
   b. A path that electricity follows during its flowing

3. Kinetic
   a. An optical instrument
   b. Movement

4. Friction
   a. Resistance due to movement
   b. Making larger

5. Hygrometer
   a. A path that electricity follows during its flowing
   b. Humidity measuring instrument

6. Barometer
   a. The intensity of sound
   b. Pressure measuring instrument

7. Humidity
   a. A quantity expressing water vapor's amount
   b. Movement

8. Pitch
   a. Findings after an investigation
   b. The intensity of sound

9. Neutron
   a. Sub-particle of an atom
   b. Findings after an investigation

10. Proton
   a. Findings after an investigation
   b. A constituent of an atom

11. Dark
   a. Categorization on a common base
   b. Absence of light

12. Practical
   a. Learning by doing
   b. A path that electricity follows during its flowing

13. Classify
   a. Categorization on a common base
   b. Findings after an investigation

14. Analyze
   a. Detail examination
   b. Resistance due to movement

15. Expand
   a. Absence of light
   b. Making larger

16. Graph
   a. A representation of data
   b. A path that electricity follows during its flowing

17. Results
   a. Findings after an investigation
   b. Sub-particle of an atom

18. Microscope
   a. Making larger
   b. An optical instrument

Environmental Health: Water Pollution

Water pollution occurs when waste, chemicals, or other particles cause a body of water (e.g., rivers, oceans, lakes) to become **toxic** to the fish and animals that rely on it for survival. Water pollution can also disrupt and hurt nature's water cycle.

Water pollution can occur **naturally** due to volcanoes, algae blooms, animal waste, and silt from storms and floods.

Human activity contributes significantly to water pollution. Sewage, pesticides, fertilizers from farms, wastewater and chemicals from factories, silt from construction sites, and trash from people littering are some human **causes**.

Oil **spills** have been some of the most well-known examples of water pollution. The Exxon Valdez oil spill occurred when an oil tanker collided with a reef off the coast of Alaska, causing over 11 million gallons of oil to spill into the ocean. Another major oil spill was the Deepwater Horizon oil spill, which occurred when an oil well exploded, causing over 200 million gallons of oil to spill into the **Gulf** of Mexico.

Water pollution can be caused directly by air pollution. When sulfur dioxide particles reach high altitudes in the atmosphere, they can combine with rain to form acid rain. **Acid** rain can cause lakes to become acidic, killing fish and other animals.

The main issue caused by water pollution is the impact on aquatic life. **Dead** fish, birds, dolphins, and various other animals frequently wash up on beaches, killed by pollutants in their environment. Pollution also has an impact on the natural **food** chain. Small animals consume contaminants like lead and cadmium.

Clean water is one of the most valuable and essential commodities for life on Earth. Clean water is nearly impossible to obtain for over 1 billion people on the **planet**. They can become **ill** from dirty, polluted water, which is especially difficult for young children. Some bacteria and pathogens in water can make people sick to the point of death.

Water pollution comes from a variety of sources. Here are a few of the main reasons:

Sewage: In many parts of the world, sewage is still flushed directly into **streams** and rivers. Sewage can introduce dangerous bacteria that can make humans and animals very sick.

Farm animal waste: Runoff from large **herds** of farm animals such as pigs and cows can enter the water supply due to rain and large storms.

Pesticides: Pesticides and herbicides are frequently sprayed on **crops** to kill bugs, while herbicides are sprayed to kill weeds. These potent chemicals can enter the water through rainstorm runoff. They can also contaminate rivers and lakes due to unintentional spills.

Construction, floods, and storms: Silt from construction, earthquakes, and storms can **reduce** water oxygen levels and suffocate fish. Factories - Water is frequently used in factories to process chemicals, keep engines cool, and wash things away. Sometimes used **wastewater** is dumped into rivers or the ocean. It may contain pollutants.

Storytime: Let Thy Hair Down| Part 2

Rapunzel had magnificent __long__ hair as fine as spun gold, and when she heard the Witch's voice, she unfastened her long braided locks and wound them around one of the window hooks above.

After a year or two, the King's Son rode through the forest and passed by the __tower__ .

He rode home, but the singing had touched him so deeply that he went out into the __forest__ every day to listen to it.

When it got __dark__ the next day, he went to the tower and cried:

Rapunzel was __terrified__ at first when a man her eyes had never seen before approached her.

When he asked Rapunzel if she would take him as her __husband__ and she saw that he was young and handsome, she thought to herself, "He will love me more than old Dame Gothel does," and she said yes and laid her hand in his.

"I will gladly go away with you, but I don't know how to get down," she added. Bring a strand of silk with you every time you come, and I'll weave a ladder out of it. When that is completed, I will come down, and you will __transport__ me on your horse."

"You wicked child!" exclaimed the Witch. "What do you say!" I hear you say. I thought I'd __separated__ you from the rest of the world, but you've duped me!"

In her rage, she clutched Rapunzel's lovely locks, wrapped them twice around her left hand, grabbed a pair of __scissors__ with her right, and snip, snap, they were cut off, and the lovely braids lay on the ground.

However, on the same day that she cast out Rapunzel, the Witch, in the evening, glued the braids of hair she had __cut__ off to the window hook; and when the King's Son came and cried:

The King's Son climbed. He did not see his __beloved__ Rapunzel above but rather the Witch, who glared at him with wicked and cruel eyes.

He __escaped__ with his life, but the thorns he landed on punctured his eyes.

So he wandered around in misery for a few __years__ before arriving in the desert, where Rapunzel lived in misfortune. He heard a voice and went toward it because it sounded familiar. When he approached, Rapunzel recognized him and __sobbed__ on his neck. Two of her tears wetted his eyes, causing them to clear and allowing him to see as before.

He led her to his Kingdom, where he was joyfully received, and they lived __happily__ and merrily for a long time.

Storytime: Let Thy Hair Down

Once upon a time, there was a man and a woman who had long wished for a **child** in desperation. Finally, the woman hoped that God was about to grant her wish.

These people had a **small** window in the back of their house to see a beautiful garden.

One day, the woman was standing by this window, looking down into the garden, when she noticed a bed planted with the most beautiful rampion (rapunzel), and it looked so **fresh** and green that she wanted so badly for it and sought to eat some.

This desire grew **stronger** by the day, and because she knew she couldn't get any of it, she looked pale and miserable.

"Rather than letting your wife die, bring her some of the rampions yourself; let it cost you what it will!" thought the man who **loved** her.

In the late afternoon, he **climbed** over the wall into the Witch's garden, grabbed a handful of rampion, and hurriedly handed it to his wife.

But when he got down the wall, he was **terrified** because he saw the Witch standing before him.

The Witch then softened her rage and said to him, "If the case is as you say, I will allow you to take as much rampion as you want, but there is one **condition** : you must give me the child that your wife will bring into the world." It will be well cared for, and I will look after it like a mother."

In his terror, the man **agreed** to everything, and when the woman finally had a little daughter, the Witch appeared immediately, gave the child the name Rapunzel, and took it away with her.

When she was twelve years old, the Witch locked her in a **tower** in the middle of a forest with no stairs or door.

Spelling Words
Crossword

Complete the crossword by filling in a word that fits each clue. Fill in the correct answers, one letter per square, both across and down, from the given clues. There will be a gray space between multi-word answers.

Tip: Solve the easy clues first, and then go back and answer the more difficult ones.

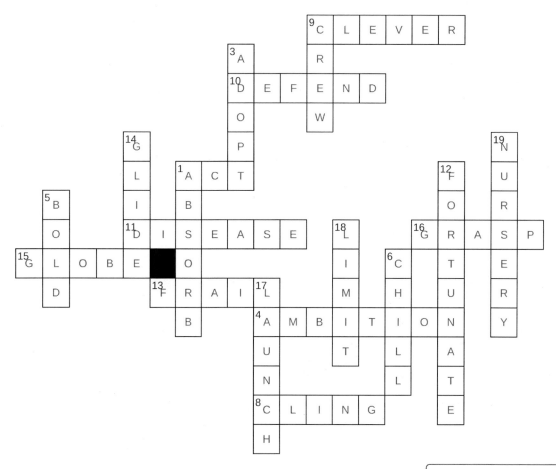

Across

1. behave in a certain manner
4. a strong drive for success
8. hold on tightly
9. mentally quick and resourceful
10. protect against a challenge or attack
11. an impairment of health
13. physically weak
15. an object with a spherical shape
16. hold firmly

Down

1. take in a liquid
3. take into one's family
5. fearless and daring
6. coldness due to a cold environment
9. an organized group of workers
12. having unexpected good luck
14. move smoothly and effortlessly
17. propel with force
18. as far as something can go
19. a child's room for a baby

ABSORB   ADOPT   DISEASE
LIMIT   ACT   CLEVER
AMBITION   NURSERY   FRAIL
BOLD   DEFEND   CHILL
GLIDE   GRASP   FORTUNATE
GLOBE   LAUNCH   CREW
CLING

Spelling Words
Unscramble

Unscramble Word Tip: Try solving the easy words first, and then go back and answer the more difficult ones.

compare	group	pond	taught	laundry	start
grade	wrap	front	stone	pardon	city
shirt	open	am	value	office	hope
highest	close	person	verb	hear	near
travel	pencil				

1. lseoc   c l o s e

2. oesnpr   p e r s o n

3. npdrao   p a r d o n

4. ma   a m

5. ntoes   s t o n e

6. earn   n e a r

7. ithrs   s h i r t

8. auevl   v a l u e

9. atelvr   t r a v e l

10. poeh   h o p e

11. tciy   c i t y

12. bvre   v e r b

13. aehr   h e a r

14. ndpo   p o n d

15. tuahgt   t a u g h t

16. adrge   g r a d e

17. ofrnt   f r o n t

18. trats   s t a r t

19. nydrual   l a u n d r y

20. enpo   o p e n

21. wapr   w r a p

22. ilencp   p e n c i l

23. gishteh   h i g h e s t

24. aempcro   c o m p a r e

25. orugp   g r o u p

26. oeffic   o f f i c e

Science Spelling Words

Instructions: Match the science words to the correct meaning.

1	C	Shadow	⇢	A dark area
2	K	Nectar	⇢	Juicy fluid within flowers
3	O	Prey	⇢	Kill and hunt for food
4	L	Gas	⇢	State of matter that can expand freely
5	G	Mixture	⇢	A combination of different things
6	M	Fossil	⇢	The remains of plant or animal
7	D	Bacteria	⇢	Unicellular microorganism
8	F	Brain	⇢	A coordinating organ of the human body
9	B	Geology	⇢	Study of earth
10	J	Atom	⇢	The smallest particle
11	A	Magnetic	⇢	Having magnetic properties
12	R	Dissolve	⇢	Solid form in any liquid
13	E	Fact	⇢	Any true information
14	I	Biology	⇢	The study of living beings
15	Q	Organism	⇢	An individual/living being
16	N	Scale	⇢	Bony plates in the fish skin
17	H	Test tube	⇢	A thin tube made up of glass
18	P	Weigh	⇢	Expression of heaviness

History Reading
Comprehension: Walt Disney

On December 5, 1901, Walter Elias Disney was born in __Chicago__, Illinois. His family relocated to a farm outside of Marceline, Missouri, when he was __four__ years old, thanks to his parents, Elias and Flora. Walt loved growing up on the farm with his three older brothers (Herbert, Raymond, and Roy) and younger __sister__ (Ruth). Walt discovered his passion for drawing and art in Marceline.

The Disneys relocated to Kansas City after four years in Marceline. On weekends, Walt continued to draw and attend __art__ classes. He even bartered his drawings for free haircuts with a local barber. Walt got a summer job on a train. On the __train__, he walked back and forth, selling __snacks__ and newspapers. Walt had a great time on the train and would be fascinated by trains for the rest of his life.

Walt's family relocated to Chicago around the time he started high school. Walt studied at the Chicago Art Institute and worked as a cartoonist for the school __newspaper__. Walt decided at the age of sixteen that he wanted to fight in World War I. Due to the fact that he was still too young to join the army, he decided to drop out of school and join the __Red__ Cross instead.

Walt aspired to create his own animated cartoons. He founded his own company, Laugh-O-Gram. He sought the help of some of his __friends__, including Ubbe Iwerks.

Disney, on the other hand, was not going to be deterred by a single setback. In 1923, he relocated to __Hollywood__, California, and founded the Disney Brothers' Studio with his __brother__ Roy. He enlisted the services of Ubbe Iwerks and a number of other animators once more.

Walt had to start all over again. This time, he came up with a new character called __Mickey__ Mouse.
The movie was a huge success. Disney kept working, creating new characters like __Donald__ Duck, Goofy, and Pluto.

In 1932, Walt Disney decided to create a full-length animated film called Snow __White__.

Disney used the proceeds from Snow White to establish a film studio and produce other animated films such as Pinocchio, Fantasia, Dumbo, Bambi, __Alice__ in Wonderland, and __Peter__ Pan.

Disney's Wonderful World of Color, the Davy Crockett series, and the Mickey Mouse __Club__ was among the first Disney television shows to air on network television.

Disney, who is constantly coming up with new ideas, had the idea to build a __theme__ park featuring rides and entertainment based on his films. In 1955, Disneyland opened its doors. It cost $17 million to construct. Although it wasn't an immediate success, Disney World has since grown into one of the world's most popular __vacation__ destinations.

Every year, millions of people enjoy his films and theme parks. Every year, his company continues to produce fantastic films and __entertainment__.

Comprehension Multiple Choice: Walt Disney

Make sure you go back and read the Disney article through to the very end. If you attempt to complete this assignment solely by scanning for answers, you will almost certainly pick the incorrect answer. Take your time. Ask questions. Get help if you need it. Good Luck!

1. Walter Elias Disney was born in Chicago, _____.
   a. Illinois
   b. Italy

2. Walter's parents names were Elias and Flora.
   a. True
   b. False

3. Walt got a summer job on a _____.
   a. train
   b. boat

4. Walt's younger sister name was _____.
   a. Ruby
   b. Ruth

5. Walt had _____ brothers.
   a. three
   b. two

6. In 1923, walt relocated to Hollywood, _____.
   a. Colorado
   b. California

7. Steamboat _____ was the title of the film, which starred Mickey and Minnie Mouse.
   a. William
   b. Willie

8. Walt spent the next year in France driving _____ for the Red Cross.
   a. taxi cabs
   b. ambulances

9. Walt and his friends created the well-known character Oswald the Lucky _____t.
   a. Dog
   b. Rabbi

10. Walt's first color animated film was_____.
   a. Bears and Tigers
   b. Flowers and Trees

11. In _____, Disneyland opened its doors.
   a. 1955
   b. 1995

12. _____ was among the first Disney television shows to air on network television.
   a. Mickey Mouse Club
   b. Mickey and Friends

13. _____ was his first major live-action film.
   a. Treasure Island
   b. Treats Island

14. Walt Disney decided to create a full-length animated film called _____.
   a. Snow White
   b. Robin Hood

Music: The Orchestra
Vocabulary Words

Who wants to attend an orchestral performance? Obviously, you do! Orchestras are fantastic. An orchestra, at its most basic, is a large musical ensemble. Traditional orchestras have sections for woodwind, brass, strings, and percussion instruments.

The orchestra as we know it today originated in the early 1600s. Instruments were added and removed over the next several centuries, and what we now call the modern orchestra began to take shape. Violins became the orchestra's primary string instrument in the 17th century. More woodwind instruments were added over time, and by the 18th century, French horns, trombones, and trumpets were commonplace.

Throughout the 17th century, orchestras were small, with only about 18-20 members, and the composer was often a performer, often on the harpsichord or violin. As a result, there was no real director. In the 18th century, composers like Johann Sebastian Bach and Wolfgang Amadeus Mozart made orchestral music famous and influential, inspiring kings and peasants alike. During this period, concert performance indeed became a respected profession.

Ludwig van Beethoven, a 19th-century composer who standardized the orchestra using pairs of each woodwind and brass instrument, took the next big step. Beethoven composed works that made full use of the entire range of instruments, from high to low, and gave each section more critical roles, rather than letting the strings carry the majority of the melody on their own.

_____

Unscramble the names of the instruments found in the orchestra.

woodwind	cello	xylophone	violin	piano	trumpet
drums	oboe	brass	trombone	flute	clarinet
percussion	conductor	saxophone	harp		

1. tulef   f l u t e

2. involi   v i o l i n

3. eoob   o b o e

4. articlne   c l a r i n e t

5. srudm   d r u m s

6. ddnwoiwo   w o o d w i n d

7. rbass   b r a s s

8. uniocrspse   p e r c u s s i o n

9. lceol   c e l l o

10. ahrp   h a r p

11. erpttum   t r u m p e t

12. rootmebn   t r o m b o n e

13. enlhoxypo   x y l o p h o n e

14. udcootrnc   c o n d u c t o r

15. oniap   p i a n o

16. heonoasxp   s a x o p h o n e

History: Thomas Edison

Thomas Alva Edison was born in Milan, Ohio, on February 11, 1847. He developed **hearing** loss at a young age. He was a creative and inquisitive child. However, he struggled in school, possibly because he couldn't hear his **teacher**. He was then educated at home by his mother.

Because of his numerous important inventions, Thomas Edison was nicknamed the "wizard." On his own or in collaboration with others, he has designed and built more than 1,000 **devices**. The phonograph (record player), the lightbulb, and the motion-picture projector are among his most notable inventions.

Although Thomas did not invent the first electric **light** bulb, he did create the first practical electric light bulb that could be manufactured and used in the home. He also **invented** other items required to make the light bulb usable in homes, such as safety fuses and on/off switches for light sockets.

As a teenager, Thomas worked as a telegraph operator. Telegraphy was one of the most important communication systems in the country at the time. Thomas was skilled at sending and receiving **Morse** code messages. He enjoyed tweaking with telegraphic instruments, and he came up with several improvements to make them even better. By early 1869, he had left his telegraphy job to pursue his **dream** of becoming a full-time inventor.

Edison worked tirelessly with scientists and other collaborators to complete projects. He established **research** facilities in Menlo Park, California, and West Orange, New Jersey. Finally, Edison established companies that manufactured and sold his successful inventions.

Edison's family was essential to him, even though he spent the majority of his life **dedicated** to his work. He had six children from two marriages. Edison **passed** away on October 18, 1931.

History: Christopher Columbus

	A	B	C	D
1.	**America**	Amerryca	Ameryca	Amerrica
2.	**spices**	spicesc	spises	spicess
3.	Eurropaen	**European**	Europaen	Eurropean
4.	**coast**	coasct	cuast	coasst
5.	abrroad	abruad	**abroad**	abrruad
6.	**sailor**	siallor	saillor	sialor
7.	**nations**	nattions	nascons	natsions
8.	explurers	**explorers**	expllorers	expllurers
9.	sylver	syllver	sillver	**silver**
10.	Spayn	Spian	Spyan	**Spain**
11.	Indains	Indainss	Indianss	**Indians**
12.	**discover**	disssover	disscover	dissover
13.	islend	iscland	**island**	issland

Health Spelling Words:
Healthy Routines

Write the correct word for each sentence.

Reading	overeat	Eating	read	fat
fresh	fruit	health	glass	chair
floss	Breakfast	Staying	daily	Sleep
fiber	enough	burn	Walking	body

1. Creating a healthy __daily__ routine is simple.

2. __Staying__ hydrated is vital for our health.

3. Exercise has tremendous __health__ benefits.

4. Exposure to the sun enables the __body__ to produce vitamin D.

5. __Walking__ is one of the most underrated healthy habits you can do.

6. Vegetables are low in calories, yet high in vitamins, minerals, and __fiber__ .

7. __Reading__ has benefits to both your physical and mental health.

8. __Sleep__ is the only time during the day where our bodies are able to relax, unwind and recover.

9. __Eating__ a variety of good foods.

10. __Breakfast__ is the most important meal of the day.

11. Drink a __glass__ of water.

12. Sitting in your __chair__ all day long isn't good for you.

13. Excess body __fat__ comes from eating more than we need.

14. Cooking the right amount makes it easier to not __overeat__ .

15. Physical activity helps us __burn__ off the extra calories.

16. Eat __fruit__ instead of eating a candy bar.

17. Make time to __read__ every day.

18. Don't forget to __floss__ .

19. Swap sugary desserts for __fresh__ fruit.

20. Get __enough__ sleep.

Grammar: SUPERLATIVE ADJECTIVES

A superlative adjective is a comparative adjective that describes something as being of the highest degree or extreme. When comparing three or more people or things, we use superlative adjectives. Superlative adjectives typically end in 'est'. Examples of superlative adjectives include the words biggest and fastest.

Unscramble Word Tip: Try solving the easy words first, and then go back and answer the more difficult ones.

prettiest	hottest	crowded	friendliest	biggest	smallest
saddest	best	worst	tallest	shortest	longest
fattest	newest	heaviest	nicest	beautiful	expensive
cheapest	comfortable	youngest	largest		

1. peehtsac   c h e a p e s t

2. talresg   l a r g e s t

3. ntogels   l o n g e s t

4. wsenet   n e w e s t

5. icetns   n i c e s t

6. tstosreh   s h o r t e s t

7. samlsetl   s m a l l e s t

8. lstteal   t a l l e s t

9. goysunte   y o u n g e s t

10. tggsbie   b i g g e s t

11. eftastt   f a t t e s t

12. ttoesht   h o t t e s t

13. adstdes   s a d d e s t

14. filtaubeu   b e a u t i f u l

15. ctlefarbmoo   c o m f o r t a b l e

16. ddrwoce   c r o w d e d

17. enpsvxeei   e x p e n s i v e

18. esdeirfiltn   f r i e n d l i e s t

19. hitvseea   h e a v i e s t

20. espttriet   p r e t t i e s t

21. bets   b e s t

22. wrsot   w o r s t

Grammar:
Contractions

Take a moment to visualize the process of blowing up a balloon. It grows larger and larger. When we let the air out, it shrinks or contracts. To contract means to shrink, reduce or get smaller.

In writing, a contraction is a word that combines two words to form a shorter word. In other words, the contraction makes the two words smaller. A contraction is simply a word that is a shortened form of two words combined.

When the words can and not are combined, the contraction word can't is formed. The apostrophe (as in this symbol: ') is a small punctuation mark that replaces the letters that have been removed. The apostrophe replaces the 'n' and the 'o' of not in can't.

	A	B	C	D
1.	**he'd**	ha'd	hh'd	hp'd
2.	yoo'rre	yoo're	you'rre	**you're**
3.	wesn't	wassn't	wascn't	**wasn't**
4.	sied	mhod	sha'd	**she'd**
5.	**they'll**	thay'l	they'l	thay'll
6.	aran't	arran't	**aren't**	arren't
7.	**let's**	latt's	lett's	lat's
8.	lad	I's	**I'd**	wts
9.	she'l	sha'l	**she'll**	sha'll
10.	wa'e	wa've	wa'va	**we've**
11.	yoo'd	yood	yuo'd	**you'd**
12.	ha'l	ha'll	he'l	**he'll**
13.	**I've**	I'vw	Ikva	I'va
14.	hesn't	hassn't	hascn't	**hasn't**
15.	thai'd	thay'd	**they'd**	thei'd
16.	**you'll**	yoo'll	you'l	yoo'l
17.	haven'tt	havan't	**haven't**	havan'tt
18.	wa'll	we'l	wa'l	**we'll**
19.	yoo've	yoo'e	yuo've	**you've**
20.	**hadn't**	hedn't	hedn'tt	hadn'tt
21.	havan'tt	haven'tt	**haven't**	havan't

Geography Words

Instructions: Match the science words to the correct meaning.

1	L	Atlas	→	A collection of maps of the planet Earth.
2	A	Atoll	→	A coral reef or an island in the shape of a ring.
3	F	Altitude	→	The measure of elevation above sea level.
4	N	Border	→	An artificial line drawn segregating two geographical areas.
5	O	Capital	→	A city exercising primary status and where the government is located.
6	I	Country	→	A political state or a nation. For example, India, Thailand.
7	M	Desert	→	A large area covered with sand, where water or vegetation is either very little or not present at all.
8	G	Earth	→	The 3rd planet of our solar system and the planet in which we all live.
9	R	Equator	→	A line drawn on the center of the earth separating the north and south pole.
10	B	Geography	→	The study of the planet Earth's physical features.
11	K	Glacier	→	A mass of ice that is slowly moving.
12	D	Hemisphere	→	The half of a sphere. Hint: Northern and Southern___.
13	J	Latitude	→	The measure of the distance from the north or the south of the Equator.
14	E	Longitude	→	The measure of the distance from the east or the west of Prime Meridian.
15	S	Meridian	→	An imaginary circle passing through two poles.
16	Q	Plain	→	A piece of land that is flat.
17	P	Plateau	→	A piece of land on high ground.
18	H	Strait	→	A narrow passage of water connecting two water bodies.
19	C	Tributary	→	A stream that flows into a large lake, or a river.

Art Words

1	D	Contrast	→	Use of opposites near or beside one another (light and dark, rough and smooth)
2	B	Composition	→	The arrangement of forms in a work of art.
3	N	Cool colors	→	Mostly green, blue, violet (purple).
4	P	Hue	→	The name of a color – red blue, yellow, etc.
5	K	Intensity	→	Brightness of a color.
6	H, M	Texture	→	Refers to the way things feel or look as though they might feel if they were touched.
7	I	Subject matter	→	The topic of interest or the primary theme of an artwork.
8	L	Tint	→	Light values of a color (adding white)
9	E	Shade	→	The dark values of a color (adding black).
10	F	Warm colors	→	Red, orange, yellow.
11	J	Variety	→	Principle of design concerned with difference or contrast.
12	G	Focal point	→	The center of interest of an artwork; the part you look at first.
13	O	Line	→	A mark with greater length than width.
14	A	Shape	→	A closed line.
15	C	Space	→	The area between and around objects.
16	M, H	Texture	→	The surface quality that can be seen and felt.

Extra Credit Question: What are the elements of art? List each of them with a description.

INDEPENDENT RESEARCH

Science Vocab Crossword

Complete the crossword by filling in a word that fits each clue. Fill in the correct answers, one letter per square, both across and down, from the given clues. There will be a gray space between multi-word answers.

Tip: Solve the easy clues first, and then go back and answer the more difficult ones.

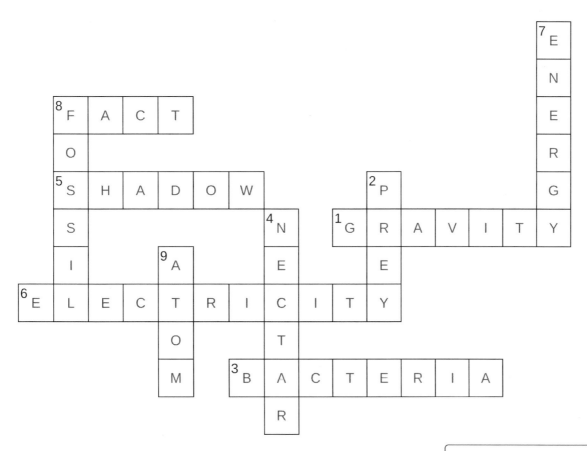

Across
1. The force that attracts mass
3. Unicellular microorganism
5. A dark area
6. Flow of electron
8. Any true information

Down
2. kill and hunt for food
4. Juicy fluid within flowers
7. Power
8. The remains of plant or animal
9. The smallest particle

GRAVITY   PREY
ATOM   NECTAR
SHADOW   FOSSIL
ENERGY   BACTERIA
ELECTRICITY
FACT

Music: String Family Instruments

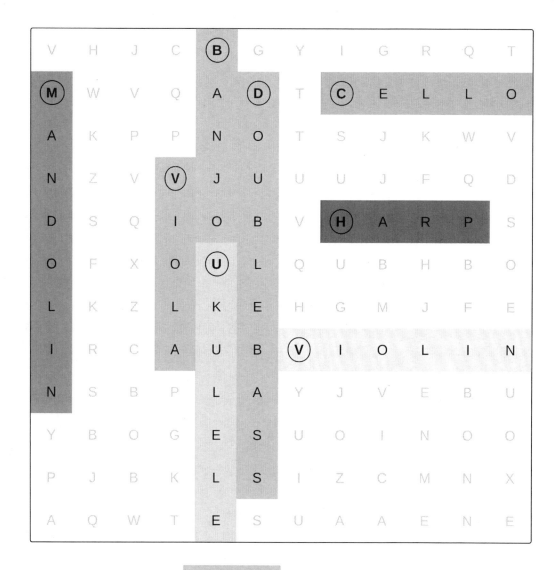

Violin → | Viola ↓ | Cello → | Double Bass ↓ | Harp → | Banjo ↓ | Mandolin ↓ | Ukulele ↓

8 words in Wordsearch: 5 vertical, 3 horizontal, 0 diagonal. (0 reversed.)

Music: Brass Instruments
List Word Search

You play a brass instrument by blowing into a mouthpiece to change the pitch, or note, of the instrument.

Breath is used by brass musicians to create sound. To play, players buzz their lips against a metal cup-shaped mouthpiece instead of blowing into a reed. Buzzing provides the sound, which is increased by the mouthpiece. In most brass instruments, there are valves attached to the lengthy pipes; the valves resemble buttons in appearance. By applying pressure to the valves, different sections of the pipe can be opened and closed.

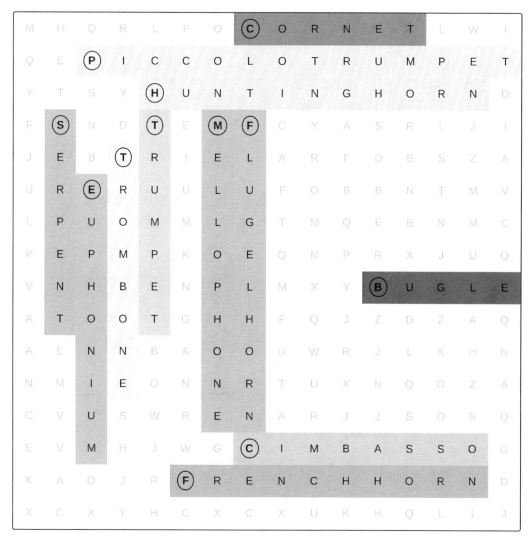

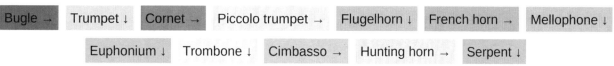

Bugle →   Trumpet ↓   Cornet →   Piccolo trumpet →   Flugelhorn ↓   French horn →   Mellophone ↓

Euphonium ↓   Trombone ↓   Cimbasso →   Hunting horn →   Serpent ↓

12 words in Wordsearch: 6 vertical, 6 horizontal, 0 diagonal. (0 reversed.)

ANSWER SHEET

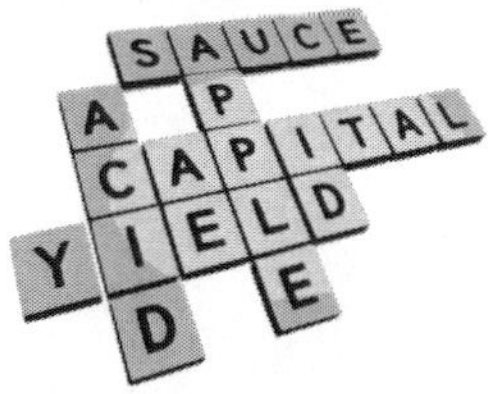

History Vocab Words

Complete the crossword by filling in a word that fits each clue.Fill in the correct answers, one letter per square, both across and down, from the given clues. There will be a gray space between multi-word answers.

Tip: Solve the easy clues first, and then go back and answer the more difficult ones.

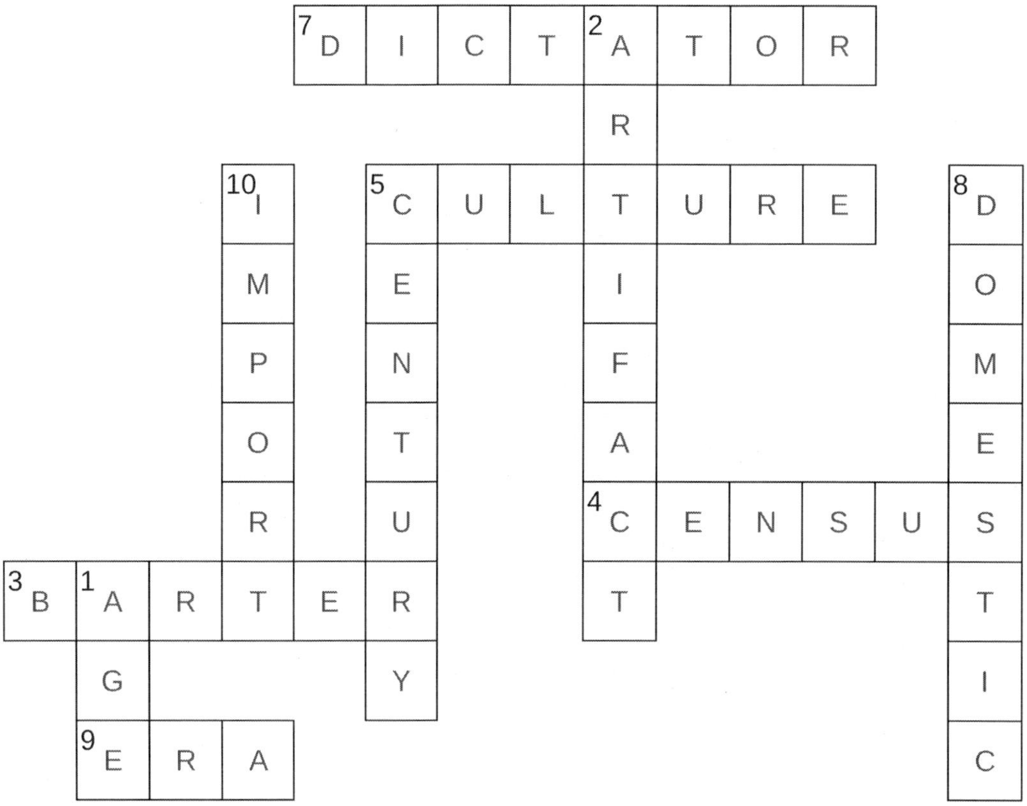

Across

3. exchange goods without involving money
4. a periodic count of the population
5. all the knowledge and values shared by a society
7. a ruler who is unconstrained by law
9. a period marked by distinctive character

Down

1. how long something has existed
2. a man-made object
5. a period of 100 years
8. of or relating to the home
10. bring in from abroad

ERA DICTATOR
IMPORT AGE
CENSUS ARTIFACT
DOMESTIC
BARTER CENTURY
CULTURE

Health Spelling Words

Instructions: Match the health term to the correct meaning.

1	Q	acute	⇢	ending in a sharp point
2	G	infant	⇢	young baby
3	J	anemia	⇢	a deficiency of red blood cells
4	E	colic	⇢	acute abdominal pain, especially in infants
5	C	brace	⇢	a device that holds injured body parts in place
6	F	dental	⇢	relating to the teeth
7	H	germ	⇢	a micro-organism, especially one that causes disease
8	K	disease	⇢	an impairment of health
9	R	fever	⇢	higher than normal body temperature
10	L	cancer	⇢	disease caused by the uncontrollable growth of cells
11	O	bedsore	⇢	wounds that develop on a patient's body from lying in one place for too long
12	D	chronic	⇢	long-lasting or characterized by long-suffering
13	A	central	⇢	in or near an inner area
14	M	biopsy	⇢	the removal and examination of tissue from a living body
15	N	injury	⇢	damage to the body
16	P	sore	⇢	painful
17	B	itchy	⇢	feeling discomfort on the skin's surface
18	I	scrubs	⇢	uniform worn by medical professionals

Grammar: Suffix

A suffix is a letter or group of letters attached to the end of a word in order to alter the meaning or function of the word. As with prefixes, the English language comes with tons of suffixes.

Consider the suffix **-ist**; by adding it to a word, you can modify it to refer to someone who performs or practices something. So, **art** becomes **artist**, a skillful performer of a particular art.

Other Examples:

The suffix **-ish** (Blueish) means relating to or resembling something.

The suffix **-ness** (Happiness) indicates a condition or quality. This suffix changes the word from a verb to a noun.

The suffix **-ship** (internship) position held.

The suffix **-less** (restless) means without something.

1. What is a suffix?
   a. A word beginning that changes the meaning of the word
   b. A word ending that changes the meaning of the word

2. What is the suffix in the word "permission"?
   a. -per
   b. -sion

3. What is the suffix in the word careful?
   a. -care
   b. -ful

4. What is the suffix in the word youngest?
   a. -young
   b. -est

5. What is the suffix in the word harmless?
   a. -less
   b. -arm

6. What is the suffix in the word cuter?
   a. -cute
   b. -er

7. What do you think the suffix -less means?
   a. Meaning: More of
   b. Meaning: Without

8. What do you think the suffix -ward, -wards means? (Towards, afterwards, backwards, inward)
   a. Meaning: Direction
   b. Meaning: Driving something

9. What do you think the suffix -ery means? (bakery, pottery, nursery)
   a. Meaning: an occupation or a way to make a living
   b. Meaning: a business or trade, a behavior, a condition

10. What is the suffix in the word breakable?
    a. -able
    b. -break

Grammar: Prefixes

A prefix is a part of a word or a word contained within another word. It is added to the beginning of another word to give it a new meaning. Additionally, it can refer to a number that is added at the beginning to indicate the position of anything inside a group.

Rules for adding prefix:

- prefix + root word = new word.

Look at the meaning of the prefix added to the meaning of the root word to get the meaning of the new word.

Meanings for prefixes vary depending on which one is used.

Example:

anti- | opposing, against, the opposite| antibiotic

com- | with, jointly, completely | combat

de- | down, away| decrease|

extra- | outside, beyond | extracurricular

1. A prefix comes at the _____ of a word.
   a. beginning
   b. end

2. A prefix changes the meaning of a root word.
   a. True
   b. False

3. What do you think the prefix re- (redo) means _____?
   a. do again
   b. not - or - opposite

4. What do you think the prefix dis- (disadvantage) means _____?
   a. add; multiply
   b. away; removal

5. If you are unable to do something, you are _____.
   a. able to do it again
   b. not able to do it

6. If you dislike green beans, you _____.
   a. really like green beans
   b. do not like green beans

7. If you disobey your parents, you _____.
   a. obey your parents quickly
   b. do not obey your parents

8. My teacher made me ___write name because it was sloppy.
   a. un
   b. re

9. My friends and I __play our favorite video games over and over again.
   a. re
   b. dis

10. Kids are __able to drive until they are 16.
    a. un
    b. re

Grammar: Nouns

A noun is a word that names something, such as a person, place, thing, or idea.

Identifying People
It might be the name of any individual, such as Jim, Ree, Tiffany, Jackie, or Tom.

The Naming of Places
It could be the name of any location, such as America, China, beach, North Dakota, or Paris.

Naming Objects or Things
Things such as a car, a hat, a bottle, a table, a cord, and a towel.

Animal Naming
A dog, a rabbit, an elephant, a chicken, and a horse.

Identifying Emotions/Qualities/Ideas
Fear, Joy, Beauty, Strength, and Anger.

1. Find the nouns: Andy likes to eat pie.
   a. eat, pie
   b. Andy, pie

2. Find the noun: The cup fell and broke.
   a. cup
   b. broke

3. A noun is...
   a. A word that describes
   b. A person, place, or thing

4. The word library is a.....
   a. place
   b. thing

5. The word window is a.....
   a. place
   b. thing

6. The word teacher is a.....
   a. thing
   b. person

7. My red bike goes really fast.
   a. bike
   b. red

8. Which answer choice is a noun?
   a. parrot
   b. blue

9. Which answer choice is a noun?
   a. lamp
   b. bright

10. Find the noun: I live in Australia.
   a. I
   b. Australia

11. Find the noun: Jackie is my sister.
   a. my
   b. Jackie

12. What are the nouns in this sentence? Ree lives on an island.
   a. Ree, lives
   b. Ree, island

Grammar: Adjectives

1. **They live in a beautiful house.**
   a. beautiful
   b. live

2. **Lisa is wearing a sleeveless shirt today.**
   a. sleeveless
   b. wearing

3. **She wore a colorful dress.**
   a. colorful
   b. wore

4. **This house is much nicer.**
   a. much
   b. nicer

5. **Jim is an adorable baby.**
   a. adorable
   b. baby

6. **Ree's hair is gorgeous.**
   a. hair
   b. gorgeous

7. **This house is bigger than that one.**
   a. bigger
   b. that one

8. **The wooden chair was uncomfortable.**
   a. uncomfortable
   b. wooden

9. **He is a funny little man.**
   a. little man
   b. funny little

10. **Did you have enough food?**
    a. enough
    b. have

11. **Kim bought six apples.**
    a. six
    b. bought

12. **The big dog chased the car.**
    a. chased
    b. big

Abbreviations ANSWERS

1	O	Ave.	→	Avenue
2	C	Blvd.	→	Boulevard
3	R	Dr.	→	Drive
4	T	Ln.	→	Lane
5	L	Rd.	→	Road
6	H	St.	→	Street
7	D	E	→	east
8	M	N	→	north
9	A	NE	→	northeast
10	U	NW	→	northwest
11	E	S	→	south
12	B	SE	→	southeast
13	V	SW	→	southwest
14	J	W	→	west
15	I	dept.	→	department
16	Q	D.I.Y.	→	Do it yourself
17	S	est.	→	established
18	K	E.T.A.	→	estimated time of arrival
19	P	min.	→	minute or minimum
20	F	misc.	→	miscellaneous
21	N	Mr.	→	Mister
22	G	Mrs.	→	Mistress

Grammar:
Abbreviations

Instructions: Match the abbreviation to the correct word.

1	L	January	→	Jan.
2	R	March	→	Mar.
3	Q	July	→	Jul.
4	B	September	→	Sep. or Sept.
5	M	November	→	Nov.
6	P	February	→	Feb.
7	I	April	→	Apr.
8	O	June	→	Jun.
9	E	August	→	Aug.
10	D	October	→	Oct.
11	N	December	→	Dec.
12	F	Sunday	→	Sun.
13	G	Tuesday	→	Tu., Tue., or Tues.
14	J	Thursday	→	Thur., or Thurs
15	K	Saturday	→	Sat.
16	C	Monday	→	Mon.
17	H	Wednesday	→	Wed.
18	A	Friday	→	Fri.

Grammar & Spelling Building

Write the correct word for each sentence.

teeth	joining	once	lion	ball
old	loved	sing	five	deep
extra	greet	clown	thank	frown
feed	away	coffee	balloons	bang

1. The circus **clown** did many silly things.

2. He tried to **frown** to make us laugh.

3. We should **thank** him for the good memories.

4. We saw a woman **sing** really high notes.

5. A loud **bang** came from a cannon.

6. The **old** man landed safely.

7. The **lion** jumped through a ring of fire.

8. The tiger balanced on a **ball** .

9. We will pay **extra** to see another show.

10. We both **loved** the elephants.

11. There was a muscle man who lifted two people at **once** .

12. We filled our **balloons** with helium.

13. My neighbor had no interest in **joining** us.

14. Let's **feed** the sheep now.

15. Keep brushing your **teeth** daily.

16. I keep **five** dollars in my pocket.

17. The river was really **deep** and wide.

18. Don't scare that deer **away** .

19. Let's **greet** the new mayor.

20. My grandma makes **coffee** every morning.

Fruit and Vegetables

Unscramble the names of these common fruits and vegetables.

apricot	avocado	kiwi	prune	broccoli	banana
pineapple	carrot	parsley	jalapeno	turnip	tangerine
raisin	asparagus	raspberry	potato	lettuce	garlic
onion	spinach	peach	cantaloupe	cucumber	radish
mango	coconut				

1. PHAEC   p e a c h

2. ABANAN   b a n a n a

3. PTAICOR   a p r i c o t

4. IKIW   k i w i

5. OMNAG   m a n g o

6. CTNOOCU   c o c o n u t

7. VOACOAD   a v o c a d o

8. EUPANTCAOL   c a n t a l o u p e

9. INLEPPEPA   p i n e a p p l e

10. ENTGNAIER   t a n g e r i n e

11. URENP   p r u n e

12. IIRANS   r a i s i n

13. BARPSEYRR   r a s p b e r r y

14. CIORBOCL   b r o c c o l i

15. CHSPNIA   s p i n a c h

16. LPRASYE   p a r s l e y

17. PRSAASAGU   a s p a r a g u s

18. LCEEUTT   l e t t u c e

19. AILGRC   g a r l i c

20. ERUCMUCB   c u c u m b e r

21. RACTOR   c a r r o t

22. IRSHDA   r a d i s h

23. OPTATO   p o t a t o

24. LPONEJAA   j a l a p e n o

25. NOINO   o n i o n

26. UIPNTR   t u r n i p

How Tornadoes Form

A __tornado__ is a violently rotating column of air in contact with and extending between a __cloud__ (often a thunderstorm cloud) and the surface of the earth. Winds in most tornadoes blow at 100 mph or less, but in the most violent, and least frequent tornadoes, wind speeds can __exceed__ 250 mph.

Tornadoes, often nicknamed " __twisters__ ," typically track along the ground for a few miles or less and are less than 100 yards wide, although rare monsters can remain in contact with the earth for well over 50 miles and exceed one mile in __width__ .

Several conditions are required for the development of tornadoes and the thunderstorm clouds with which most tornadoes are associated. Abundant low-level __moisture__ is necessary, and a "trigger" (perhaps a cold front or other low-level zones of converging winds) is needed to lift the moist air aloft.

Once the air begins to rise and becomes saturated, it will continue rising to great heights and produce a thunderstorm cloud if the atmosphere is __unstable__ . An unstable atmosphere is one in which the temperature decreases rapidly with height. Atmospheric instability can also occur when dry air overlays moist air near the earth's surface.

Tornadoes usually form in areas where winds at all levels of the atmosphere are not only strong, but also turn with height in a __clockwise__ , or veering, direction.

Tornadoes can appear as a traditional __funnel__ shape, or in a slender rope-like form. Some have a churning, smoky look to them. Others contain "multiple vortices" -- small, individual tornadoes rotating around a common center. Even others may be nearly invisible, with only swirling dust or debris at ground level as the only indication of the tornado's __presence__ .

Tornadic phenomena can take several forms.

__Supercell__ Tornadoes

Some of the most violent tornadoes develop from supercell thunderstorms. A supercell thunderstorm is a long-lived thunderstorm that has a continuously rotating updraft of air.

These storms are the most impressive of all thunderstorms and can produce large hail and tornadoes, although less than half of all supercell thunderstorms produce tornadoes.

Supercell thunderstorms and the tornadoes they sometimes produce are most __common__ in the central part of the United States.

Waterspout

Resembling a tornado, a __waterspout__ is usually less intense and causes far less damage. Rarely more than 50 yards wide, it forms over warm tropical ocean __waters__ , although its funnel is made of fresh water from condensation, not salt water from the ocean. Waterspouts usually dissipate upon reaching __land__ .

State Capitals 1 - 10

1	A	Alabama	⇢	Montgomery
2	E	Alaska	⇢	Juneau
3	J	Arizona	⇢	Phoenix
4	B	Arkansas	⇢	Little Rock
5	G	California	⇢	Sacramento
6	C	Colorado	⇢	Denver
7	F	Connecticut	⇢	Hartford
8	I	Delaware	⇢	Dover
9	H	Florida	⇢	Tallahassee
10	D	Georgia	⇢	Atlanta

Pronouns, Common Nouns, Proper Nouns

teacher	boy	desk	they	mom	table
pen	girl	dad	Spot	it	Monday
Superman	she	cat	us	John	he
Charlie	we	his	computer	I	chair
October	them	car	November	McDonald's	dog
their	him	Friday			

Common Nouns	Proper Nouns	Pronouns
teacher	October	he
dog	November	him
cat	John	I
car	Spot	she
pen	Charlie	it
table	Monday	we
chair	Friday	them
computer	McDonald's	they
desk	Superman	us
boy		his
girl		their
mom		
dad		

Plural or Possessive

secretaries'	its	libraries	secretary's	nieces
hers	crow's	theirs	witness's	witnesses
niece's	libraries'	country's	nieces'	ours
witnesses'	library's	crows	countries'	countries

1. All the **secretaries'** desks are covered with file folders.

2. My young **niece's** birthday is next month.

3. All the **witnesses** to the crime agreed on what they'd seen.

4. My two **nieces'** bedroom has a window overlooking the park.

5. There were **crows** in the trees outside my window.

6. I found a black **crow's** feather in the woods.

7. It is a **witness's** duty to tell the truth.

8. I have three nephews and two **nieces** .

9. The **secretary's** job is to help the president with her appointments.

10. There are two **libraries** in my town.

11. Many **countries** sign treaties with one another.

12. My local **library's** book sale was full of bargains.

13. A **country's** prosperity depends on its economic strength.

14. Our state **libraries'** computer systems are all linked together.

15. Many **countries'** flags have stripes.

16. My sister has a doll that is **hers** .

17. My dog has a ball that is **its** .

18. My neighbors have a house that is **theirs** .

19. My family has a house that is **ours** .

20. All of the **witnesses'** accounts of the crime were the same.

WEATHER

1	C		→	rainy
2	E		→	stormy
3	B		→	sunny
4	F		→	partly cloudy
5	D		→	windy
6	H		→	cloudy
7	A		→	snowy
8	G		→	foggy

It's Lab Day Scrambler!

Venipuncture	Cholesterol	Prothrombin	Hemostasis	Hemoglobin	Influenza
Infectious	Antecubital	Nitrile gloves	Phlebotomist	Tourniquet	Technologist
Bandage	Capillary	Urinalysis			

1. NPCVUERITEUN   Venipuncture

2. SMAITSHOES   Hemostasis

3. OQUETTINUR   Tourniquet

4. TOSEHROCLLE   Cholesterol

5. LBAETIACUNT   Antecubital

6. YALLRIACP   Capillary

7. SLYARSINIU   Urinalysis

8. GANADBE   Bandage

9. ORRTPMOHINB   Prothrombin

10. HNCOOGLESITT   Technologist

11. LIZEUAFNN   Influenza

12. LEIRTIN VSLEGO   Nitrile gloves

13. EMLTSTOOBPHI   Phlebotomist

14. OINESFCIUT   Infectious

15. BEGOOHINLM   Hemoglobin

Vocabulary: Community Services

Directions: Read the words. Sort the words into the community services in which they belong.

insurance	sick	injured	emergency	firefighter	doctor
driver's license	video	adult education	nurse	ticket	EMS worker
Principal	students	teacher	magazines	officer	return
loan	learning	junior high	borrow	newspapers	librarian
medicine	books	pharmacist	911	high school	pharmacy
elementary school					

Hospital (8)	Library (8)	Police/Fire Department (7)	School (8)
doctor	librarian	officer	teacher
nurse	books	firefighter	Principal
pharmacy	video	EMS worker	students
pharmacist	magazines	911	elementary school
sick	newspapers	ticket	junior high
injured	borrow	emergency	high school
medicine	loan	driver's license	adult education
insurance	return		learning

QUANTITATIVE CHEMISTRY

Conservation of Mass

In __1789__ , Antoine Lavoisier, a French chemist, first proposed the Law of Conservation of Mass. To do this, he had to carry out thousands of experiments, making very careful __measurements__ . he found that in any chemical reaction or physical change, the total mass after the reaction was __exactly__ the __same__ as the mass before. His law can be summarised as follows:

"Matter cannot be __destroyed__ , or __created__ , just changed from one form to another."

If you mix lead nitrate solution with potassium iodide solution a yellow solid is formed called __lead__ iodide. If you measured the mass of products (the chemicals formed) you would find that it is __exactly__ the __same__ as the mass of the reactants (the chemicals that were mixed).

Mass is never __increased__ or __decreased__ in a chemical reaction - particles cannot just be lost! Sometimes it may look like mass is lost, but in that case, it is usually a gas that has been produced and __escaped__ into the air. The same can happen when the chemicals made have a mass more than the mass of the products started with. You may have guessed, that in this case some gas from the air has been added to the __products__ !

For instance, if you heat zinc in the air you get a white powder. The mass of the white powder is greater than the mass of the __zinc__ you started with. The zinc has combined with __oxygen__ from the air to form zinc oxide. The mass of the zinc and the oxygen that reacted would be the same as the mass of the zinc oxide.

Which President?

Match each president to his description

1	A	Zachary Taylor	→	"I was a U.S. Army General in the Mexican-American War."
2	H	Jimmy Carter	→	"I was a peanut farmer from Georgia."
3	G	John Adams	→	"I was the first Vice-President. I signed the Declaration of Independence."
4	D	Ronald Reagan	→	"I was the first television and movie star to become president."
5	E	Andrew Jackson	→	"I was a lawyer and the 7th president. People called me 'Old Hickory'."
6	B	Barack Obama	→	"I was born in Honolulu, Hawaii. I was elected president in 2008."
7	C	Franklin D. Roosevelt	→	"I was the only president to have been elected for four terms. I was in office when Japan attacked Pearl Harbor."
8	F	Donald Trump	→	"I was born in New York to wealthy parents. I became president in January 2017."

Sustainability - Global Warming - Climate Change

This is a spelling worksheet to check your spelling and then your understanding of keywords to do with sustainability, climate change and global warming,

	A	B	C	D
1.	Ozone Layerr	Ozone Leyerr	Ozone Leyer	**Ozone Layer**
2.	**Sustainability**	Sustianability	Susstianability	Susstainability
3.	**Deforestation**	Defforestation	Defforestasion	Deforestasion
4.	Renewablle Resources	Renewablle Resoorces	**Renewable Resources**	Renewible Resources
5.	**Non Renewable Resources**	Non Renewablle Resoorces	Non Renewablle Resources	Non Renewible Resources
6.	Cllimate chanje	**Climate change**	Climate chanje	Cllimate change
7.	Habitat lous	Habitat los	**Habitat loss**	Habitat louss
8.	Trropical rian forest	Trropical rain forest	Tropical rian forest	**Tropical rain forest**
9.	Recicling	Reciclling	Recyclling	**Recycling**
10.	**Carbon dioxide**	Carrbon dioxide	Carrbon doixide	Carbon doixide
11.	Mathane	Metthane	Matthane	**Methane**
12.	Grenhouse gas	Grenhoose gas	Greanhouse gas	**Greenhouse gas**
13.	Hydrroflurocarbons	**Hydroflurocarbons**	Hydrophlurocarbons	Hydrrophlurocarbons
14.	Sulphur hexophluoride	Sullphur hexofluoride	Sullphur hexophluoride	**Sulphur hexofluoride**
15.	Nittrous oxide	**Nitrous oxide**	Nitroos oxide	Nittroos oxide
16.	Foussil Fuels	Fosil Fuels	Fousil Fuels	**Fossil Fuels**
17.	Trranspurt	Transpurt	**Transport**	Trransport
18.	Indusstry	**Industry**	Indostry	Inductry
19.	Agrricolture	Agrriculture	**Agriculture**	Agricolture
20.	Palm Oyl	**Palm Oil**	Pallm Oil	Pallm Oyl

WEATHER

1	C	..→	rainy
2	E	..→	stormy
3	B	..→	sunny
4	F	..→	partly cloudy
5	D	..→	windy
6	H	..→	cloudy
7	A	..→	snowy
8	G	..→	foggy

Holocaust Word Scramble

One of the most heinous events in human history is the Holocaust. It happened during World War II when Hitler was Germany's leader. The Nazis were responsible for the deaths of six million Jews. As many as one million Jewish youngsters were affected. Millions of other people who Hitler despised were also slaughtered. This included Poles, Catholics, Serbs, and individuals with disabilities. It is estimated that the Nazis killed up to 17 million innocent people.

Hitler despised Jews and blamed them for Germany's defeat in World War I. He did not consider Jews to be fully human. Hitler also believed in the Aryan race's superiority. He sought to employ Darwinism and breeding to produce a perfect race of humans. In his book Mein Kampf, Hitler stated that he would banish all Jews from Germany if he were to become the leader. Few doubted he would do it, but as soon as he became Chancellor, he began his anti-Semitic campaign. He passed legislation declaring that Jews had no rights. He then orchestrated attacks on Jewish businesses and residences. Many Jewish homes and businesses were burned down or vandalized on November 9, 1938. The Kristallnacht, or "Night of Broken Glass," was the name given to this event.

Ghettos	Propaganda	Liberation	Captured	Typhus	anti-Semitism
Swastika	Surrender	Starvation	Jews	Gestapo	Executed

1. errnrudse   S u r r e n d e r

2. askwatsi   S w a s t i k a

3. ewsj   J e w s

4. ptsuhy   T y p h u s

5. eaptcdur   C a p t u r e d

6. dueceext   E x e c u t e d

7. heogstt   G h e t t o s

8. stoatanvri   S t a r v a t i o n

9. airtlenbio   L i b e r a t i o n

10. stmeains-itim   a n t i - S e m i t i s m

11. noaragpdpa   P r o p a g a n d a

12. gaopset   G e s t a p o

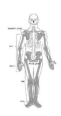

The Lymphatic System
Unscramble

There is a part of the immune system called the lymphatic system. It maintains a healthy balance of body fluids and protects the body from illness. Lymphatic (lim-FAT-ik) veins, tissues, organs, and glands collaborate to drain a watery fluid known as lymph from the body.

When there is a lot of extra lymph (LIMF) fluid in the body, the lymphatic system drains it and sends it back to the body's bloodstream. Lymph contains lymphocytes (LIM-fuh-sites), white blood cells, and chyle (KYE-ul), which is made up of fats and proteins from the intestines.

This is critical because water, proteins, and other substances constantly leak out of microscopic blood capillaries and into the surrounding bodily tissues. This additional fluid would build up in the tissues and cause them to bulge if the lymphatic system did not drain it.

lymphatic	antivirals	cytotoxic	leukocyte	phagocyte	immunology
lymphoma	pathogen	lymphedema	tonsillectomy	thymus	capillaries
spleen					

1. yhmtcalpi   l y m p h a t i c

2. muloinmoyg   i m m u n o l o g y

3. tcgayphoe   p h a g o c y t e

4. mehdeaplmy   l y m p h e d e m a

5. ottcyxoci   c y t o t o x i c

6. tvalriinsa   a n t i v i r a l s

7. nymseltooiltc   t o n s i l l e c t o m y

8. stumyh   t h y m u s

9. nlsepe   s p l e e n

10. aomlmhyp   l y m p h o m a

11. uekloytec   l e u k o c y t e

12. lecasiriapl   c a p i l l a r i e s

13. hgetpnao   p a t h o g e n

ADDITIONAL ASSIGNMENTS PLANNER

○ MONDAY

GOALS THIS WEEK

○ TUESDAY

○ WEDNESDAY

WHAT TO STUDY

○ THURSDAY

○ FRIDAY

EXTRA CREDIT WEEKEND WORK
○ SATURDAY / SUNDAY

ADDITIONAL ASSIGNMENTS PLANNER

○ MONDAY

GOALS THIS WEEK

○ TUESDAY

○ WEDNESDAY

WHAT TO STUDY

○ THURSDAY

○ FRIDAY

EXTRA CREDIT WEEKEND WORK
○ SATURDAY / SUNDAY

ADDITIONAL ASSIGNMENTS PLANNER

○ MONDAY

○ TUESDAY

○ WEDNESDAY

○ THURSDAY

○ FRIDAY

EXTRA CREDIT WEEKEND WORK
○ SATURDAY / SUNDAY

GOALS THIS WEEK

WHAT TO STUDY

ADDITIONAL ASSIGNMENTS PLANNER

○ MONDAY

GOALS THIS WEEK

○ TUESDAY

○ WEDNESDAY

WHAT TO STUDY

○ THURSDAY

○ FRIDAY

EXTRA CREDIT WEEKEND WORK
○ SATURDAY / SUNDAY

GRADES TRACKER

Week	Monday	Tuesday	Wednesday	Thursday	Friday
1					
2					
3					
4					
5					
6					
7					
8					
9					
10					
11					
12					
13					
14					
15					
16					
17					
18					

Notes

GRADES TRACKER

Week	Monday	Tuesday	Wednesday	Thursday	Friday
1					
2					
3					
4					
5					
6					
7					
8					
9					
10					
11					
12					
13					
14					
15					
16					
17					
18					

Notes

End of the Year Evaluation

Name: _____

Grade/Level: _____ Date: _____

Subjects Studied: _____

_____

_____

Goals Accomplished: _____

_____

_____

_____

Most Improved Areas: _____

_____

_____

_____

Areas of Improvement: _____

_____

_____

Main Curriculum Evaluation	Satisfied	A= Above Standards S= Meets Standards N= Needs Improvement	Final Grades
_____	Yes No	98-100 A+ 93-97 A	_____
_____	Yes No	90-92 A 88-89 B+	_____
_____	Yes No	83-87 B 80-82 B	_____
_____	Yes No	78-79 C+ 73-77 C 70-72 C	_____
_____	Yes No	68-69 D+ 62-67 D	_____
_____	Yes No	60-62 D 59 & Below F	_____

Most Enjoyed: _____

_____

Least Enjoyed: _____

_____

Made in United States
North Haven, CT
19 September 2024

57552468R00217